John & Jane[?]
all ever w[?]
and rememberin[?]
happy times.
John

More Lees Than Cheshire Fleas

and

Tinker, Tailor, Soldier, Restaurateur

John Howard

© John Howard 2011

Published by The Princess Street Press, Knutsford

ISBN 978-0-9564362-0-7

Cover design by Clare Brayshaw

Prepared and printed by:

York Publishing Services Ltd

64 Hallfield Road
Layerthorpe
York YO31 7ZQ
Tel: 01904 431213

Website: www.yps-publishing.co.uk

Acknowledgements

A thank you to the following people for their help and encouragement, mostly given unwittingly and probably unknowingly in the production of these two books.

To Jim and Marilyn Rait for their belief that the content was important in the context of local social history. To Glyn Stockdale whose lovely Courtyard Restaurant was the backdrop for much early discussion. To Sharon and Matthew Fay an apology for monopolising space and time in the same said Courtyard and a thank you for their endless patience and friendliness. To the gentle Janette Drake who had to persevere with my sad attempts at English Grammar and endless changes to the copy. To Joan Leach who was unknowingly, since our liaison in the presentation of "Knutsford in Portrait" been a source of inspiration. I may even have borrowed some of her photographs. Finally, but far, far from least, has been the faith, encouragement and real help given by my old friend David Naylor who, when in my cups latterly, has kicked my backside and brought about what I hope is a successful conclusion.

A Memory

Shortly before going to press my old friend and former colleague Joan Leach, local historian and founder of The Gaskell Society sadly died after a short illness. We were both born in the town in 1933, lived not too far away from each other, travelled on the same trains to schools in Altrincham. We went on our ways in midlife and work brought us together as co-presenters of Peter Wildin's excellent video "Knutsford in Portrait". Joan of course providing the bulk of the historical content.

Though we often cross referenced on the history (of the town); Joan's knowledge and research work was simply awesome and I owed her far in excess of what I was able to provide her with, though I suspect she was just a trifle envious of my access to my family's long and controversial association with Knutsford.

No one will ever take the place of Joan, Knutsford was in her blood. She will be sorely missed but never forgotten by those privileged to know her.

Author's Preface

I realised, not too far into my scribblings, that what I was actually and unwittingly writing was something that could be considered approaching the shape of an historical novel. The huge difference being that the location was not that of a fictionalised country town, but a real one noted for its beauty and its history and one populated not by a novelist's cosmetic characters but one with a fair share of original if somewhat eccentric natives.

Knutsford was made famous in the literary sense by the town's own dear and adored authoress, Elizabeth Gaskell, who drew heavily on the town and its residents to provide the ideal backdrop and characters for her classic novels "Cranford" and "Wives and Daughters" set as they are in the kind, genteel late Georgian and Regency periods.

My book moves Knutsford on some fifty to eighty years, through mainly the mid to late Victorian and Edwardian periods and ends much later. The people in the book are real. I have made little or no attempt to glamourise them, which would anyway have been a difficult thing to do. They are presented "warts and all" as being possibly representative of their time. The Lees, in the main, were an aggressively ambitious and opportunistic breed. They strode the Knutsford stage as if it was theirs of right, though it must be said they contributed much to the town that was good in the political and economic sense. The nigh on joint sixty year period that Robert and Fred Lee served the town during its time of expansion and development must be taken into consideration. In particular Robert's decision making was a considerable factor. However, what fatally attracted me were their quirky private lives. Had it not been for these lives, this book would, of course, not have been written. Who anyway wants to read about the more boring aspects of Victorian and Edwardian life?

Many good and more formal books have been penned about Knutsford and the many various aspects of its history and development. What I have produced is a book which I believe truthfully and realistically portrays the town over a certain period and gives a glimpse into the lives of the real people that were influenced by it. Thank heavens that the skeletons in the Lee cupboards rattled about as furiously as they did, and that recklessness and foolishness surfaced frequently and that ill fortune lurked around every Knutsford corner when it was least expected.

The brothers, Robert, George and Fred Lee all died between 1930 and 1934, all were in their seventies and had long ceased to play any part in Knutsford's affairs. In 1904 Richard Harding Watt brought his all important executive leather buyer, Albert Howard, my paternal Grandfather, from Manchester to Knutsford and built a house for him – Cranford Gardens, in the belief that his sickly children would benefit from living in the clean Knutsford air. By 1913 Watt was dead. My Grandfather had by then left Watt's employ and failing leather goods business to reluctantly enter the licensed hotel trade by taking the licence of the 17th/18th century former coaching inn, The White Bear, thus joining a local trade once monopolised by the Lees whose involvement with it was, by then, on the wane.

In 1928 Albert Howard died, and my Father, a young draughtsman engineer had little or no alternative but to take over the licence of the inn to protect his vulnerable Mother. I was born there, in the early thirties, and my earliest recollections are of a young life lived in Knutsford during the Second Word War of 1939 – 45. These memories and many more have prompted my second self-indulgent book "Tinker, Tailor, Soldier, Restaurateur" which centres largely on a restaurant life lived in Knutsford with, I hope, a few lively and interesting diversions either side of it.

More Lees Than Cheshire Fleas

Introduction

On resigning his position as custodian of Arley Hall in 1996, and to all intents retiring from a life lived full and variously, John Howard was at a loss for something to occupy his time and attention. History had long been a major interest which had been stimulated by his time at Arley when it was necessary to become conversant with the history of the Egerton-Warburton family in order to relay it on an almost daily basis to the visiting general public.

Tongue in cheek he thought it might be fun to research that of the Lee family, his maternal ancestors. It had long been a matter of considerable curiosity, aroused during the second 1939-45 World War, when as a small boy, with a vivid imagination, growing up in his Father's ancient inn, he had eavesdropped on the lurid and colourful conversations between his recently demobilised Indian Army uncle, Major Kenneth Lee and his cousin, the author's mother. These were riotous, totally outrageous and barely believable, so much so, they were etched deeply into his memory.

The result of his research discovered that there was indeed a terrible truth in the stories, not only that, but that there were deeper and darker truths yet to be revealed, so much so that he decided to take the subject further and compile it into a lecture or talk with good relevant photographic slides and then peddle it around Cheshire and Greater Manchester hoping to both amuse and shock a selected audience comprising mainly of members of history and heritage societies, probus clubs, women's institutes, townswomens guilds and all manner of other clubs. The talks went extremely well and were watched and listened to by an estimated audience of over 5000 over a very short period. So well, in fact, that encouraged by this "More Lees than Cheshire Fleas" a play on words of an old Cheshire saying, which tells the story of the Lee family from when the astute and ambitious early Victorian Stockport publican, Tom Lee, followed his uncle Joseph to Knutsford and bought two adjoining main street inns – The Hat and Feather and The Rose and Crown, married the daughter of a local innkeeper, produced a family of four boys, made plans for their future careers, which involved the two youngest being willed the two inns at the tender ages of eleven and fifteen making them, surely, the youngest public house owners recorded, at the same time ensuring that the eldest twenty-one year old son would carry on with his intended plan to become Knutsford's first wine merchant, all this before dying at the early age of fifty-six. This is mainly the story of the fortunes of these four young men and their families and their aspirations to establish themselves in the inn-keeping and wine business and also with the local politics of the bustling, thriving and in those late Victorian and Edwardian days, the important Cheshire country town that Knutsford was.

The story tells firstly of the eldest son Robert and his success in realising his father's ambition to become a leading wine merchant. So successful that the business was soon purchased by a large Manchester brewery with which he soon became a director and major shareholder. It tells of Robert's involvement in the town's political affairs as a big player on the Knutsford Urban District Council and on the Knutsford Royal May Day Committee – all this leading to, on his eventual death, having a town thoroughfare named after him. It goes on to tell of Robert's two finely reserved and genteel spinster daughters who lived their sad reclusive lives only for each other, behind closed and affluent doors.

There is a downturn in the story with the second son, the ill-starred John, who with no room for him in the family business, ploughed a defiant and lonely furrow with much of his business career misguidedly placed in the clumsy and selfish hands of an older longtime loser of a business partner, who ruthlessly exploited his vulnerability, leading to failure and poverty and a life further stricken by the tragic misfortunes of his children.

All then bursts into frenzied action with the riotous story of the barn storming number three son, George, who ignored his father's plans for him to eventually manage The Rose and Crown Inn. He never did and eventually sold it to a brewery but not before becoming a teenage horse dealer, property dealer, fire brigade superintendent, short time KUDC councillor, Boer War Cavalry Sergeant, professional barefist pugilist, boxing ring master of ceremonies and not least, a supposed murderer. He married, died childless, much feared and hated.

The story of Tom Lee's sons ends with that of the fourth young man, Fred, who with apparent early wealth at his disposal and continuing vast disposable income, contrived to live a wasteful and ill managed private family life, marred by the tragic accidental death of a loved but alcoholic wife. So profligate a life did Fred Lee live that he contrived and succeeded in taking his own life, the cause of which became obvious when his safe was opened and found to be full of IOU's. He was penniless. However sad and wasteful his private life was, it did not prevent him from serving thirty loyal years on the Knutsford Urban District Council, many years on the Knutsford Royal May Day Committee, riding at the head of the procession as Marshal, this also for thirty years. He was survived by three sons, two of whom were to bring further controversy and disgrace to his family name.

Contents

sweet Annie Duffy – the bonny Irish lass – Bessie and
Geoffrey born – the emerging drunken bully – a wartime
respite – the gallant refuse lorry driver – the Chester pub
crawl – the stumbling drunk – Tom's bad Good Friday
– head versus door handle – the handle of God?

10.   **Neville and Brian Lee**   **132**

Neville career-less due to war – called up in 1940 – North
Africa and Italy with Desert Rats – King Street Gentleman's
bookmaker – marries Kay – moves to Wakefield – theatre
restoration – theatre heart attack – the Lee jinx.

Brian joins brother's Berkeley Square business – devastated by
his early death – moves to Chilterns – establishes Industrial
Cleaning Company – Consultant to Oxfordshire Health
Authority – Territorial Army Commission with Green
Jackets/Rifles – retires to North Wales and dies there.

CHAPTER ONE

Tom Lee

Illegitimate in Alderley Edge – Farm servant Mother Mary – Father Joshua a surrogate Father – early visits to Knutsford blacksmith Uncle Joseph – A Norbury Wife – The Forresters Arms – purchases ancient but dilapidated Hat and Feather and The Rose and Crown Inns – ale and porter merchant – wine merchant ambitions – the four sons, Robert, John, George and Fred – an early death – family plans – youngest Inn owners in England? – Robert Lee as twenty-one year old head of family.

~

My great great maternal grandfather Tom Lee was illegitimate, born in 1818 he was the son of Mary Lee, a young servant girl who at the time was in service at a farm at 'The Hough' which is very near to Alderley Edge, a pretty little town made notorious in recent years as the home of Neil and Christine Hamilton, David and "Posh" Beckham and many other of Manchester United's footballing millionaires. I am unsure as to whether they appreciate the beauty of the place, but past generations of immensely wealthy gentle folk built wonderful houses on the edge itself to take advantage of the splendid views over the Cheshire Plain. 'The Hough' is to the rear of the edge and the commencement of the gently rolling countryside leading to the Cheshire hills.

Mary, like a vast number of poor young girls in the 19th century, was a house servant living with her employers family. All were vulnerable and unwanted pregnancy not uncommon. Sadly, in the tradition of such a situation, the work and money were of more importance than the child. It could have meant dismissal, if however the employers were sympathetic to a girl who's work was satisfactory and was well integrated with the family then the girl was shipped briefly home to her family to have the child and for the family to bring that child up. Many a child was mothered by a Grandmother and not the worse for it, at least the vital income would still be available and assist in the bringing up of the child.

Such was the case with Mary Lee, but with a slight difference in that young Tom was cared for by Mary's fathers family in Stockport. Joshua Lee was an overseer in a Stockport mill and was a twin brother to Joseph Lee, a blacksmith and farrier living and working in Knutsford having arrived circa 1810. Joseph proved to be the catalyst to the Lee involvement in Knutsford life. Mary did return to her agricultural employers, but we lose sight of her very soon. She appears for a time in Knutsford, more than likely visiting her uncle Joseph and then disappears from sight, it is thought dying unmarried at an early age.

Young Tom living in comparative poverty with his surrogate father, Uncle Joshua in Stockport, appears to have either been extremely fortunate or very bright in that he prospered quite early in his short career, becoming a Stockport inn keeper by his early twenties. Was he clever and ambitious enough to have earned himself the management of the inn? He certainly proved to be a shrewd customer as he made his way through life. Did he own the inn? If so, how did he acquire the funds to purchase it? Was his unknown father sufficiently well off to bankroll his illegitimate son? Regretfully I have never had the time to research the Stockport period of Tom Lee's early career.

As a boy, his Uncle Joshua would have taken him to visit his twin brother Joseph. In so doing, over the years he would have become well acquainted with old Knutsford, and like so many people over the centuries, come to love it, and eventually want to live and conduct business in it. Nothing has changed over the centuries, it is still the case. It was during one of his visits that he met and courted his future wife, Margaret Norbury. The Norburys proliferate in Cheshire and were positively tribal. They were and still are very much evident in the Knutsford and adjacent Mobberley area. This particular branch of the Norburys were innkeepers, keeping The Forresters Arms, which more accurately should be described as an ale house, in the Old Market Place and sadly long gone, and The Church Inn at Mobberley.

Margaret was the daughter of the landlord of The Forresters Arms, Sarah Norbury, and was assisting her mother managing the inn, her father John Norbury having died earlier. Tom could have met Margaret from across the bar, and as a visiting publican may have even assisted the two women in their busier periods of business, perhaps on race days when there was a meeting at the racecourse on the Knutsford Heath. At the mature age of thirty three, he eventually popped the question and he and Margaret were married in Knutsford Parish Church in 1851. He would have by this time of his life become an assured, confident and experienced individual. He had achieved a certain amount of success and with it money in the bank. He also arrived with a positive plan of action.

His marriage to Margaret gave him considerable financial elbow room. Bringing his widowed surrogate father Joshua with him, he moved into The Forresters which was a large handsome Georgian building, one of many surrounding The Old Market Place. Sadly all are now gone. These fine buildings fell victim to ruthless and aggressive landlords long before the necessary laws were introduced to prevent such wanton destruction. Today's planners and developers would most certainly have produced a much more sympathetic scheme which would have saved, preserved and integrated the facades of these lovely buildings, allowing The Old Market Place to retain it's architectural dignity.

With his financial powder kept dry, Tom Lee then put into action the plans he had in mind for some years. This was the acquisition of two adjoining inns in Knutsford's main thoroughfare, King Street or the 'Bottom Street' as the natives prefer to call it. Public houses in the early Victorian period were largely privately owned. The sundry brewery companies had not yet become too acquisitive and were selling their now advertised products to these individual licencees, who in many cases had been brewing their own ales, this being prevalent in the Knutsford area.

The breweries were also building their own large Victorian beer houses in surburbia, but unable to do so in picturesque towns like Knutsford. The inn trade was highly competitive and Knutsford had always had a very large number of inns and ale houses since the 17th Century. By the 1850's there were considerably fewer but there were still thrice as many as there are today. As you would expect in an ancient market town most properties were very old indeed, and most innkeepers were not doing sufficient business to maintain these old inns of which many were falling into further disrepair, many eventually closing as did The Forresters Arms at a later date.

Such was the case with the two inns that Tom Lee purchased. The Hat and Feather was a tall Georgian inn not too dissimilar in size to The Forresters Arms, but with a stuccoed white façade. The Rose and Crown was a delightful black and white timbered jumble of a building of great age and could have been three hundred years old at the time Tom Lee bought it. The Hat and Feather is long gone, in it's place stands The Gaskell Memorial Tower and the Kings Coffee House, now the home of the celebrated La Belle Epoque restaurant. A Lee family saga revolves around this property and is related in further chapters. The Rose and Crown, the Lee's eventually sold to a brewery who promptly demolished it and replaced it with a typically tasteless concoction purporting to be a black and white timbered Cheshire inn.

Trade at both these inns had become so dismal that the tenant innkeepers and their landlords felt obliged to stop trading and move on. The licences were allowed to lapse and the only recourse for the property owners, ill prepared as they were to restore the inns, was to then rent them as domestic dwellings, most probably this at extremely low rents given their dilapidated condition and their unsuitability as houses. Tom, paying his Uncle Joseph frequent visits over many years would have seen this situation evolve, become interested, made his plans accordingly, and duly purchased both inns, probably for a song, and having done so and used all his capital in acquiring them, would have had to continue renting them, eventually raising the rents in an effort to rid himself of his impoverished tenants. He could then commence the process of restoring the inns to something like their former glory. To achieve this aim he would need to fill his empty coffers once more.

It was doubtful whether the income from The Forresters Arms would have contributed greatly in this direction, anyway that was no concern to him, and he would have known this from the outset. No! Tom had other ideas about the licensing trade. In fact the two inns were pretty low on his agenda. He had long known where he was going to place the emphasis on his business venture, he would have to bide his time with the development of the two inns. His immediate concern was with increase of the turnover and the development of "off sale" trade in the ale and porter shop, which was situated in the other main thoroughfare, Princess Street or "Top" Street, and at the entrance archway which had led to The Rose and Crown stables and coach house.

The late Georgian Knutsford described in Mrs Gaskell's books was still largely intact. The wealthier, self important and highly sophisticated citizens of the town still resided in their fine town houses in the Victorian 1850's. Princess Street in particular, higher up the Knutsford hill was most refined, this despite being the main road through the town and providing access to the rear of King Street inns for their carriage and stage coaching trade. The houses on the west side of the street overlooked Tom Lee's rather ramshackle ale and porter off licence premises. Was there though much demand for this rather working class product in classy Princess Street? Tom did not think so. He reasoned that his enlightened and worldly neighbours and potential customers might prefer to do business with a wine and spirit merchant and cut his cloth accordingly. His turnover would increase highly and if well managed so would the profitability. The downside of course being the desperately poor condition of the shop and building. He resolved to address that problem at the earliest opportunity. Much work and endeavour however would be the order of things before he had sufficient capital to do so.

From the day he purchased the two inns with the off licence, to the day he died Tom Lee would trudge from the Old Market Place, along King Street up and through The Royal George coaching yard and along Princess Street to his premises. He would certainly on numerous occasions have passed through The Rose and Crown and The Hat and Feather, either to collect the rents from his impoverished tenants or at the same time evaluate the situation and formulate plans for the day when both inns could be re-activated, re-licensed and managed. They would certainly have needed refitting, to what extent would be subject to the profits from the wine and spirit business. In the evenings he would either return to The Forresters Arms and assist his wife and mother-in-law with the running of the ale house or considering the late opening off licensing hours remained to manage the shop. Whichever it was a hard life.

Despite the continual daily graft, Tom and Margaret managed to produce a largish family of four boys. All were born in the ten year period between 1853 and 1863. Robert in 1853, John 1855, George 1859 and Fred 1863. When Fred the youngest was born, Tom Lee was a mature forty-five years old. As the boys grew up his plans would change to accommodate them within the framework of the family licensing business. However this depended on it's success and the willingness of the young men as they grew up to comply with their father's plans. This book is principally about the lives of these four young men and what part they played in the affairs of the town and the way the town influenced their private lives. Robert the eldest boy was to become a paragon of virtue and a pillar of success and respectability fulfilling both his own and his fathers ambitions. Poor John the second eldest son it is very sad to relate achieved very little, ill luck and tragedy dogged his every footstep. For sons number three and four, George and Fred, life in late Victorian and Edwardian Knutsford was a controversial roller coaster ride which titillated the traditional Knutsford appetite for gossip and scandal with a rich and varied diet of stories of fortune and misfortune.

Sadness loomed large over the family when Tom Lee fell victim to meningitis in his mid fifties. Frustratingly success was near to hand and towards the end of his life the Lees had become a close knit and loving family. By the time of his death in 1874 at the age of fifty six, he had changed his business plans to accommodate his sons within it and so influence their future lives, hopefully for the good. Robert at the time was a fully matured young man aged twenty one, who had loyally and enthusiastically served his apprenticeship under his father and was fully aware of his father's ambitions. John aged nineteen had played no part in the family business, it simply could not afford two apprentices, and was apprenticed to a King Street earthenware dealer. George had only recently left the Knutsford Grammar School, which all the Lee boys attended, situated below the Parish Church in King Street, it is now a wine bar and was the site of the former Chapel of Ease which was demolished in 1741 and the church built on the hill opposite. Young George was showing disconcerting signs of being of a headstrong nature. The youngest boy, Fred, was still a schoolboy aged eleven.

The certain knowledge of his impending death prompted Tom to draft a will which he hoped would secure the future lives of his family and was an exercise in family planning the like of which had not been seen before in Knutsford. He simply divided his business interests up between the boys. The twenty one year old Robert was willed the wine and spirit business, and would go on to develop it in a way that may have been beyond his father's wildest dreams. Unfortunately, for poor John there was no place in his father's plans. He was though a junior partner in William Peer's earthenware business and was soon to be married. The revelation contained in the will concerned the fifteen year old George and the eleven year old Fred. George was given The Rose and Crown Inn which was to be developed and managed until he reached his seniority age of twenty one whence he would be able to take up the licence. Similarly Fred aged eleven was willed The Hat and Feather with the same circumstances being applicable. It was an eye popping moment when researching the licensing records in the Chester records office to find that my great grandfather Fred Lee was an inn owner at the tender age of eleven and my great uncle George one at the age of fifteen. George never took up the licence of The Rose and Crown and never lived in it. This madcap fellow had other ideas about the way he wanted to live his life and by heavens they were frantic ones. Fred Lee did take on the licence of The Hat and Feather and remained faithful to the licensing trade, which after very many highs in his lifetime, subsequently brought him down, eventually leading to his tragic death.

When my great, great grandfather Tom Lee died in 1874, his loyal and loving eldest son Robert was by his side. I would like to think that his last words were "look after your mother and your brothers". Robert thus assumed the position of head of family and did just that for as long as was necessary. He buried his father in Knutsford Parish Churchyard at the same time reserving a plot next to his father's grave. He would eventually be buried there, and be as close to him as he was in life. I can see the two graves from my Lee built cottage, in no way does this make me morbid, rather the opposite. Tom Lee from his almost disastrous start in life had grafted his way through it. A highly ambitious, forward thinking family orientated man, he was not to see his ambitions fulfilled. He would have certainly been well pleased with the manner with which Robert conducted himself, the business and the affairs of the family.

CHAPTER TWO

Robert Lee & His Daughters

His Father's apprentice – a good marriage – Nelsie, Maggie and Flo Flo – The Lord Eldon – the refurbished wine merchants – well educated young ladies – an acquisitive brewery – the sell out – a Directorship – an advantageous marriage – Ralgarth built – retirement – local Government – the Royal May Day Committee – reunited in death – Flo Flo and Arthur Harlow – the early death of Arthur – a reclusive Flo Flo – a mourning Nelsie – a mauve shrine.

~

Robert would have served a strict apprenticeship under his father's guidance and supervision. A telling photograph of 1865 shows father and son outside their still decrepit premises, the twelve year old Robert holding a shopping basket. The photograph, taken on a Saturday afternoon being one of the first pictures of life in mid-Victorian Knutsford, and one of many taken that day in which scores of it's working inhabitants posed in front of their businesses. The young Robert was obviously running errands that afternoon for his father and probably on most Saturday afternoons.

Even though on the death of his father he assumed the mantle of head of family, his mother Margaret then only forty-seven years old would have been party to her late husband's plans, and still able to manage The

Forresters Arms, the licence of which was transferred in her name, life would have been difficult for her then. The dedicated Robert would have presented few problems, it is quite likely that he assisted her whenever he was able. The sulky and rebellious John would soon leave home and marry. The volatile and independent minded George would have needed constant supervision. Young Fred, quiet by nature was still in Grammar school, and presented few difficulties.

However within two to three years of their father's death Robert and John had married and left home. Robert had met Anne, a lovely lady from Croft near Leigh on the Lancashire-Cheshire border, the newlywed's taking a cottage in nearby Tatton Street where they produced two baby daughters, Nelsie in 1879 and Florence in 1880. They continued to reside in Tatton Street until in 1881 when the twenty-seven year old Robert obtained the licence of The Lord Eldon inn, just across the road from his home.

This of course was no part of his father Tom's overall scheme of things. The maturing Robert, now fully confident was able to make his own plans for the future, on the face of it the move looked rather hazardous. Progress was being made by the blossoming wine and spirits business, he was working extremely hard to obtain success, he knew however that to attain total success, he would have to upgrade the Princess Street premises. This would mean high capital investment in bricks and mortar. To achieve this he would have to increase his turnover and profitability. The move to The Lord Eldon was made for just that purpose. He was prepared to work the two business's together for as long as it took. From 1881 to 1889 for eight tough years day and night he worked diligently, doing exactly as his father did before when he was similarly involved with the retail premises and The Forresters Arms.

By 1890 the now thirty-six year old Robert had knocked down the old and ruinous building and built by late Victorian standards a modern building which stretched along Princess Street from the corner of Silk Mill Street to the side of the Methodist Church. The development had retained the old coaching access to the rear of The Rose and Crown, by then no longer a Lee owned inn, to either side of the archway were retail shop premises including the wine and spirit merchants. Crucially above these retail premises was the living accommodation that Robert and his growing family had so long desired. Spacious rooms stretching the length of the block in which to bring up his three daughters, for during his sojourn at The Lord Eldon, a third baby girl, christened Maggie had been born in 1883. She was to play an important role in the future affairs of the family.

With regard to the development of the whole new block of shop premises, I am unsure as to whether Robert had any financial assistance in say partnership terms, but I think not. The whole has the hallmark of one man. I feel sure that he had somehow, over many years acquired the whole run down block. He would then have been able to lease the adjoining retail outlets, the rental income further adding to his growing wealth. It is interesting to note that on relinquishing the licence of The Lord Eldon in 1889, it was re-licenced in the name of his younger brother, the thirty year old George, who still owned The Rose and Crown which the wine merchants premises had been part of. There would have been considerable insider wheeler dealing within the family to bring about these changes. The Lee's worked as a close family unit, but at what stage the retail wine merchants had been prised away from the inn, only the Lees would know after all they owned both and could do as they wished.

Whatever, the new buildings now represented a statement which declared that Robert Lee had really arrived as a business man. The town which must have watched with considerable interest and great sympathy, the struggle of a young man who had lost his father and mentor when he was twenty-one years old and now sixteen years after was the owner of a large slice of Knutsford real estate. Those sixteen years had been a considerable struggle, head of the family, responsible for his younger brothers and their affairs, keeping an eye on his mother as she continued to manage The Forresters Arms and bring up her young men, work long hours and care for his own young family of little girls. At long last he could rid himself of the problem of bringing up a family in the oft times unsavoury environment of a public house. His youngest brother Fred was to do this with his family to deadly effect many years later. The Lee girls at a crucial time in their formative years could now go to private schools, and Robert could afford the very best education for them. They may have attended Miss Egerton's School for Girls on the edge of Tatton

Park, this is guesswork. It is now Knutsford Golf Club. Wherever they went to school, it produced three very fine and genteel young ladies.

The now streamlined wine and spirit business, made an immediate impact and the business flourished to such an extent over the next five years that it attracted the attention of an acquisitive Manchester brewery. Taylors Eagle Brewery seeking to expand on it's beer brewing base, and most probably anxious to improve it's image, beyond providing ale for the working man, sought an outlet for it's own wine and spirit business, what better place than pretty and historic Knutsford. The town was booming, the late Victorian developers were expanding the boundaries of the town, building many avenues of terraced houses, the population was growing, the demand for fine wines by the wealthy occupants of Knutsford's greater houses was increasing many fold. For the Taylor's of the Eagle Brewery, it was a must buy situation. Robert was wooed and an offer made for his business which he could not refuse. This included a Directorship with the brewery. Robert accepted the offer with alacrity. It was a get rich quickly opportunity that he was not prepared to miss.

The sale of the business now meant that he had more than ample funds to achieve further ambitions, one of which was to build a fine and large house well away from the town's busy and noisy main streets. He bought the end plot of land in St Peter's Avenue, a cul-de-sac on the furthest western boundary of the town and commenced to build "Ralgarth". He also acquired a row of terraced cottages in King Street which he rented. He moved out of his Princess Street apartments and took the licence of The Legh Arms in Brook Street on a temporary basis at the same supervising the building of an extension to this 18th century inn. The Legh Arms had recently been acquired by Taylors Eagle Brewery as part of their expansion programme, and stood at the extremely well heeled end of Knutsford, enjoying the custom of a wealthy local clientele. Robert obviously enjoyed life at the Legh Arms, remaining there for over five years before in 1902 he finally moved into 'Ralgarth', now like The Legh Arms fully built.

Robert's young daughters had by the turn of the century, blossomed into very fine young ladies. Maggie (or Molly) in particular was a winsome young thing approaching her majority age. Robert's directorship had brought the Taylor and Lee families into close contact, so much so that young Jack Taylor, the heir to the brewing business, having met the Lee girls, fell in love with Maggie and duly married her. This of course meant further wealth and opportunity for Robert. His was now a world of director and shareholder meetings and he soon became a major shareholder in the company, and was never to get his hands dirty again. He probably felt that he had deserved his financial reward for all the time and effort that he had subscribed to the family business since the age of fifteen when he started life as his father's apprentice, and for thirty years had worked strenuously to promote his business, now by the turn of the century he had achieved all that was possible within the boundaries of his profession and more besides.

He was still in his late forties and virtually retiring from business needing only to take the train to Manchester to attend board and shareholder meetings. However a life of leisure did not appeal to the energetic and creative Robert, who maybe became a little self regarding. In the eyes of his fellow townsmen he had become an important fellow. They had witnessed his rise to local fame and fortune and were well aware of his integrity. So when he decided to dabble in the politics and the development of the town they whole heartedly supported him by voting him onto the Knutsford Urban District Council, as they did his younger brother Fred at approximately the same time.

If you pass through Knutsford on it's main road, you could be impressed by the assembly of the quite serious and extremely large and self important buildings to either side of the road, all within a couple of 100 metres of one and other. They are all of considerable architectural interest and speak volumes for the fact that Knutsford at one time was indeed a major Cheshire town. Going south on the right hand side of road is the formidable and neo classical Knutsford Sessions House, built it is largely assumed by Thomas Harrison renowned for his work on Chester Castle and Crown Court. Behind the Sessions House once stood Knutsford Gaol which could accommodate up to seven hundred inmates, and was demolished in 1930. Opposite can be seen architect Alfred Waterhouse's Victorian gothic Town Hall, commissioned by Lord Egerton in 1871, his Lordship chose to use the services of the man who designed both Manchester Town Hall and the Natural History Museum in Kensington, London. Behind the Town Hall, in 1893 Lord

Egerton built the Egerton School for boys and girls, with the building echoing the grandeur of Waterhouse's magisterial edifice. Opposite the school is the Georgian parish church built in 1744. It is impossible not to be impressed by this group of solemn yet imposing group of buildings, which in a way are at odds with the rest of the town with it's narrow winding streets and alleyways and it's conflicting yet harmonious mix of ancient buidings.

Possibly inspired by all this architectural grandeur, Robert along with his youngest brother Fred, between them, were to serve the town for a joint period of fifty seven years, Robert for twenty seven and Fred for thirty years. A natural business man he would bring a huge degree of business know how to the council chamber, a quality I think is sadly missing in many of today's modern councils. He served the council and town in many ways, during his twenty-seven year involvement being variously on the "finance and office committee" which he would have been suited for, and the "cemetery committee". The Parish churchyard now being choc full of the Lees and Norburys and of course many more distinguished Knutsfordians there was now the need to locate fresh accommodation for the town's deceased. Robert helped to find Knutsford's Boot Hill and to administer to it in it's formative years. His three brothers and their families were eventually to become it's customers as would two of his daughters, one of them in melodramatic circumstances. He also served on the quaintly named "technical instruction committee". The modern progressive man that he was made him the ideal choice for this committee. In all probability he was responsible for the procurement of the first mechanised council refuse lorry which his disgraced nephew, my grandfather Tom, was to drive so appropriately as you will discover. It was however rumoured in Knutsford at that time, that there was something approaching a cabal within the council chamber. Joining the two Lee brothers on the council were another pair of brothers, the Wildgooses, whose drapery business was sat cheek and jowl next to the two Lee owned public houses, The Rose and Crown and The Hat and Feather. Over the years the two sets of brothers had become great family friends, now they all served the town in committee. Apparently much council business was discussed in a Lee pub prior to a council meeting, all four men agreeing as to how things would be discussed and agreed beforehand. Given the integrity of these men, I personally could see little wrong with this, but it was said that the Lees and the Wildgooses governed the town. What is likely is that the Lords Egerton of Tatton Park who owned a great deal of property within the town, and had known the Lee brothers for a number of years, so much so that they were allowed to exercise their horses within Tatton Park itself and were frequently invited to do so. In particular Alain de Egerton was quite friendly with Robert's brother George being his troop officer in the Tatton Troop of the Cheshire Yeomanry. George as his Troop Corporal, had ridden with him in the escort column that accompanied the Prince and Princess of Wales through Knutsford in 1887 on their way to stay overnight at Tatton Hall. With the Lords Egerton owning so much of Knutsford it was convenient for them to know what was being discussed and decided in the council chamber. The Lees acted as a conduit through which relevant information could be passed.

Robert's interest in the towns affairs did not stop there. There has been a May Day celebration in Knutsford since it was officially organised in 1864. It was probably celebrated in some ways centuries before. It became a much grander affair having a procession through the town and a May Queen who was crowned with great ceremony on the Knutsford Heath. It became even grander in 1887 with the aforementioned visit of their Royal Highnesses the Prince and Princess of Wales, later Edward VI and his Queen who ordained that from then on it should be dubbed "Royal". There are many May Days celebrated the length and breadth of the country but I do believe that Knutsford's May Day celebration is the only "Royal" one. Coincidently and perhaps appropriately in the context of this book that is, my uncle Geoffrey's daughter Victoria Lee was crowned Queen in 1965. Queen Victoria indeed!

With the event being so prestigious, it needed a grand committee to oversee the event. To serve on this committee was a privilege, an early photograph shows it to have been twenty-one strong, with seventeen of it's members being men. Many of the town's great and good vied for positions on it, including Robert and Fred Lee, who were duly elected, it is possible that George Lee also flirted with the committee, and it is no surprise to know that William Wildgoose was a treasurer.

The Lee brothers went on to serve on the Royal May Day Committee for nearly sixty years between them. Robert's input was considerable and his influence crucial. He had at some time been a co-founder member of the Mid-Cheshire Farmers Association, in those days there was a closer bond between the townspeople and the farming and rural community than there is today. The farmer and the townspeople knew each other well. Robert had little difficulty in persuading his farming friends to dress their splendid shire horses with brasses and plumes, adorn their farm carts with flowers and allow the committee to make these into nursery rhyme floats that carried the appropriately dressed children through the town.

Throughout this volume it will be assumed that the reader will become aware of the Lee family involvement with horses. Of course the horse in their day was almost the sole source of travel. In a country town like Knutsford, it was essential to own a horse if you were in business. The Lees though were more than just owners, they loved their horses. Fred Lee as May Day Committee man and Procession Marshall, rode his white horse at the head of the May Day parade for thirty years. The horse would also be instrumental in his tragic death in 1933. Robert took his interest in horses to a much higher plain. His love of the equine world was such that he became "Judge, Steward and Referee" and could be seen on all the county show rings where it was said that he was never happier, and was most conspicuous in his white bowler hat.

Family life at "Ralgarth" would have been a contented affair, Maggie of course had fled the family nest and was now living the high life with her wealthy husband, Jack Taylor. They produced a family of which I know only very little, grandchildren it would be assumed visited Knutsford and made Robert and his family ever happier for reasons which I will shortly explain. His two other daughters never married and lived out their lives as spinsters of the parish. When their mother Anne died in 1924 aged sixty-nine, the two genteel ladies chose to look after their father. They were then both in their mid forties, the marital boat having sailed away many years previously. They then took it upon themselves to look after their father for the rest of his life. Robert died in 1930 aged seventy-seven, he had a long and distinguished innings. Many, many tributes were paid to him, deservedly so, amongst those were that "he had a marked ability for local government", that he "spent a lifetime of active and enthusiastic participation in local affairs", and that "he always sought to maintain the privileges of the public", but the reader may have deduced that already. On his death the Knutsford town council stood for a minute's silence in his memory and later paid him due respect by naming a road after him, Lee Close which appropriately runs parallel along the side of "Ralgarth" and it's long garden. I called at "Ralgarth" some years ago, the Lee family having long left it. The then owners did not even know it's name was "Ralgarth", I did not stop to relate the stories of those that previously built and lived in it until 1959, almost sixty years. How soon are we forgotten.

Robert having been instrumental in the creation of the new Knutsford Cemetery chose not to be buried in it. He became possibly the last person to be buried in the Knutsford Parish Churchyard, and was laid to rest in the plot that he had reserved so many years previously, next to his father Tom Lee. This was rather poetic and apt, after all he had been alone at his father's side when he died at The Forresters Arms fifty-six years earlier. The bond that existed between father and the number one son was finally restored. Appropriately the epitaph on his tombstone reads "he rode straight", the obvious reference being to his character and his love of horses, it was of course in the Lee tradition for being somewhat flamboyant, it does make him sound like some latter day Wyatt Earp, perhaps his brothers were responsible. Their lives were to be lived more audaciously and controversially, perhaps less so with the hapless number two son, John. But before his story what of the lives of Robert's two home loving daughters.

The eldest Nelsie, we will refer at length later. It is Flo Flo, born Florence whose story captures the imagination. Born in a Tatton Street cottage in 1880, she was soon to move, along with her sister across the road to the Lord Eldon inn, where Maggie the youngest was born in 1883. Robert would certainly have ensured that their early education was a good one, and in all probability private. With the re-development of the Princess Street wine and spirit merchants business, the three girls were at last able to enjoy the spacious accommodation that provided, and with their fathers increasing wealth, enjoy further education opportunities, becoming even more refined. During the six year period of life in

Princess Street, the impressionable young Flo Flo met Arthur Harlow, a young man four years older than herself, dashing and handsome and one of two sons working for their father at his greengrocery, fish mongering and poulterer's business up the street at number 37 Princess Street. A word about the Harlow family is appropriate here. Their family grave lies not far from the Lee graves in the Parish Churchyard. In the grave are buried seven members of the family, five of whom are children all under the age of seven. You will be immediately aware that the longevity of life in the Harlow family was somewhat uncertain.

Flo Flo, a pretty girl by reputation, though a May Day picture of her in her early teens does not support this, she is supposed to have contracted a skin disease at some early stage of her life which necessitated her wearing a veil over part of her face. If she did and I'm sure that this was the case, I believe there was another reason for doing so, which will be referred to later. It is unclear just how much Arthur Harlow felt for Flo Flo. She was obviously very much in love with him. Arthur somehow comes over as somewhat of a "Jack the lad", a little unwilling to get involved and a fancy free character who loved life and was perhaps grateful to be living it considering the early deaths of his brothers and sisters. A relationship did exist and which certainly blossomed. Flo Flo having high hopes of eventual marriage, whether they were ever engaged to be married, it is not known.

In 1900, Flo Flo was twenty years old by then having moved to The Legh Arms, Arthur was twenty-four and now a part owner of the family business, a member of the de Tabley Masonic Lodge and most significantly a volunteer trooper with The Tatton Troop of the Cheshire Yeomanry. The year 1900 was an immense year in the affairs of the nation. The second Boer War in South Africa was continuing and it became necessary to raise a cavalry army to help suppress the Boer nation, this entailed recruiting horse mounted units from the Yeomanry detachments that existed in almost every Shire county. The whole then becoming known as 'The Imperial Cavalry Yeomanry'. The Cheshire Yeomanry provided 250 men in two detachments the 21st & 22nd companies, and the restless adventure seeking Arthur joined the 21st company commanded by Major Arthur Grosvenor, the later Duke of Westminster. The adoring Flo Flo was left weeping and wondering. After a year and a half soldiering, catching and surviving dreaded enteritus, and a skirmish in which a patrol of four horsemen including Arthur, and commanded by Lt Richard Grosvenor, no relation to the future Duke, was surprised by 200 Boers but luckily out ran them to escape. He returned home in the June of 1901 as did Robert Lee's younger brother George who served as a sergeant in the same 22nd company. George may very well have kept watch over the young Arthur Harlow.

Arthur would have been welcomed home enthusiastically by his adoring boyhood sweetheart, the ever emotional Flo Flo and resumed his position as co-owner of the family business. Arthur appearing not to want to rush into marriage, enjoyed life to the full for the next six years. He worked hard, enjoying the hospitality of the Lee family in their fine new home 'Ralgarth' and maintained his connections with the local Cheshire Yeomanry. He had a fine voice and sang lustily at Yeomanry re-unions and concerts held at Lord Egerton's Knutsford Town Hall. By the age of thirty in 1906 there was still no indication of his willingness to marry the twenty-six year old Flo Flo. Perhaps there was an inner fear of his own vulnerability, always remembering his family's tendency to meet their maker at the tenderest of ages. Tragically this proved to be the case, the grim reaper did make his early call and that very year Arthur Harlow suddenly died, whether there was any early indication through illness I am unaware. I have not researched medical records or attempted to locate a death certificate. He survived conditions in South Africa which stronger men did not, surviving even the bout of the deadly enteritus. In all probability this infection further weakened an already suspect constitution and it may have been just a matter of time. Photographs do show Arthur as being slight in stature and far from robust, they do however indicate the gaiety and vibrancy of his character.

For some reason Arthur died in Timperley. Perhaps he was visiting family who lived there. A brother, being a clergyman, and a vicar of one of the churches in the Altrincham area, presided over the service in his own church and from there the funeral cortege moved to Knutsford, for burial at the new cemetery for which Robert Lee had had considerable influence over. It would also appear that the grief stricken Flo Flo, had a huge say in the funeral arrangements at this juncture. After a graveside service conducted by both the Reverend Harlow and the Vicar of Knutsford,

Arthur was laid to rest in possibly the most prominent position of all in what in 1906 was an almost empty cemetery. It is located in the centre of the very first row as the cemetery is entered. There is little doubt that Flo Flo was responsible for the creation of the memorial to her lost love, it would have been a testing work for a stonemason being heavily inscribed with words and quotations appropriate to her grief including a short inscription reading "Who holds you now – Not death but love". This beautiful tombstone is not raised high in the direction of heaven and is a full length horizontal grave, which is flat on the surface, which was highly suitable for an emotionally charged lady to prostrate herself on from time to time. It is almost as if Arthur had not been buried at all, but perhaps lies just inside the stone walls of his tomb and is thus just inches away. The grieving Flo Flo would also be able to picture the face of a young man in death, and not one who died in old age.

The tragedy was sufficient enough to affect Flo Flo for the rest of her life. She had no need to work for a living, being extremely well cared for by her father's wealth. Perhaps a job of work might have been what she needed to take her out of her mournful existence. Instead the family closed ranks around her, she became somewhat reclusive spending most of her time in the bosom of her loving family and the walls of 'Ralgarth'. She and her sister Nelsie cared later for their mother and father when they aged and after they died, Nelsie looked after her delicate sister. If and when Flo Flo did leave the sanctuary of home and visit the town, then this I believe is when she chose to wear a veil, it was further indication of permanent mourning for Arthur Harlow. I may add that this is mostly hearsay and an impression gained from conversation, it could have been quite different in that, the Lee girls, had wonderful opportunity to have led quite a sumptuous existence given their father's associations and activities. Surely their lifestyle and wealth would have attracted some speculative suitor, but no. After the death of their father in 1930 and for the next five years, Nelsie chose to look after her increasingly delicate sister, albeit with the help of house maids, one of whom proved to be of lesbian leanings. That however is a road that it would be better not to go down. Flo Flo died in 1945 aged sixty-five, and as was pre-ordained, was laid to rest next to her long lost love, Arthur, in their sad and beautiful tomb, Nelsie overseeing the funeral details.

The melodrama does not quite end here. In 1948 my sister, then aged eleven and with a little girl friend, accidentally arrived at 'Ralgarth's' door to deliver a parcel, mistakenly going to the correct house number but not the right road. The maid answering the door being of the town, recognised my sister, and took the liberty of ushering her in to show her to Nelsie as a relative. Now my sister was an extremely pretty girl who eventually was to become a leading fashion model. A characteristic of the Lee family was from time to time to produce an auburn haired member including Robert's brother George and my son Clive, so too was Flo Flo. More importantly at that moment in time stood my auburn haired sister with waist length hair tied in plaits and being in Nelsie's eyes a reincarnation of her beloved sister. My sister was in fact christened Jeannette Lee Howard, my mother, formerly Bessie Lee, was a fiercely proud and independently minded woman and apparently had chosen not to have contact with Robert Lee's wealthy family in case this was interpreted as currying favour, which was hardly gracious of her.

Shortly after my sister's accidental visit to 'Ralgarth', my mother, her brother Geoffrey Lee, my sister and myself, then a very surly fourteen year old were asked to take tea with Nelsie at 'Ralgarth', for a boy of fourteen this was a particularly boring exercise. After tea it suddenly became extremely interesting when we were taken to a door, which for some reason was locked. Nelsie with great solemnity ushered us all into a heavily scented room which transpired to be the room that Flo Flo had died in three years earlier. The room had not been used since then, and from that moment it had been closed off and become a shrine of sorts for the still grieving Nelsie to worship at. It had become something of a time capsule, nothing had changed from that sad day. Flo Flo's favourite colour had been mauve, a funeral colour if there ever was. Everything in the room was mauve, carpets, curtains, the walls, everything. Over a mauve bedspread was draped a mauve nightdress that she wore at the time of her death.

My memory of the accompanying Nelsie is dimmed by the great number of years that have passed since that day and I was never to see her again. Surly I may have been but in the corner of the mind of the over imaginative boy that I was, lingers the image of a dear old lady who was reminiscent of a mix between the old ladies portrayed in the

Boulting Brothers films of the time, and, Miss Haversham in Dicken's classic 'Great Expectations', the whole scenario having a Dickensian overtone. Imagination or not, what was very real were the mauve envelopes presented to us as we departed, this of course was Flo Flo's personal stationery, and in them as if it were a gift from the deceased Flo Flo herself, were amounts of money totalling several thousands of pounds, which amounted to a small fortune in the late 1940's.

Nelsie Lee died in 1959 aged eighty. She left a sizable will in favour of her youngest sister Maggie's family, who of course were particularly well placed, Maggie being the only one of Robert's three daughters to marry and have a family. This was a right and proper decision, Maggie's family would have brought great cheer over the years to 'Ralgarth's' sad walls. There had been no 'Great Expectations' of another windfall by my mother who still stubbornly refused to visit 'Ralgarth', more so after the 1948 visit, again in case this was seen as patronising and with a view to seeking further financial gain. Neither was my sister allowed to visit, a sympathetic and intelligent girl, she could have brought considerable pleasure into Nelsie's lonely life.

Nelsie Lee was buried with her beloved Flo Flo and Arthur Harlow in their beautiful monument to eternal love. A further inscription was added and reads: "Her Life was lived – for those she loved", the perfect epitaph. 'Ralgarth' was sold and stands today owned by families living their lives unaware of the melodramas that occurred within it's walls for over sixty years.

CHAPTER THREE

John Norbury Lee

No room at the Inns – earthenware shop apprentice – marriage and a Junior Partnership – Hannah and Harry born – an unwanted pregnancy – the business fails – a Silk Mill Street home – Knutsford station porter – Harry's tragic death – a lonely end to a sad life.

~

The fortunes of Robert's younger brother John, differed to such an extent as to verge on the ridiculous, seemingly always in the shadow of Robert in his climb to success and prosperity. John's career appears to have been one long slow decline into eventual obscurity. Robert's potential was obviously perceived in it's early stages. He was enthusiastically running errands for his father after school and on Saturdays and learning the business at the same time, all this from at least the age of twelve, and was apprenticed immediately he left Grammar school. John, just two years younger, also went to the King Street Grammar School, but was not as academically inclined, and early comparisons would have been made which would have affected his young confidence.

By the time John had left school, Tom Lee's Princess Street business had been trading for some dozen years or so. It would have begun to take shape and prosper a little, but not yet flourish. Father and son Robert were all that were needed to manage the business. There was no need or room for another pair of hands. He would have to forge a career outside the licensing and wine and spirit trade. We know that when his father died in 1874 and aged only fifty six, that Robert took up the reins in his twenty first year. It is likely that Tom Lee's brain tumour was not a sudden illness and therefore Robert may very well have been managing on his own, possibly even a year or two earlier, and when in his late teens. This surely would have been the time to bring John into the family business. No! For whatever reason be it a matter of economy or John's apparent lack of potential and known tardiness, Robert decided to persevere on his own, just like his father had done. It could also have been that he was a tad canny, realising that this might have meant partnership and subsequently shared profitability.

Since leaving school John had had to find other and quite different work in the town, and in so doing bring some additional income home which would help with his upkeep. Just around the corner from The Old Market Place was the King Street business premises of William Peers. He had been an earthenware dealer for some years, everything points to the fact that Peers was no high flying purveyor of the finer porcelain and china products from the nearby Staffordshire factories, but rather that he supplied basic ceramic products to the town. In 1869 the fourteen year old John was taken on board as an apprentice. William Peers was by then a man aged fifty-six and the business almost certainly beginning to reflect his advancing years and like him be tired, jaded and generally run down. Peers would have certainly needed a young pair of legs at this stage, whether he could have afforded an apprentice was another matter. He would most probably have been placed under considerable pressure to do so by Tom Lee due to Peers being a peripheral member of the Lee family circle since circa 1840, when he married Hannah Lee the daughter of Joseph Lee the Knutsford blacksmith and the uncle to Tom Lee and great uncle to his four boys. Sadly Hannah Peers had died in 1853 at the tender age of thirty-one and Peers had been on his own for sixteen years by the time he took young John on board the business, hence it's decline. In 1877 the then twenty-two year old John married Sarah Jane Littler, daughter of a deceased local blacksmith, and as ever with the Lee family, were married in Knutsford Parish Church. They were then able to make their home above the King Street earthenware shop, unfortunately they had to share it with the ageing William Peers. They would continue to do so for much of their lives, and it would certainly have been a long and trying experience, reducing what little opportunity there was for romance. For Peers himself, things could not have been better. He was sixty- four years old and had cared for himself however badly, for over twenty years, now there was a young woman in the house who could attend to his needs. As for John and Sarah what mattered most was that they had a roof over their heads. That same year Peers made John Lee a junior partner in the business in the fond hope that this would help restore the fortunes of the ailing shop. John had brought neither experience, wisdom or money with him, only energy and youth, it was not going to be enough to resurrect matters, he simply was not of entrepreneurial ilk and the business would continue to slide into eventual oblivion.

The small profits generated by the business were sufficient enough to keep John and Sarah in relative comfort but very very far from luxury, and they were happy enough with their lot. They were more than happy when they produced children, a girl Hannah being born in 1881 followed eight years later by a son Harry John in 1889. These relatively happy years ended in 1900 with the first of the family misfortunes when the then nineteen year old Hannah was made pregnant by one Charles Buckley, an itinerant local labourer, and a man ten years her senior. He had the decency however to marry her. The product of their liaison was a girl, loyally named after her mother, Hannah. Imagine the dent to the Lee family pomp and pride. John's brothers all being well established and respected by their fellow citizens for the roles they were then playing in the town's affairs. What a scandal this was for Robert Lee to endure. He above all was at the height of his local fame and was about to move into 'Ralgarth'. Trivial this may sound but this was gossipy old Knutsford, a community that thrived on scandal and rumour. The brothers may well have distanced themselves even further from John and his family, as there is little evidence that they attended any of John's family celebrations. Even the marriage appears to have been snubbed.

This unfortunate event precipitated the final decline in John's low key commercial affairs. The earthenware business was now on it's last legs. William Peers now turning ninety years of age was still living with the family, imagine the depressing effect that this would have had on their lives, though long officially retired he would have been unable to stop meddling in their private lives and business matters, and John not strong enough mentally to deal with the situation. By 1902 all was over and the business simply ceased to trade, it is unlikely that it had a saleable value and if so for a pittance. John had not put money into the business and was unable to take any out, there was no grand home for John, Sarah and young Harry John to move into. The very year that Robert moved into 'Ralgarth', John Lee's little family moved into a rented property in Silk Mill Street, a street once of some commercial importance, but by this time becoming full of semi-derelict properties that were over-crowded and occupied by some of the town's poorest families. John was then aged only forty-six and very much in need of a job of work. Without a profession and due to his age, there were few opportunities for him. Sarah was unable to work, having to look after Harry John, their daughter Hannah had long fled the nest and was busy bringing up her own family.

He found work with the Cheshire Lines Railway Company at Knutsford Station as an 'outside station porter', a job which entailed meeting passengers as they arrived and carrying their bags and baggage to and from the platform. These were the golden days of the railway, and Knutsford Station a shining example of it's glory, a photograph shows a staff of twenty. Knutsford by then was home to numbers of very rich and important people, amongst whom would have been Robert Lee on his way to Manchester to attend Taylors Eagle Brewery board and shareholders meetings. Would there have been any sign of recognition between the two brothers? Would Robert have distanced himself and been too aloof to speak to his poorer brother? Would John have been too embarrassed, or proud and too pigheaded to acknowledge Robert as anything other than a passenger? Was this the final humiliation for him?

It was though not the end of John and Sarah Lee's misfortunes. Tragedy was about to strike again. At about the time of the demise of the earthenware business in 1902, their son young Harry John, then aged twelve had a fall in the Egerton Boys School playground, landing heavily on his head. According to the medical practitioners, the fall "weakened his heart" and caused him to suffer periodical epileptic fits from then on. On one hot August afternoon in 1906, Harry John then aged seventeen had been playing football in the street with other boys. Minutes after doing so, his mother Sarah "heard a noise" at the door and on opening it, found him lying on the doorstep, and with only time for him to say "Oh mamma" and die. The exertion of the football had been "too much for his heart to bear". At the inquest a Dr Fennel said that "he had been hovering between life and death" since his playground fall. Of all the sad events in the lives of the Lee families, I find this the most touching.

I am sure there would have been some sympathy from the other Lee families. However, Robert's family was still grieving over the death in the May of that same year, of Arthur Harlow and you will remember just how much he was mourned by the heart broken Flo Flo Lee, whose family would have been stretched to the limit in trying to sustain her in her grief. I doubt that there would have been much time to sympathise with John and Sarah. In 1915 Sarah died at the age of sixty. John lived on alone in retirement from the Cheshire Lines Railway Company. A neglected and half forgotten figure, he died in 1924 aged sixty-nine, the first of the four Lee brothers to die. All would follow him within ten years. He is buried in Knutsford Cemetery with Sarah and Harry John. The grave is simple and stands not a metre or two away and looking on over the grand and elaborate tomb and memorial to Robert's two daughters, the caring Nelsie, the love-lorn Flo Flo and her lost love Arthur Harlow. The two graves reflecting the huge disparity in the fortunes between the two families.

So died the least colourful of the four Lee brothers. John seemed to have merely been caught up in and carried along in the slow flowing stream of life. Possibly he was unaware that he was in it, though he only had to look around to see the success his three brothers were enjoying and the oft times sensational and controversial affairs that surrounded them. Robert of course did not seek notoriety, success and respectability were his gods. The two younger brothers, George and Fred would become the source of much local gossip and controversy, George in particular seemed determined to walk on the wilder side of life. John and his sad little family lived on the outside of the Lee family circle. Whether it was his brothers who chose not to include him in it, or whether John himself, stubborn, independently minded, pigheaded and possibly socially ill at ease, chose not to belong we will not know. The limelight that his brothers basked in, would have made him feel inadequate and introspective, possibly making his judgement all the more suspect and this contributing significantly to his luck, for he was an extremely unlucky, if somewhat hapless man.

CHAPTER FOUR

George Lee

The Rose and Crown owner at fifteen – horse dealing age fifteen – the young cavalry Yeoman – Uncle Joseph the Peterloo Veteran – Trumpet Major Smith of Balaclava fame – cheating in Ireland – a fight and a death – skeleton alley – The Lord Eldon licence – The Rose and Crown sold – property dealing – fire brigade superintendent – The Boer War Sergeant – action at last – the barefist pugilist – the Blackpool tower M.C. – May Day boxing booths – retirement and confession.

~

When his father Tom died in 1874 aged only fifty-six, George was only fifteen, Tom Lee had made every provision to ensure the future of his four boys. At least that is for three of them, John having chosen what he hoped was a successful career in the retail earthenware business, George having been willed The Rose and Crown inn in King Street in 1872 at the tender age of fifteen prior to leaving Knutsford Grammar School. Certainly a 17th century inn and in all probability much older, it had lain fallow since Tom purchased it in the early 1850's. He then let the inn as cottage accommodation. George would have to wait until his twenty-first birthday before he could take possession of it. In the meantime his eldest brother the astute Robert kept a wise eye on it, maybe renewing the lapsed licence and making some attempt to clean up what was then a near derelict property, one however with huge business potential. George though would never ever take possession, but never the less as he matured and with Robert's help he would ensure that it was well managed and profit making. It was his ace card and he would play it when he was good and ready. Meanwhile there were other more exciting fish to fry. On leaving school he would have to serve some sort of apprenticeship to tide him over until at least he was eighteen years old, then he could have dabbled with the management of the inn without getting in his manager's hair.

He found employment in the livery stables in Stable Street now Tatton Street, working for the stable keepers. Not a job one suspects that his father would have approved of. There he would have rubbed shoulders with the horse dealing fraternity not among the most salubrious of business people, with it's fair share of country rascals. Never the less George developed a yen for the trade and by the age of eighteen, was trading under his own name, the name of Lee would have helped him in his local dealings mainly through the growing reputation of Robert Lee. He was far from stupid and realised that there was good money to be made in the business. The horse was still the nation's principal mode of travel. In the cities, the trams were horse drawn, the railway system was still largely on the drawing board. Though the Cheshire Lines Company had linked Manchester to Chester and Knutsford was a major stop on the line, it was the horse and carriage that met the trains and took their many wealthy and important passengers to their homes in the area.

The great estates surrounding Knutsford, the numerous farms, the increasing number of fine houses being built, the town's business community, the local Yeomanry and most self respecting individuals all would need horses and would continue to do so until the end of the first Great World War in 1918, and George Lee was just the man to cater for their needs. The 1914-18 War in fact sounded the death knell of the horse trading business. Then, unless horses could be proved to be essential to their owners, they were requisitioned for military use. It took only two weeks in August 1914 to boost the army's horse establishment from 25,000 to 165,000 by this method, and by the end of the War this figure had risen to 468,000 with roughly the same number being purchased from the U.S.A. it is estimated that by the end of the War, four million horses had been killed. A dreadful figure. By then George Lee had long left the horse dealing business. However, back in 1881 he was trading very successfully. Then aged twenty one he had declined the option to take control of the management of The Rose and Crown and had appointed his own manager to do just that. Three years earlier in 1878 as an eighteen year old, he had joined the Tatton Troop of the Earl of Chester's Yeomanry, the 'A' squadron of which was based in Knutsford. As a small boy he would have been enthralled by tales related to him by his great uncle Joseph Lee, the Knutsford blacksmith who from 1810 had been both trooper and farrier with the Tatton Troop, and had been on parade with the Cheshire Yeomanry that infamous day in 1819 in St Peter's Fields, Manchester, when cavalry units were used to crush the peaceful rally being held in support of industrial reform. Fortunately the Cheshire Yeomanry were not used to charge the crowd estimated at 50,000. The dirty work being done by their comrades in the Manchester Yeomanry and even more so by a regular cavalry regiment. This incident of course going down in history as "The Peterloo Massacre" it is strange but true to relate that among the huge throng that day were members of my own family, the Howards, who lived and worked in Bow Lane on the extreme edge of St Peter's Fields.

George's early introduction to soldiery would have been further titivated as he grew up. What young man, particularly one like George with an aggressive and martial attitude, could fail to be excited by military events around the British Empire as they were reported in The Times or Guardian? The soldiers of Queen Victoria were variously in action on most continents during her reign, I did once read that they were so, in every year of it.

The Crimean War had ended in 1855 shortly before George was born. It was still very much in the memory of the nation in 1864, only ten years afterwards, particularly as Alfred Lord Tennyson's epic poem celebrating the Charge of the Light Brigade at Balaclava was on everyone's lips. It was in 1864 that a hero of that courageous cockup arrived in Knutsford in the shape of trumpet Major William Smith late of the 11th Prince Albert's own Hussars, nicknamed "the cherry pickers" because of their scarlet breeches. William Smith was credited with the sounding of the charge, but as all of the five cavalry regiments that charged the

Russian guns that fatal day had their own trumpet majors, including the 4th Queen's Own Hussars, who I served my national service with in Germany a hundred years later. William Smith however was the field trumpeter to the Brigade Commander, Lord Cardigan, and if anyone did so, it would have been him. Smith was one of the 198 survivors out of the 607 who made the charge, he had his horse shot from under him, and was injured when it fell on him, but still found time to bind up a thigh wound of one of his fellow soldiers and carry him to safety.

On arrival in Knutsford, after his discharge from the army at the retirement age of forty, and after having served for twenty-five years, he promptly joined the Cheshire Yeomanry and retained his rank of trumpet major with them. His first home in the town was in The Old Market Place, becoming a near neighbour to Tom Lee and his young family of boys at The Forresters Arms. He and Tom Lee were of a similar age, and would have exchanged many words over the bar counter, Smith having the old soldiers thirst for the hard stuff. George Lee was only a small boy at this time, but would have been made aware of the local fame of the Balaclava veteran through his father and his former Yeomanry uncle Joseph. All would serve to fire George's imagination, and surely influence his future life.

William Smith loomed large in Knutsford's affairs, becoming variously the town crier at the quarter sessions and manager of the Tatton Gentleman's Club which still exists, and of which my father was a member. Smith acted as Marshall in the 1867 May Day parade, and served it briefly as a committee member, he was however more well known as the star entertainer at local events, giving poetry recitals, including his own poem relating to the Charge of the Light Brigade. He also had a fine singing voice and was very much in demand. Imagine then what influence he would have had within the ranks of the Tabley and Tatton Troops of the Cheshire Yeomanry, especially at their social and mess gatherings when he would have been the life and soul of the party. The camaraderie would have been something to behold, such men breed esprit de corps.

With young George Lee horse trading with individual Yeomanry members, and all fired up with stories of Smith, he could hardly wait to join, and did so at the age of eighteen, in 1877 and possibly earlier than that. As a young Trooper, he would then serve with and be very much influenced by Smith. Unfortunately this was to last only two years. In the November of 1879, Smith, probably suffering from depression and drinking heavily at the Red Cow inn, deliberately took a heavy overdose of laudanum and went home to his wife in Love Lane where he died. The inquest was at the White Bear inn and returned a verdict of "death by apoplexy accelerated by laudanum taken by the deceased whilst of unsound mind". He is buried in the Parish Churchyard. Strangely coincidently my father much later in time held the licences of both the Red Cow and the White Bear inns, and I was born in the latter.

George's involvement with the Cheshire Yeomanry manifests itself on a painting showing Edward, the Prince of Wales, with Princess Alexandra, in an open carriage passing along King Street on their way to Tatton Hall to stay overnight with Lord Egerton prior to opening an industrial exhibition in Manchester the following day. The Prince and Princess are shown being escorted by the Tatton Troop of the Yeomanry, commanded by the honourable Alan de Egerton. The heir to the baronetcy and includes the then twenty-eight year old Corporal George Lee. To my delight the painting depicts the entourage passing directly in front of the two Lee owned inns, The Hat and Feather recently occupied by George's young brother Fred and The Rose and Crown owned by George himself, what a moment of triumph to be savoured by the two young Lee brothers. The year was 1887.

That same year was indeed a momentous one for George, but ended in a far from glorious manner. If the stories about his escapades were true, you will remember yours truly as a youthful eavesdropper listening to Lee stories exchanged between my Indian army major uncle Kenneth Lee and his cousin my mother Bessie Lee (Howard), many of which appertained to George. The events of 1887 are difficult to digest as the truth, but if you read on and absorb more of the events surrounding the man you may come to believe that what was supposed to have happened actually did.

The now tougher and more experienced horse dealing George invariably had to journey to the Irish Republic to purchase their very fine animals making the trip to Dublin and returning with small herds of horses, many of which he had orders for. He is reputed to not have honoured a deal struck with an Irish counterpart and left Ireland without paying. As you may imagine this did not exactly please the Irishman who was determined to obtain his just rewards for the transaction, and possibly some retribution at the same time. His determination was quickly apparent and within days he was hot on the trail of George, following him by the same Dublin – Liverpool route, eventually tracking him down to Knutsford. Luckily for George he did not have his private address. What he did discover were the horses that he had supplied George with in the stables of The Hat and Feather and which George had supplied his brother with. The hapless Fred being unaware that they had not been paid for. It is worth mentioning at this juncture that most inns of any consequence had stables in which not only horses were kept but also small carriages, gigs and traps and the like. This was because the inn keepers of the day performed the role that taxi cab owners and the car hire companies do today, you could hire your horse or horse and trap from them.

The Irishman now had the bit between his teeth, if you forgive the pun, and had tangible evidence of the attempted fraud. He demanded that Fred contact George and advise him where he was and that he expected to see him that evening in The Hat and Feather, also that he expected to be paid there and then. Fred duly sent the message to George who in fact was only a couple of hundred metres away at his home, The Forresters Arms in The Old Market Place. He was the last of the Lee young men to leave the inn and to his credit, along with his new wife Isabella, was looking after his ailing mother Margaret, who was soon to die and relieve him of that responsibility.

George sent a message back to his brother to say that he was busy but would come later. In the meantime would he keep the man happy, meaning keep plying him with drink. The man of course duly obliged with traditional Irish gusto. However in assuaging a terrible thirst he became impatient and aggressively tipsy, you could say that "his paddy was up". George in the meantime had cannily left his visit to the last possible moment, near midnight, by this time the Irishman was extremely and near riotously drunk.

In those late Victorian days, landlords obeyed the licensing laws to the letter. They decreed a closing time of 10.30pm and that public houses should be empty by 10.45pm. The local constabulary was out and about to ensure this. Knutsford had a tradition dating from Georgian days of being a quiet town in the late evenings. In those days, owners of late travelling horse drawn transport were encouraged to muffle the sound of their horses hooves by covering them with sacking, this to ensure the genteel residents of the town were not disturbed. So narrow, winding, King Street at near midnight, on that fatal night was ghostlike, with only George's footsteps to be heard as he made his way to The Hat and Feather.

He arrived of course to find as he anticipated, only Fred and the Irishman, the latter who apart from being exceptionally drunk, was by this time hopping mad with impatient frustration at the time he had been kept waiting. George of course was stone cold sober and ready for any eventuality. Angry words were addressed at him and were followed by punches to his head. This of course was a terrible mistake to make, the twenty-eight year old George was at the peak of fitness, an outdoor life trading horses coupled with his part time soldiering had honed him into a near perfect physical specimen. He was immensely strong and very tall. Add this to his red haired aggressive nature, reckless lack of fear and a more than handy pair of fists, he was the wrong man to throw a punch at. George of course losing his temper retaliated and struck back with considerable venom.

The outcome was disastrous, the force of his punch to the head was so great that due to probable additional factors, they were sufficient to kill the poor man. What then? The two Lee brothers were now alone with a dead man. What to do? You could not dial 999 for an ambulance in 1887. You could however call a doctor who would confirm that the man was dead. Then of course the police would become involved. Here though we had two young men at the early stages of their careers, belonging to a family becoming quite well respected in the town. If this came to light they would be ruined. It was a terrible accident. George didn't mean to kill the man, how could they explain the situation? It could look like murder. They deliberated at length. The twenty-four year old Fred was somewhat gauche and lacked the forcefulness of his elder brother and was easily influenced by the commanding George, who reasoned that as no one else had witnessed the incident, if they could dispose of the body successfully, they might get away with it, after all the man had arrived in Knutsford alone and unannounced. He was a stranger and a citizen of another country. Maybe he had not made his intentions known at home before leaving Ireland. George anyway would have known something of the Irishman's background, it was worth the gamble. They removed all means of identity, and came up with a reasonable plan for disposing the poor man's body. This was to bury it in the nearby moor. Wrapping it in a blanket they quickly and quietly crossed the narrow unlit King Street and entered the covered alley conveniently and directly opposite the front door of The Hat and Feather all a matter of just a few short metres and seconds in time, they were now totally invisible and then no more than a very dark 100 metres to the moor itself.

A word here to the stranger that has never visited our glorious little town. Today it is an ancient market town on two sides of a valley divided by a wide grassed area. A small Cheshire mere and a large marshy expanse through which a tiny stream "the Lilybrook", now narrowly confined, flows in a northerly direction into Tatton Mere in Tatton Park, and then on again where it assumes another identity. A thousand years or so ago all this good order did not exist and it was less than a hundred years ago that some order was obtained. The little Lilybrook stream rises in the hidden sanctuary moor and in ancient times flowed widely through the valley a few inches deep over a sand base creating a much bigger marsh, with the sand in places becoming quicksand, an extremely dangerous place, and which needed to be carefully forded if one was to cross from one part of the town to the other. Legend has it that circa 1017, King Canute, not wishing to get his feet wet again, led a Mercian army north to deal with a warring Northumbrian Prince and had to ford the Knutsford marshes to do so. The Danish name for Canute is Knut. Hence the ford which Canute crossed. Knutsford an obvious explanation to those of us who prefer a simple solution as to how the town obtained it's name. To the more academic amongst us the explanation causes a great gnashing of teeth.

Thus on that dark night in 1887, the two Lee brothers carried the body of the poor Irishman to the Knutsford marshes and deposited him in an area of deadly quicksand hoping that it would disappear forever. The manoeuvre would not have been an easy one in the dark but it must be remembered that these two young men were born and bred in The Old Market Place not a stone's throw from the marshes and as adventuresome boys growing up there, would have known every wet inch of it. The story goes on to relate that in the 1920s possibly during one of the many attempts by authorities and their engineers to reclaim the moor and make it a safer and dryer place, that a skeleton was found. The Lee brothers would have known this was their man, they were now in their 60th plus years, and there was nothing to remotely connect them with such a thing.

What would the forensic departments of the day make of the skeleton if it ever got as far as that? Nothing except establishing approximate age and sex, the cause of death would have been impossible to determine. These after all were the remains of a foreigner, it wasn't a local person, no one had significantly been reported missing in the town. It could have been a drunken vagrant wandering haplessly at night into the Knutsford marshes. Horse dealers had and may still have an air of the virtually permanent outdoors about them. They are nomadic, a visit to the delightful Appleby Horse Fair will confirm this. The Irish version is a little different to his British counterpart. He possibly had no family or at least an indifferent one, well used to their relative disappearing for weeks or months on end. They might eventually have mentioned it to the local Garda, who could have taken note but shrugged their shoulders possibly believing that the poor chap had fallen in a drunken stupor into any bog across Ireland.

Many stories about the Lee family which I overheard as a youth have proved not to be wholly true, subsequent research has revealed many inaccuracies, and certainly considerable embellishments have occurred over the years with the telling of the stories. However there has always been more than a grain of truth at the heart of each one. In many instances though, I have found the truth to be far more terrifying. I have never seen or heard a word regarding the skeleton on the moor which would have given the story credence. In my own mind set though, having delved so deeply into the Lee psyche, I believe the story to be true. Certainly I have never attempted to research records as to whether a skeleton was ever found, for me the story feels right, I am comfortable with it. The players involved, the locations, the situation, the timing, the necessary secrecy. Obviously it was George himself who eventually then in his seventies in the 1930's, related the story to his nephew Oliver Lee, one of his brother Fred's three sons and a former First World War Artilleryman who could relate to George's soldierly and martial attitude. It was then related to Oliver's eldest son Major Ken Lee from whom I overheard it. The narrow covered alley opposite the site of the old Hat and Feather, formally the Kings Coffee House and now La Belle Epoque restaurant, still stands menacingly there today, it has never been considered important enough to be given a name. Whenever Lee family members gathered to gossip and reminisce, they always refer to it as 'skeleton alley'. This whole episode seemed to unnerve George and had a salutary affect on his horse dealing career. He felt ill disposed to travel to Ireland to buy fine horses, thus disrupting the supply of the better animals, and this bringing about a serious loss of business. He was also not to know whether his accidental victim had family or friends who might have reported him missing, recognise his face and connect him. For the next two years he scaled down his business and turned his attention to the Lee's traditional line of work, the licensed public house trade. Two years later in 1889 he had ceased to horse trade and was totally involved in Lee family affairs.

This did not mean he was at last going to take control of his own inn The Rose and Crown. This he still preferred to keep managed and making him reasonable profits. The year 1889 was a key one in the affairs of the family, Margaret, mother to the Lee brothers died that year. George and his wife Isabella had stayed with her at The Forresters Arms looking after her in her failing years, and at the same ensuring that business was still conducted properly. Her death relieved George of all responsibility to the inn, it had after all been licensed in the Norbury name and there appeared to be no one in the family prepared to renew the licence. Little is then heard of The Forresters Arms and in all probability it ceased to trade at this time. Coincidently in that same year his older brother Robert had completed the redevelopment of his Princess Street wine and spirit business and moved into the apartments above it with his wife and three daughters, vacating the Lord Eldon inn. Neatly as you please George and Isabella Lee then moved in the moment that Robert left. This being as smooth an example of Lee clansmanship as one could wish for. The simplicity and arrogance of this move, I find to be breathtaking. This did not mean that George had become less active, and a domestic being, far from it. He was still a part time soldier with the Cheshire Yeomanry, and used his Lord Eldon licence to obtain occasional licences at the Town Hall for Yeomanry re-unions when the squadron could let it's back hair down in the tradition that trumpet major William Smith had initiated so many years earlier.

For the next nine years he played his part in the town's affairs serving for a while as a member of the Royal May Day Committee, becoming the third of the four Lee brothers to do so. In 1896 George at long last played his trump card and sold his only one great asset, The Rose and Crown inn to Groves and Whitnall, a Salford based brewery. By this time all ambitious brewers were extremely acquisitive competing with each other for the country's privately owned inns. In Cheshire there was an abundance of quite delightful and desirable hostelries and Groves and Whitnall were determined to obtain their share. Thus went the ancient Rose and Crown and also, amongst others, my eventual home, The White Bear. The Rose and Crown was to suffer later at the hands of Grove and Whitnalls's architects, who demolished the beautiful old pile, replacing it with the abject apology for the traditional Cheshire black and white building that we see today. Why is it that brewers have so recklessly destroyed so many lovely inns and systematically replaced them with tasteless reproductions? To answer my own question, it is for further volume of trade and greater profit. There are of course many exceptions to my generalisation. A notable one being my old home, The White Bear.

With his capital windfall, George bought local property acquiring houses in Manchester Road and Brook Street in the town, these he could then rent thus doing exactly what his brothers did, Robert who bought a row of houses at the southern end of King Street and Fred who had actually built a terrace of houses on his land behind The Hat and Feather and called it 'Church View'. George and Isabella moved into "Roselea", one of his own Manchester Road properties, which is in close proximity to the newly built Conservative Club of which he was one of the original members. He also served as a committee member of the Knutsford Freeholders Association. That same year 1898, on behalf of the Knutsford Council, he became superintendent of the Knutsford Fire Brigade and was paid the princely sum of £30 per annum for doing so. The fire engine at this time being housed just around the corner from "Roselea" and next to the quaintly named "Night Asylum" on the heathside. One must presume that the horses that pulled the engine were stabled on the other side of the fire station and not with the inmates of the "Night Asylum", though I imagine they would have kept the poor overnight residents a lot warmer. The fire bell was also located at the fire station which would have had to have been tolled by George after he had been aroused and advised of the location of the fire. There is a wonderfully sweet item listed in the minutes of the Knutsford Council to the effect that the fire bell sounded remarkably like the sound of the workhouse bell and when that was rung mayhem ensued, as firemen in various forms of undress needlessly turned up for duty, priceless! Pure Cranford, Mrs Gaskell would have relished the occasions.

It was at this time that other bells were ringing, but these were warning bells and were loud in George's head, at long last there was a whisper that the soldier in him might soon see some action. The one great love in his life was soldiering. George was now approaching forty years of age and coming to the end of his part time career with 'A' squadron of the Earl of Chester's Yeomanry which was now Knutsford based. From a very early age he had listened to tales told by his great uncle Joseph, the Yeomanry farrier of the Peterloo Massacre, and other attempts to contain industrial unrest. Then shortly after he had joined the Yeomanry at eighteen years of age, trumpet major William Smith strode large into his life, with his vivid stories of his part in the Charge of the Light Brigade at Balaclava and the Crimean War battles at Alma and Inkerman. All these yarns being related by Smith when he joined the Yeomanry and was then a comrade in arms with the young George.

Since Smith's death in 1879, George's imagination would have been further stimulated by the campaigns being fought world wide by "the Soldiers of the Queen". Wars were fought in Afghanistan (sound familiar?) in South Africa with the Zulu nation, in Egypt and in the Sudan where General Gordon was killed. Again in South Africa the Jamieson raid in 1886 had served to cause resentment with the Boer nation, this had simmered until 1899 when war eventually broke out.

By this time George would have been hopping with frustration at these events. However his prayers for action were answered.

In 1880/81 Great Britain had fought a near disastrous war against the Boers which was won at great loss of life and world prestige, but had not subjugated the Boers completely. They were now fighting a war known as the second Boer War, and which the British were trying with little success to contain. To do this it was necessary to increase the strength of the army. This was done by mobilising the nation's volunteer Yeomanry cavalry units and naming the whole as the Imperial Cavalry Yeomanry. Most Shire counties fielded their own Yeomanry regiment which, if possible, was made up of four squadrons of approximately sixty volunteers. In this instance they surrendered their county titles to become numbered detachments, they would however never lose their county identity which was, and is always, precious to a regiment. The Cheshire Yeomanry provided two companies each 125 men strong. These were the 21st company made up of men from the Chester area and the 22nd company made up of mid Cheshire men including many Knutsford Yeomen.

George was now approaching forty-one years of age which when reached would have made him ineligible for military service. He would have held his breath and crossed fingers and toes. By hook or by crook he was going to make the trip. However George's company the 22nd decided that they would take their own Cheshire horses with them, all 400 of them. This would have made the tough, experienced and resolute Sergeant George Lee's services indispensable. How could a man who had spent much of his working life as a horse dealer be left behind? He would have been one of the most valuable members of the company, and almost certainly have helped to procure many of the animals that made the trip. In retrospect the decision to take the Cheshire horses proved to be the wrong one. The poor animals were totally unsuited to the South African veldt and desert and sadly all would eventually die. The 21st Cheshire company did not take Cheshire horses, relying instead on the more sturdy local cape ponies which of course were more suited to the South African terrain. Did they know something that the 22nd company did not? If they did they did not pass the information on.

The two companies paraded outside Chester Town Hall for their honorary colonel the Earl of Harrington, and their colonel Piers Egerton Warburton, and in front of a huge ecstatic and patriotic crowd, prior to departure from Liverpool on the S.S. Lake Erie on the 30th of January 1900 and arriving in Capetown on 26th of February. They were one of the best equipped Yeomanry detachments to leave Britain. The cost of sending them was £5,000 which was raised by public subscription and which was over subscribed. It even allowed each man a pair of binoculars, a luxury indeed. The appeal for volunteers was also in excess of requirement. A strict medical examination was enforced as was the age limit of forty. The 21st company was commanded by Captain Lord Arthur Grosvenor the future 2nd Duke of Westminster, who put both his life and title on the line, he was not to be confused with his namesake Lt Richard Grosvenor whose escape with three Troopers including Trooper Arthur Harlow from a raiding Boer commando of some 200 men has already been mentioned. Harlow though a Knutsford man had been drafted into the 21st company to make up their strength. He was subsequently transferred to the 22nd where George Lee would keep a watchful eye open for his brother Robert's daughters fiancé.

It is fascinating to look at the peacetime occupations of the volunteers in the Chester company. It was comprised amongst others of 26 farmers, 13 clerks, 6 gentlemen which leads to the assumption that the rest of the company were not, in today's terms these might be described as mercenaries or adventurers, 5 grooms, 3 tailors, 2 land agents, 2 gamekeepers, 2 under graduates, 1 architect, 1 cotton broker, 1 valet, 1 auctioneer, 1 brewer, 1 park keeper and 1 jockey. It could be deduced in analysing the composition of the Chester company that Lord Arthur Grosvenor had been rather active in encouraging those involved in any way with his Eaton Hall Estate to volunteer. "Dragooned" might be a more appropriate word, it is interesting that the land agent, the architect and one gentleman were all members of the Parry family and all joined as lowly Troopers.

The major battles had been fought at considerable loss of lives to the British, in every sense the war had been won, but the Boers had not been conquered. Forming themselves into small highly mobile "commandos" they were now fighting a guerrilla war which was extremely difficult to defend against and deal with, hence the need to form the Imperial Cavalry Yeomanry from the county Yeomanry regiments and to meet like with like by having equally mobile units. The Boers though were on home ground and had a decided advantage, the Yeomanry operating eventually like rapid reaction police or fire brigades.

The two Cheshire companies joined a large column commanded by Colonel Thorneycroft which made a forced 200 mile march across the Karroo Desert which was part of a 500 mile march which lasted 21 days and in one day completed 46 miles, a standard days march being 36 miles. This was to deal with a large Boer column led by Christian De Wet, a widely respected Boer Commander, but a column forced to operate on the wide fringes of the British dominated central areas. The march proved disastrous for George's 22nd company, the Cheshire horses were much of the time short of water and feed with many dying and more having to be destroyed through physical exhaustion. The 22nd lost 280 of it's remaining 360 horses, 40 having died at sea in transit. Tough old George would have been a very sad man indeed at the loss of so many of his beloved horses.

With De Wet's threat thwarted, the Yeomanry then settled into a pattern of patrolling and protecting supply columns, ferrying food and ammunition to the sundry outposts and blockhouses that proliferated and that were part of the system needed to subdue the Boers. Even this extensive and highly concentrated system of small forts failed to suppress them. It was after all a defensive and protective system designed to keep an uneasy peace and protect British interests. The Boers knew that if they raised an army it would be defeated in the field as it eventually had been in the first part of the Boer War. In simplistic terms it was easier to challenge the British by forming local commando units drawn from the same farming communities. These could be quickly raised and easily dispersed back to their farms and homesteads and ready for another sortie, it brings a new meaning to today's phrase "working from home". Eventually this proved to be the Boer's Achilles heel, the British had by now devised a counter measure which would close down their modus operandi. This was to reduce their local supply bases and camps, which in reality were their homesteads. So began a systematic campaign of descending on each and every one of them, driving off their livestock, killing every animal that could not be driven, destroying grain by either burning it or throwing it into local streams and rivers. It did not stop there, the Boer families then without provisions were removed from their homes and concentrated in tented camps and hutments which were then heavily defended, thus were born the first "concentration camps" a system which our former perverted adversary Adolf Hitler and his Nazis brought a new more devastating and hideous meaning to in the 1939-1945 Second World War.

There are figures that indicate that 4000 horses, 9000 cattle and 35000 sheep were rounded up and that all pigs and poultry were slaughtered. The Yeomanry which included a huge percentage of men with rural background, farmers, estate workers and the like would have been largely adept in this role. What I am pretty sure of is that this was a considerably distasteful business that they were involved with. These men were not hardened professional soldiers, but volunteer citizens who had enlisted to fight their country's enemy. Many would have had a troubled conscience about the role they were being asked to play. This was not the kind of warfare they had anticipated, in particular their involvement with the uprooting of whole families of elderly men and women, wives and children would have been hard to stomach.

The system however proved to be hugely successful as it was bound to be. The roving Boer men now without homes and bases, food, ammunition and worst of all without parents, wives, sweethearts and children, soon capitulated and the second phase of the Boer War, the "commando" war, was over. The British did not cover themselves with glory by their methods, we were castigated world wide, but collective international bodies did not exist at the turn of the 19th century, no League of Nations, no European union, no action, the empire was mighty, Amen. At least no further blood was shed. The Yeomanry sailed home for England on S.S Tingagel Castle, arriving in Southampton on the 16th of June 1901 and were back home in Cheshire the following day. Less than half of the 250 officers and men that had left England one and a half years earlier came back. Only four officers and ninety-six other ranks returned home, of the 150 that did not, 17 were casualties, many dying of the deadly enteric fever. The greatest number, being single men, chose to remain in South Africa and seek their fortune there, no less that 61 men joined the police forces.

The family men and those with business interests returned home as local heroes. George to his wife and rented property business. Arthur Harlow to his family business in Princess Street and the welcoming arms of Flo Flo Lee. George's long suffering wife Isabella had occupied herself with the business in his absence, and with the Primrose League which she was actively involved with, representing the Knutsford branch on many occasions at the Annual General Conference in London. Unfortunately the marriage was a childless one and the very good reason that both were able to pursue their own interests.

George now aged forty-two was still a very fit and active man. Further toughened by his South African experience, he was also a man of leisure with much spare time on his hands and with income and funds to support a more casual lifestyle. He was a prosperous man and could have indulged himself. Not for George Lee though, he was a man of action. A countryman to the very core, who valued his fitness and freedom. The numerous country estates surrounding Knutsford afforded him the opportunity to involve himself with country pursuits. They were owned by men with long connections with the Cheshire Yeomanry, almost all having been officers with the regiment at some time. There had been Yeomanry troops at Arley, Tabley and Tatton. George and his brothers had long been allowed to ride in Tatton Park, George was also allowed to rough shoot and took time out there to visit gamekeeper Kingham and his two sons both of whom had served with him and the Yeomanry in South Africa. One of the Kingham boys also went on to become a superintendent of Cheshire police. He also loaded guns for the game shoots on the estates, including the Arley estate, the home of his former commanding officer Lt Col Piers Egerton-Warburton, an estate I was privileged to work for, for five happy years as custodian of Arley Hall. There was too, still some involvement with the Knutsford May Day committee and the Freeholders Association.

There was however a dark side to George Lee's character to be considered. The huge strength of the man needed an outlet, there had always been a violent streak in his nature, a bully lurked within him. The affair with the Irish horse dealer was a terrible thing to have happened, but he had put that behind him. What he was aware of was his ability to hurt with his fists and his need to do so. Fortunately for him, there existed not too far away, the very platform on which to perform his now favourite physical occupation or sport, blood sport if you prefer it. That of pugilism.

There was and still is, just a couple of miles out of Knutsford on a quiet back road leading to the neighbouring village of Mobberley, an inn called "The Chapel House", which then had a barn with an upstairs room in which were held bare fisted boxing matches. George became the leading local protagonist of this violent and bloody, and I am sure illegal black art, this due to the money that was exchanged in betting form. Here George could fulfil his need for ferocious physical action, his need to cruelly dominate an opponent, all with an apparent lack of fear and the ability to absorb punishment. He very soon gained a reputation which extended far beyond the Knutsford and county boundary.

In delving into George's life, I came across information that confirmed that somewhere between 1905 and 1910, and possibly after that, he was master of ceremonies at Blackpool Tower Ballroom. This for me was a totally startling revelation. My image of the rough, tough all action gung-ho George Lee was shattered. What possibly could a hell fire man like this be doing supervising the sedate dancing activities that Blackpool Tower Ballroom was famous for at that time. Then late one Sunday afternoon watching a BBC television programme called "The Great Antiques Chase" I discovered the answer. The programme involved two teams of two people, chasing up and down various parts of the country seeking out bargains. A further feature of the programme was to visit a noted local landmark and look into it's history. That afternoon the BBC was visiting Blackpool, Mecca to millions of working lads and lassies from the North of England and the Midlands and immortalised by cheerfully smutty postcards. The obvious venue of course was Blackpool Tower and it's ballroom. All then was revealed. At the end of the summer season, the ballroom was converted into a boxing arena and remained so until the spring. George in fact was the master of ceremonies in the boxing ring, in his element. Doling out justice according to the Marquess of Queensbury rules. Gladly stepping in between the exponents of the ignoble art of fisticuffs, possibly administering the odd cuff of the hand and not minding the odd spot of blood on his white shirt, revelling in the action and an atmosphere created by thousands of chaps baying for blood. This would make up for them taking his war away from him!

A further classic example of George's need to impose his physical presence was during the Knutsford Royal May Day festivities, these were and still are accompanied by a large travelling fun fair. A component part of which was the traditional tented boxing booth, outside of which a seedy looking promoter who touted the entertainment that could be obtained within the booth. Along side of him stood two equally seedy and impoverished older gentlemen clad in the brightest of silk boxing gowns, which soon proved to have been hiding their ageing physiques. These were introduced as "Gladiators". When eventually the booth was full the entertainment began. The audience was largely comprised of local wags and cynics who knew the type of fare that was going to be dished up to them, and as a young man I belonged to that particular variety. There was too, always a fair sprinkling of callow country lads, who with the Knutsford public houses open all day for May Day, were invariably much worse for drink.

The show began with a bout between the two "Gladiators" who when stripped of their silken finery, revealed themselves as being far from the finest physical specimens on earth. What followed was an exhibition of boxing which was of the slow foxtrot variety, in which the two men slapped feebly at each other with open gloves, apparently locked in some male bonding embrace. One must though remember that the poor chaps by late Saturday evening, had been performing this ritual for two days, and were all but dead on their feet. This could too, have been an energy conserving exercise for the second half of the programme. By this time the hoots of derision and cat calls of the "give him a kiss" variety would be reaching fever pitch. This was the moment for the promoter to silence the noise emanating from the discontented clientele. The winner of the exhibition bout had been declared. This usually was by a knockout which was no more than a gentle cuff to the cheek which had brought further derisory comments. The promoter then invited any member of the audience to step up into the ring and take on the listless "champion". This had the effect of silencing those members of the crowd who had been the most critical and who were not prepared to make an exhibition of themselves, particularly as they were dressed in their May Day best. They though, were not the targets. These were the rather drunken and foolish country lads who liquored up as they were, were full of Dutch courage, and really fancied their chances, usually they were quite strong young men, but who at that particular moment in time, were brain dead. The "Gladiators" on the other hand now came into their own. They had been stung by the uncomplimentary comments and verbal abuse aimed at them during the course of the evening, were seething with anger and anxious for revenge. Now they were Gladiators and the lads anxious to show their drunken courage were the Christians about to enter the arena. The promoter then selected his victim who was then given a thoroughly good hiding by someone who earlier had appeared to be a toothless has been, but who in fact, though well past his sell by date, had been a fairly useful professional in his day.

The boxing booth was nearly always located in the corner of the Knutsford Heath adjoining Manchester Road where George Lee's house 'Roselea' was situated. It would take him a mere minute to cross the road to watch the type of entertainment that was being provided. The humiliating treatment being handed out to unsuspecting Knutsford boys was a far cry from his idea of fair play. On one famous evening it all was far too much for him to bear, he managed somehow to convince the booth promoter that he was the fair game he was looking for. He should have been aware that this tall, lean man with the mean look, might present a few problems. Perhaps George play acted, and appeared drunk, perhaps it was his advancing years, whatever, what happened then was sheer murder. The upright George, with his long reach, hard hands and deadly intent proceeded to give the old pro a beating to remember. He was never invited into that ring again, it was escapades of this type that earned him the nickname "crackers" Lee.

In 1910 at the age of fifty-one, George was in full pomp, his high profile appointment with the famous Blackpool Tower coupled with the fact that it had not been too long before that he had returned as a local hero from the Boer War, established him as a character of some substance. In that same year he joined his younger brother Fred as joint Marshall at the head of the Royal May Day procession and milked the applause obtained by his new found fame. There is a photograph of the two mounted Lee brothers appearing round the corner of Adams Hill, like two Marshals in a western movie, arriving in town to settle some local unrest. High noon indeed. This golden period in George's life was to last only a further four years, events in Europe were gathering momentum and would lead to the 1914-1918 Great World War. Soon the young men who had packed the Tower ballroom to watch the boxing were called to serve their country, mostly as members of the ill fated "Pals" battalions. The boxing soon stopped and George was jobless. He returned home to fret at the action taking place in France and Belgium and his inability to play any part in it. By the end of the war he was sixty years old. He sold most of his rented property and began to live a relatively quiet existence. When his nephew Oliver returned from fighting an artillery mans war, he was delighted. Oliver was the middle son of the three boys that his younger brother Fred had spawned. Of the four Lee brothers only Fred had produced male family members, who would be comparatively long lived. We of course know that the unfortunate John had tragically lost his only son Harry when the boy was seventeen years old.

To George, Oliver Lee was manna from heaven, childless himself, Oliver was the son he had never had. He was twenty-six years old at the end of the war, having survived he was then able to regale the old Boer War veteran with stories about his experiences and views about the first great war. The two men became very close and it was to Oliver that he himself at last opened up and confided to him his part in the death of the poor Irish horse dealer. Oliver passed the story to his Indian army son, Major Ken Lee. The story then I was to overhear in my early youth when living at The White Bear inn.

Isabella Farmer Lee, that most patient and understanding of wives, died in the December of 1933, George Lee gave up the ghost at last only six months later in June 1934. They lie together in Knutsford Cemetery amongst a group of Lee graves, strangely enough almost next to that of former trooper and Boer war comrade in arms, Arthur Harlow and his sweetheart Flo Flo Lee. Knutsfordians of the day were supposed to have suggested that "he should be buried face downward so that he could dig his own way to hell" A saying which has given me much cause to reflect on, was he that bad? I doubt it. What would Mrs Gaskell who based some of her fictional characters on the real life ones of a Knutsford of genteel Georgian times, made of him had she been born some years later, and chosen then to write about Knutsfordian characters. Shock? Horror? George's stage was the rumbustious hurly burly of a growing late Victorian and Edwardian town. He would have been a subject that Charles Dickens would have been more interested in. He strode the Knutsford scene in his uncompromising and oft times violent manner. He was a man's man to the core, like him or loathe him, dare I say it?, but maybe there was considerably more backbone to him than many of his contemporaries. They don't make them like that any more. Did somebody whisper thankfully?

A final thought. The Knutsford Conservative Club was built on the corner of the Knutsford Heath at the turn of the 19th century, it is a huge and imposing edifice. Like most Knutsfordians of the day, George was a staunch Tory and one of the club's original members. In the General Election of 1997, the Knutsford constituency was contested, amongst others by the unpopular Conservative candidate Neil Hamilton and the well liked Martin Bell, the former War Correspondent, the "knight in shining armour" and the independent candidate. There was a much hyped televised confrontation on George's Heath, possibly because of this Martin Bell won the seat by a country mile. One of the largest Conservative majorities in Great Britain, that of tens of thousands, was overturned, it was a miraculous result. Let us imagine that George Lee had been buried face down and that it was possible for the election result to have been communicated to him by some supernatural medium. He would have then most certainly "turned over in his grave" and thus be happily then face up, looking at a starry sky which would have extended not just over the Knutsford Heath but also over the South African Veldt.

Tom Lee the ambitious and farsighted Stockport licensee who came to Knutsford in 1851 and bought the adjoining dilapidated Hat and Feather and Rose and Crown Inns.

The old Rose and Crown and Hat and Feather inn's purchased by Tom Lee circa 1850.

The historic Old Market Place where the Forrester's Arms was situated.
Disgracefully and sadly demolished after the Second World War.

Knutsford Racecourse circa 1870. A magnet for Tom Lee and others like him
who later in the day filled Knutsford's inns.

Tom Lee with his twelve year old son Robert photographed on a Saturday afternoon in 1865. Behind them and to the right of the picture can be seen the run down ale and porter licensed off sales premises belonging to The Rose and Crown which was to be the source of Robert's wealth after it's conversion to a wine and spirit merchant's premises. (Robert with Basket)

Robert Lee. The hugely successful wine merchant.

The sign of success. A Robert Lee stone jar.

The Peterloo Massacre 16th August 1819. The authors great, great, great uncle Joseph Lee, the Farrier to the Tatton Troop of the Cheshire Yeomanry was riding with the Regiment on this infamous occasion. The Cheshire Yeomanry were not drawn into the affray. The 15th Hussars, a regular Cavalry Regiment, supported by the Manchester Yeomanry were used to disperse the crowd of 50,000 peaceful citizens assembled in St Peter's Fields.

Florence "Flo Flo" Lee in May Day fancy dress circa 1894.

Returning Home on the "Tintagel Castle."

Left to right —Troopers Rigby, Taylor, J. K. Cooke, Knott, Geo. Cross, Foster, Harlow and Buchannan.

All of the 22nd except Taylor, who was of the 21st Co.

Arthur Harlow, third from right with pipe, returning from South Africa with Yeomanry comrades aboard the SS Tintagel Castle in 1901.

The romantically inscribed tombstone in Knutsford cemetery where are buried Arthur Harlow, his sweetheart Flo Flo Lee and her loving sister Nelsie.

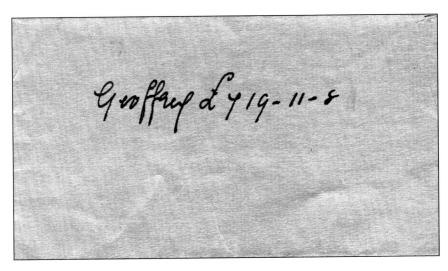

One of Flo Flo's mauve envelopes gifting monies to Bessie Lee's family in 1948. Not a lot of cash by today's standards but a tidy sum then and down to the last penny at that.

*Knutsford Railway Station staff, all 20 of them in 1906.
Outside Station porter, the impoverished John Lee aged 51,
is seen standing fifth from the left.*

THE PRINCE AND PRINCESS OF WALES AT KNUTSFORD, NEAR MANCHESTER.

*The Prince and Princess of Wales passing the Lee owned Rose and Crown
and Hat and Feather inns in 1887 on their way to stay with Lord Egerton
at Tatton Hall, prior to opening an exhibition in Manchester the following
day. Corporal George Lee, owner of the Rose and Crown is riding with the
Cheshire Yeomanry escort commanded by Lt the honourable Alan
de Egerton. Fred Lee owner of the Hat and Feather would be waving
from his inn's windows.*

Trumpet Major William Smith, hero and veteran of the Crimean War "Charge of the Light Brigade". A market place neighbour and customer of Tom Lee's at the Forrester's Arms, he had a huge influence on George Lee's Cheshire Yeomanry career.

Skeleton Alley. The Lee named alley opposite the long gone Hat and Feather now La Belle Epoque restaurant where George and Fred Lee carried the body of the allegedly murdered Irish horse dealer in 1886.

The Knutsford Fire Brigade circa 1900, for whom George Lee was Superintendent at a salary of £30 per annum, prior to him resigning to join the Imperial Cavalry Yeomanry in the Boer War.

The Cheshire Yeomanry now as the 21st and 22nd companies of the Imperial Yeomanry being addressed by their honorary colonel the Earl of Harrington outside Chester Town Hall in 1900 prior to embarking from Liverpool to South Africa

THE RIGHT HON. THE EARL OF HARRINGTON, Hon. Col.
of the Earl of Chester's Yeomanry Cavalry,

Addressing the two Companies in front of the Town Hall, Chester, on Monday, the
29th January, 1900, prior to their departure the following day for South Africa.

GROUP OF No. 1 SECTION OF THE 22ND COMPANY, TAKEN AT DRACHOENDER

No 1 section 22nd company Imperial Yeomanry at Drachoender, South Africa in 1900. Sergeant George Lee is seen standing 4th from right in the slouch hat.

Manchester Royal Infirmary in 1845 and where the 17 year old Sarah Jones was made pregnant by the in-house pharmacist in 1865.

The young Sarah Margaretta Jones. Nurse at Manchester Royal Infirmary.

A mature Dr James Livingstone. It is hoped photographed long after he seduced Sarah Jones

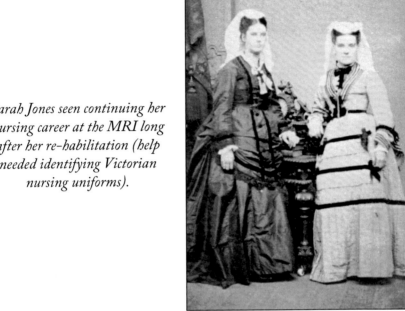

Sarah Jones seen continuing her nursing career at the MRI long after her re-habilitation (help needed identifying Victorian nursing uniforms).

Jeanette Livingstone Jones, Sarah and James Livingstone's daughter, sits prettily for the photographer prior to her marriage to Fred Lee in 1884.

THE KING'S COFFEE HOUSE. KNUTSFORD.

The Gaskell Memorial Tower and Kings Coffee House circa 1909. Built on the site of the Hat and Feather, sold by Fred Lee to Richard Harding Watt to enable him to erect the buildings. The formerly George Lee owned Rose and Crown is shown still in it's gloriously ancient condition.

Church View. The row of eight cottages was a present from Fred Lee to his wife Jeannette in 1886. They are built along the side of the former carriage way leading to The Hat and Feather stables. The Gaskell Memorial Tower 1907 can be seen in their place.

Fred Lee as marshal of the Royal May Day procession and was so for 32 years. His horse was witness to his sad end.

Fred Lee outside his inn The White Lion.

Knutsford prison. Built in 1817 and demolished in the 1930's. It could hold 700 inmates. It is now the site of Booths Supermarket.

John Henshall. A warder at Strangeways Prison, Manchester who married Sarah Jones. He obtained a position at Knutsford on learning of the good fortune enjoyed by Sarah's daughter. They lived in a warder's house in County Terrace.

The White Lion stable seen from the Courtyard Restaurant and where Fred Lee committed suicide in 1933.

The horse feed on the wall of the courtyard restaurant is possibly the one that penniless Fred Lee hung himself from.

Fred Lee and family outside The White Lion. Tom Lee, the eldest boy at the back, can be seen scowling, possibly at the prospect of being banished to America for un-named family crimes. He was only 15 years old when he was dispatched.

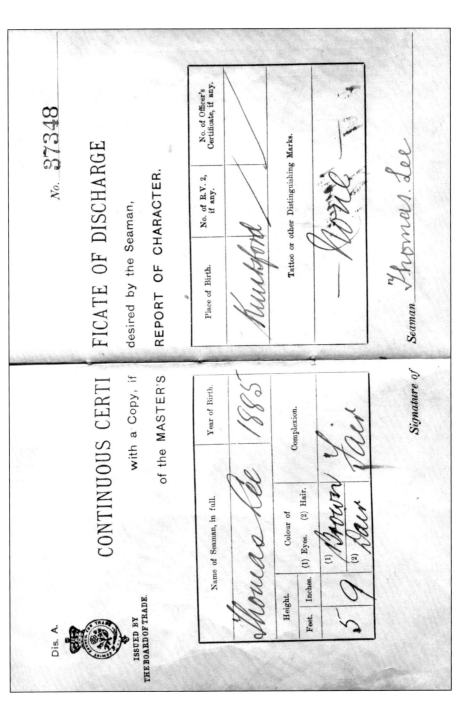

Young Tom Lee's seaman's certificate of discharge after working his passage to New York on the SS Oceanic which sailed from Liverpool in 1900.

The Eastgate, Chester, where in 1935 an inebriated Tom Lee emerged from Huxley's Vaults just behind the left hand archway and in blindly crossing the street contrived to headbutt the handle of a passing motor car and die of a fractured skull.

Oliver Lee who did much to restore the good name of Fred Lee's family, with his wife Dorothy bringing up their charismatic sons.

Maurice Victor Lee, the youngest son of Fred and Jeanette Lee, seen here as Royal May Day crown bearer in 1914.

The dinner suited Maurice Lee partying with friends. The foolishly ever generous Maurice would no doubt be picking up the bill. It will be observed that he is without a partner.

The dashing Major Kenneth Lee, Indian army. Seen somewhere in Italy 1943/44. At the time he was serving with a joint Anglo–American field intelligence unit.

Oliver Lee's three sons, from the left, Kenneth, Neville and Brian.

24 Berkeley Square, London. The exclusive offices housing Ken Lee's executive recruitment company.

CHAPTER FIVE

Fred Lee

The eleven year old inn owner – a long apprenticeship – The Hat and
Feather at last – a necessary wife – Sarah Margaretta Jones – Manchester
Royal Infirmary nurse – Dr James Livingstone – a pregnancy – Jeannette
Livingstone Jones – The Cross Keys servant girl – marriage, children
and prosperity – Church View built – Richard Harding Watt's offer to
buy – the move to The White Lion – the alcoholic Jeannette – fell to
her death – the inquest – Fred a long serving councillor and Royal May
Day committee man – a stable death by hanging – another inquest – the
IOU's – foolish generosity.

~

Born in 1863 Fred Lee was the youngest of Tom and Margaret Lee's
four sons, like his brothers he was born at The Forresters Arms in The
Old Market Place. He was only eleven years old when his father died
in 1874, his eldest brother Robert and his mother were then responsible
for his education and his upbringing. We know of course, that according
to his father's grand plan for the careers of his sons, he was earmarked
to take on the licence of The Hat and Feather when he reached the
age of seniority. Without a father from such an early age and being the
youngest child, he would have received much love and affection and was
probably considerably spoilt. I believe that this early period in his life

was to affect Fred's personality and judgement in his later years. He was to become a man with a much more amiable and genial nature which eventually led to an overall weakness in his character which seriously affected his judgement, which when translated to the management of his family affairs and the upbringing of his own three sons, brought unmitigated disaster and ultimately stark tragedy.

Like his brothers he was educated at the Grammar School just along King Street two minutes away from The Hat and Feather. On leaving school he was apprenticed to the ironmongery and blacksmithing business which was located to the rear of the King Street premises which is now the home of the Knutsford Heritage Centre. The smithing business would help to further his interest in horses. The reader must surely by now be aware of the part that the horse played in the lives of the Lee men. They were to play a final and fatal part in Fred's life.

He duly took the licence at The Hat and Feather in 1884 as pre-ordained. He was not, however a young novice, he had lived all his life in a public house, the business would have been the subject of family conversation. Robert by then had married and been living in and managing the Lord Eldon inn for several years. George, though owning The Rose and Crown but having it managed on his behalf, was helping his mother run The Forresters Arms. It was therefore more than likely that Fred was itching for the day when he could take over the licence from the man who had been managing the inn for him, he would have been actively involved helping the manager and performing the numerous tasks like the cellar work, bottling up, clearing empties, stocktaking et al. There is little doubt that he was ready and capable when the time came, in fact there is evidence that he already had capital at his disposal which would indicate that the inn was an efficient and profitable one and that an immediate good living was to be had from it.

However it was obvious that a man so young could not manage a public house business without the help of a wife who could cater for his domestic requirements and provide the loving support that was and is necessary in the variable and somewhat theatrically volatile atmosphere that is part and parcel of the licensing business. As for being strong in the face of difficult situations that were and still are an almost every day occurrence where alcohol is involved, it must be remembered that his much feared brother George, living a stone's throw away at The Forresters Arms, could place a protecting arm around his shoulders. This would prove the most effective deterrent.

Fred was to marry in 1884, the very same year that he obtained the licence for The Hat and Feather, one Jeannette Livingstone Jones, and it now becomes necessary to put an immediate but temporary hold on his story in order to meet the Jones family. Of considerable interest and importance was Fred's future mother-in-law, Sarah Margaretta Jones, mother to the said Jeannette. We are now referring here to my maternal great great grandmother and her daughter my great grandmother.

Sarah Margaretta Jones was born in the tiny hamlet of Bowling Bank, close to the North Walian town of Holt which sits prettily across the River Dee and opposite the Cheshire border village of Farndon sometime home to that loyal (?) Royal servant to the late Princess Diana, Paul Burrell, and of course to many much more distinguished citizens. Sarah's home was a small agricultural holding where the Jones's lived frugally by keeping and selling a few pigs and chickens. Photographs show Sarah as an extremely pretty young girl and one that was obviously not meant to continue in the rustic family business. She and her parents decided that like so many border welsh youngsters, that there were greater career opportunities and a brighter future to be had in the nearby great English cities of Chester, Manchester and Liverpool. Strangely enough this situation was to repeat itself again when my paternal great grandmother, Kathryn Williams moved to Manchester to meet and marry my grandfather Albert Howard, so many Cheshire families are well laced with Welsh ancestors.

Sarah chose nursing as a career which meant that if she was going to succeed in her profession, she needed the best in tuition. She certainly obtained that when she joined the staff of that great medical institution, Manchester Royal Infirmary, a Georgian building then dominating what is now Piccadilly Gardens in the centre of the City. Early prints show a wonderfully classical edifice surrounded by beautiful gardens and ornamental lakes. It was demolished in the latter part of the 19th century, nothing that has ever been attempted to beautify Manchester's Piccadilly has achieved that degree of classical elegance.

She would have joined the infirmary at the age of fifteen, a young raw welsh country girl abroad in that heaving mass of humanity. It was to be hoped that the job entailed living accommodation of some sort and that she did not have to find lodgings for herself. Assuming she did live within the confines of the infirmary, then this was to prove to be her undoing, for lurking in the corridors was the occasionally predatory Doctor, looking for a little dalliance with young trainee nurses. In Sarah's case she had the early misfortune to meet one such Doctor, a certain Dr James Livingstone, the in-house pharmacist. This particular dalliance could have proved fatal for both parties, for the then seventeen year old Sarah became pregnant in 1865 to the good Doctor, thus replicating the earlier instance when Mary Lee became pregnant, resulting in the birth of my great great grandfather Tom Lee. What going's on!

As with Mary Lee, the need to retain the job was paramount. Sarah loved nursing and was determined to continue with her profession. Mary was "in service" and the money which was needed at home was the over riding factor. Sarah of course was in a dreadful predicament. The pregnancy was now a considerable threat to her nursing career, if the truth were to be revealed, the ramifications for her and Livingstone were too terrible to contemplate. She would have been sent home in disgrace and have to bring up a child in an impoverished environment. At the infirmary, should the truth come to light, his future career and the excellent position he held was surely in jeopardy. Something had to be done to avert the impending disgrace and disaster. Should Sarah have an emotional breakdown and reveal all to the hospital authorities, then all was lost for both of them. It would be presumed that because of his medical knowledge that the pregnancy had been recognised at an early stage, and that it was not obvious. He surely with so much to lose, had to take the initiative, he did not need a near hysterical girl on his hands. The situation called for a calm and reasoned solution that would suit both parties, if that were at all possible. It would appear that she was a lot calmer in the face of this adversity and recognised the predicament that her seducer was in. She would have been aware of his vulnerability and might have conceivably played on it. She would surely have known that he was married, had a family and was living a respectable life in the Macclesfield area, and holding such a post in one of the greatest hospitals in the country, did not want his future life threatened by a distraught young girl, who would certainly have commanded a deal of sympathy from the hospital authorities. They would also not have welcomed any ensuing scandal that would have tarnished its reputation.

An arrangement had to be made to resolve the situation that would suit them both. That I believe was along the following lines. An abortion was far too risky and I do not believe was a consideration anyway, she wanted to keep the child. If the infant was to be born, then it would have to be born far far away from Manchester and in a safe, healthy and loving environment. The obvious place was back at home on the small holding at Bowling Bank on the rural Welsh border. A situation had to be invented that would necessitate temporary compassionate leave that would allow Sarah to return and take up her earlier position again. Let us say, unsettled domestic circumstances involving her mother's health which would require her to return home to look after both parents. Conveniently there were not other members of the family in Wales that could have performed this duty. Had it been an actual situation this is exactly what would have had to happen. Thus was born a baby girl who one day was to become my maternal great grandmother, whether Livingstone was ever consulted I know not, but she was christened Jeannette Livingstone Jones. Jeannette was then to be brought up tenderly over the following fifteen years by her grandparents in the peace and tranquillity of Bowling Bank.

Almost immediately after the birth, Sarah returned to Manchester to resume her nursing career. Again self important photographs would indicate that her career prospered. What then of her relationship with Dr Livingstone? Did they resume their affair? The answer I feel is certainly yes, but with considerably more discretion. Did he fulfil, under extremely difficult circumstances, any responsibilities towards his offspring? Did he ever even see his little girl? Possibly, but it is doubtful. This did not appear to perturb the Jones's who clung proudly and tenaciously to the Livingstone name. There is every suggestion that some financial arrangements were made by him towards Jeannette's upbringing, and for which the family were grateful which maybe was why they revered the Livingstone connection, and that he was not just the man who had disgraced and embarrassed them but the man who may have helped them in their difficult time. I do not suggest that he lavished money on them, but did whatever he could under the circumstances and with the Jones family being so impoverished, any financial assistance at all would have been most welcome. Though Sarah's affair with Doctor Livingstone may have continued secretly for some years, nothing was ever going to lead to any eventual coming together. By the early 1880's and with her now thirty plus years old, she met and formed a relationship with John Henshall, a prison officer at Strangeways Prison in Manchester, a grisly and formidable looking individual as per available photographs. This was to lead eventually to marriage. As for Livingstone, some score years older then Sarah, he would either have moved his career on elsewhere, retired or possibly died.

Jeannette Jones, carefully nurtured by loving grandparents, completed her education in a local school in Holt and by her early teens and school leaving age would have had to find work. Unfortunately, job options in such a small rural area were few and far between. If she was to find a decent job of work she would have to seek it further afield. She did what her mother Sarah had done so many years before, packed her bags and moved to one of the more affluent Cheshire towns. In this case to Knutsford, perhaps one of the fairest, which also meant that because of the rail link between Knutsford and Manchester, she would have easier access to her mother and vice versa. Holt becoming virtually in-accessible.

Some time ago I was spending a few idle minutes trawling through the microfilm records at the Knutsford Library, when I came across an entry in the 1881 census that showed one "Jeannette Livingstone" working as a sixteen year old servant in The Cross Keys inn on King Street, without doubt I had accidentally found Jeannette Livingstone Jones, with Jeannette conveniently ridding herself of the populous Jones title. Not much of a job one is forced to say and more in keeping with that of Mary Lee who was "in service" so many years previously. Now The Cross Keys was only next door to the old Hat and Feather in which the then eighteen year old Fred Lee was eagerly and assiduously applying himself to learning the tricks of the licensing trade. We have already established that The Hat and Feather was in more than good shape and appears to have been making decent profits. This would have largely been due to the efforts of the manager that the family had engaged, no doubt Robert Lee was instrumental in his appointment. The manager would have known that he had to perform well under the professional gaze of the whole family, not only Robert, but George Lee's presence would have been felt, running as he was between his own managed house, the next door Rose and Crown and The Forresters Arms where after his days work dealing in horse flesh, he assumed responsibility at night. Though the licence was in the Norbury name, George was no doubt in charge and taking care of his mother at the same time. The position that the manager was in, was not to be envied. He had to endure the burgeoning presence of the young and thrusting Fred, knowing that three years hence, he was due to be made redundant, this when the young man he was teaching the trade, took control.

Fred Lee was a tall well built upright man, and throughout his life was quite handsome. At eighteen years of age he was a good looking youth, with in local terms, a bright future in front of him. This would not have been lost on the quite beautiful sixteen year old Jeannette. They could hardly have avoided noticing each other and have become attracted to each other, so began a courtship that was to last three years until 1884, the year that Fred attained his seniority and was able at last to take over the licence and control of The Hat and Feather. To crown a triumphant year, he led nineteen year old Jeannette to the altar of Knutsford Parish Church, just a few metres around the corner where they were duly and happily married and ready to meet the rigours of the public house business. A year later in 1885 my grandfather Thomas Livingstone Lee was born and more than likely was highly cherished in those happy formative years, was this period in any way to have been instrumental for the deadly and destructive man that he was to become in later years? Certainly, as has been already established the family appeared to enjoy early prosperity, due to the previous excellent management of the inn.

In 1886 the twenty-three year old Fred as a gesture of his love for Jeannette, built a row of eight terraced cottages on the largish plot of land which he owned and which extended to Princess Street. These were built along the carriage approach to the stabling at the rear of the inn and had an unrestricted view of the Knutsford Parish Church. Even the fact that Baron Wilbraham Egerton built his Egerton School for

Boys and Girls in 1893 behind his magnificent Victorian Gothic Town Hall has failed to obscure the still extremely impressive view that I obtain from my cottage, and I enjoy even as I write these words. This particular cottage has always been retained by my family give or take the odd Norbury incumbent. Etched into the brickwork by the door are the initials J.L which is extremely appropriate, my sister Jeannette Lee Burdon, stays with me from time to time, what her emotions are on those occasions one can only guess. The initials F.L are stamped into the brickwork of number 8.

The whole terrace cost £1750 to build in 1886, less than £220 each. At the time of writing they are fetching around £200,000 each on the property market. If the family had continued to rent from 1886 until today and retained ownership they would have been extremely wealthy but that is not the way of the world, and the Lee family, though exceedingly ambitious were also equally cavalier in their dealings having owned quite nice slices of the Knutsford property cake, namely Robert owning rows of cottages in King Street and retail premises in Princess Street, George properties in Brook Street and Manchester Road and Fred in Church View, add that to the ownership of both The Rose and Crown and Hat and Feather inns. There is nothing left now that indicates their former wealth or presence in the town. Fred however was to prove to be the most wasteful of all. The obvious aspiring and well off young man of the late 1880's and early 1890's would eventually become the very worst possible manager of his financial affairs which would all end in a final and tragic disaster and one that to this day still beggars belief.

1887 was an eventful year for the young couple. The visit of the Prince and Princess of Wales to the town had engendered great excitement in the Lee owned inns. The two Lee brothers dressed their adjoining inns overall with flags and buntings and celebrated. Matters though took a serious and potentially ruinous downturn later in the year when George involved Fred in the dire episode resulting in the alleged death of the poor Irish horse dealer in the Hat and Feather. Subsequent years brought further wealth and happiness and another son, Oliver was born at the inn in 1892. All appeared to go swimmingly well until circa 1895 when considerable upheaval took place and a certain Richard Harding Watt made an offer to Fred Lee which he could not refuse, and that was to purchase the inn from him. Richard Watt in 1895 was formulating his plans for the introduction in the town of a number of Italianate buildings, which when he actually did so, caused considerable furore and controversy. Watt was to eventually demolish The Hat and Feather and by 1907 had built the Elizabeth Gaskell Memorial Tower and the first phase of the Kings Coffee House, later to house La Belle Epoque restaurant. The second phase of the project was completed in 1909. More of Richard Harding Watt in the second part of this book. This mainly due to my own Howard family involvement with this intriguing man.

Fred's financial affairs were still healthy, the inn was thriving, large amounts of capital were accruing from either the renting or selling of his Church View cottages. He could ask a high price of Richard Watt for a going business concern. Fred was still only thirty-two years old and at the summit of his career. He may have had sufficient capital to retire on, move into one of his own, or his brother's properties and then wisely invest his money. No! He and his brothers were still at the heart of the licensing business in the town and all three brothers engaged in the trade were flourishing. By being in the business their profile was being given the maximum amount of exposure, and this they enjoyed. Fred took another inn, he didn't move very far, merely along the street to The White Lion, a more ancient hostelry than The Hat and Feather and certainly a 17th century building. He did not purchase it, he never intended to, he and his family were going to continue to enjoy their prosperity boosted as it was by Watt's money. In any case The White Lion was not for sale. The licensing trade was in a state of transition. The brewers were buying the privately owned public houses, many of which were owned by the sundry lords of the various local manors, who in the Knutsford area were manifold. They owned much of the property in the town and possibly no longer wished to be associated with the sordid business of owning premises which sold a commodity which could result in anti-social behaviour and sustain the poverty levels which existed in the town. Fred's decision to sell may have been influenced by Robert's deal to sell his wine and spirit business to Taylors Eagle Brewery. That appeared to cause a chain reaction in the family for within a year, George Lee sold The Rose and Crown to the Salford Brewers, Groves and Whitnall. Fred's decision to move to The White Lion meant that he was then engaged as tenant/manager by the owners, Walker's Brewery of Warrington.

What the financial terms of his tenure involved cannot be established. He was probably paid for his management skills, which may have been profit related. What is for sure is that the family were extremely well off. They were however, and always had been, somewhat self indulgent. Now that self indulgency seemed to gather pace and with it went much more of the family discipline. Fred's easy going nature and love of his family was going to be badly abused by certain members. I am afraid this has to include Jeannette's mother, Sarah Margaretta Henshall as she then was, who having attended her daughter's wedding, had very soon established that her daughter had done particularly well for herself in the financial sense, and decided that there were benefits to be had if she could be nearer to her. This was achieved by her prison warder husband, John Henshall, applying for a similar position at the awesome, extremely large and impressive Knutsford prison. This he obtained and along with it, a very pretty terraced cottage owned by the prison authorities and utilised by married warders, the row stands just as prettily today and is known as County Terrace. This quite obviously meant that the couple were now living off one salary, with Sarah having or wishing to give up her nursing career and leave Manchester Royal Infirmary. There were however rich pickings to be had at The White Lion which would more than compensate any financial discomforts.

Photographs of Jeannette Livingstone Lee, at the time of her marriage to Fred in 1884 at the age of nineteen, show a girl of rare beauty, dark with classic and finely defined facial features which were quite obviously those of the Livingstone family. However, a family group photograph circa 1900 with Jeannette then in her mid thirties, shows a very different lady. She had thickened and coarsened which I suppose given a fifteen year advancement in time might be expected, however there is much evidence to hand of the good living that the family enjoyed and could well afford. There was though something else that was contributing to the deterioration in Jeannette's appearance, she had taken a strong liking to that so available and friendly social aide to the landlord and his wife, the demon drink.

By the year 1910 there was little doubt that it could be medically proven that she was an alcoholic. Her condition was such that it was constantly demanding much of the attention of their local G.P Dr Phelps Fennel working from his Princess Street surgery. She could have also had the benefit of the undivided attention of a loving mother with her vast nursing experience, though Sarah Henshall herself appeared to be rather enjoying her visits to The White Lion and availing herself of the many treats it had to offer. At lunchtime on Sunday the 30th of October of that year, according to official accounts "she felt faint and retired to bed", this should read "retired to bed drunk". She did not get up until Tuesday evening, which will give some indication as to her condition, then when on her unsteady way to the bathroom, she missed her footing at the top of the stairs and plunged headlong down the staircase, landing on her face, this caused a large wound to her nose from which she "bled profusely", sadly she died the following day. There is no indication as to whether she died in The White Lion or had been hospitalised. At the ensuing coroners court, the verdict supported by the damning medical evidence of Dr Fennell, was that her death was caused by alcoholism accelerated by shock and this had weakened her heart. She was forty-five years old. It is interesting to note that in giving evidence, Fred, though aware of his wife's addiction and hopefully doing everything in his power to prevent this, said that he had never actually seen her drinking. This was rather ludicrous, in a public house this is an impossibility. She must many times have, when being in the front of the house, accepted drinks from customers. The alcoholic however can be a furtive and cunning creature and develop squirrel like tendencies preferring to hide the substance in the most unlikely places. My mother who was also a former landlady, and who sadly took to drink in her advanced years, caused me and my family much anxiety. It is interesting that in his summary the coroner said, and I quote "when a woman takes to drink it is ten times worse than a man, because she would have it at all risks and hazards", all in all a very sad episode.

Though Jeannette's life was a comparatively brief one, it was a fulsome one. It would have been a busy life, which is the lot of a publican's wife, and she had brought up a family of boys in the hurly burly way of the licensing trade. There was of course though, no shortage of money, on the contrary, there was an abundance of the stuff, and she and Fred enjoyed an extravagant life style, which may have been the root cause of the family's later troubles. The money that was lavished on her boys, led to their being spoiled to their very death, which was almost the truth. With regard to Tom the eldest boy, who in 1900 at the age of fifteen, committed some terrible act which brought disgrace to the family, and which they dealt with in the most drastic manner, but which unfortunately, ultimately failed and he went on to cause further family mayhem, all of which will be referred to in later pages. In 1901 Jeannette produced another baby boy, Maurice Victor, who was only nine years old when his mother died. The lack of a good mother at a crucial stage in his development, proved to be the catalyst to his future life which became a sad, lonely and tragic one. Only the middle boy, Oliver, who was eighteen at the time of his mother's death was displaying any sign of independence of mind and character. Outside influences, totally opposite to The White Lion way of life, were later to inspire him to attempt more. Again the lives of this generation of male Lees I will refer to later. I hope you will find them as interesting as that of Fred and his brothers. Before departing from Jeannette's sad story and referring once more to the content of the coroners report, it was noted in the body of the report that Tom Lee, the eldest son, aged twenty-five was at the bar in The White Lion at the time of his mother's death, so what! you may think. Tom was married with two very young children at home with their mother. The reason I make this point will be related shortly.

Fred then aged forty-seven, had to get on with his life as best he could. This life was a fulsome one. He had been elected as the independent councillor for Knutsford's Nether Ward in 1901 and continued to serve on the council until 1931, a massive thirty years of dedicated involvement. He served it in many ways and as Vice Chairman on many occasions. He out served his older brother Robert by three years, if you add Fred's thirty years to Robert's twenty-seven, it adds up to a fifty-seven year period of dedicated service to the town. He was to continue to serve on the Knutsford Royal May Day committee for a similar number of years, again in tandem with his eldest brother Robert, George Lee joining them in committee for a shorter period. He also was a highly visible member of the May Day event, acting as Marshal at the head of the procession, he looked magnificent in black frock coat and top hat sat proudly on his white horse. This he continued to do for another twenty years making it thirty-two years in all and Knutsford's longest serving Royal May Day Marshal.

He also continued to serve on the committee of the Knutsford Freeholder's Association, a necessary body in this town and very active at this time. He was also the branch treasurer of the Unity of Odd Fellows which knowing what I am going to relate about Fred's financial affairs, will I am sure, bring a wry smile to the reader's face. Managing money was to prove not to be his forte. He was a member of the Knutsford Flying Club. No he had not yet obtained his wings or taken up flying model aeroplanes, anyway the Wright brothers had not long taken to the air. He flew pigeons from the loft he had built on his small holding, located at the bottom of Marble Arch, that much admired and beautiful corner of old Knutsford. On his allotment he grew flowers and vegetables for The White Lion dining table, invariably he chose to take a longer route home which would allow him to call at Argyle House near to the old Forresters Arms, where he could enjoy the company of the widow who resided there, and who he saw frequently after Jeannette's death.

Good horsemen that the Lee family were, they enjoyed riding in the then very private Tatton Park, this at the invitation of Baron Alan de Egerton with whom they shared both very strong Yeomanry and political associations. It is more than likely that council business affecting the large Egerton property ownership in the town, was passed on. The Lee's were also given the opportunity to shoot the game in the park, supervised by head gamekeeper Kingham whose two sons had served with George Lee in the Yeomanry in the South African Boer War. To maintain good and close links with the Egerton family, Fred would open The White Lion at a very early hour of the day and provide blue Cheshire cheese and porter to Tatton employees on their way to work in the park, The White Lion being the last real inn before the Knutsford gate. You will perceive that Fred lived a full, varied and active life for many years after his wife's death. However, as the years advanced and he grew older, he began to lose the plot. Events involving two of his sons, Tom and Maurice, had caused him considerable personal pain and much local shame in the community and within the town council, and which because of his age he had difficulty in coming to terms with. Oliver, his middle son, had married the very sweet Dorothy Jackson, and had produced three fine sons. However, misfortune had overtaken Oliver and his family, and they felt obliged to leave Knutsford, which was another personal blow. Much more significantly, his judgement with regard to money matters, suspect as it had been through the afore mentioned self indulgence of previous years, now was spiralling out of control with deadly and disastrous effect.

Which brings us to that ghastly morning of Wednesday the 27th of September 1933, the day Fred Lee chose to end his life. According to the evidence given at the ensuing coroner's inquest, Alice Robinson, the housekeeper who had worked at The White Lion for fifteen years, said Fred, who by then was rising at 9.30 in the mornings came into the kitchen at 8am and that "he was not fully dressed" what ever that means, refused a cup of tea, said that "he did not feel too well" and went into the rear courtyard and into the stable. Some quarter of an hour later she alerted a neighbour who found him dead and hanging by a rope attached to his neck and to the horse's hay feed attached to the inside wall of the stable. Fred's legs were touching the ground, he had merely let his body weight take the strain. Artificial respiration was unsuccessfully applied and he was taken down by a Mr Ditchfield who ironically was Fred's neighbourly local butcher. Some short time after his death, his safe was opened and was found to be full of IOU's. Fred, then seventy years old was in fact penniless, and depressed by this had committed suicide. The headline in the local paper called it "Tragedy of Generosity". None of us can help our nature, and it was Fred's nature to be foolishly generous.

How could Fred have ended his life in such a needless way, with all the advantages that he had at his disposal throughout it? Let us once again look at the wealth he had enjoyed through both good fortune, but mainly hard work. He had a flying start to his business career, inheriting the buoyant business that had been generated for his benefit at The Hat and Feather, comprising the sale of liquor on and off the premises, guest accommodation, and the proceeds from the hire of the horses and cabs kept in the stables. There is clear evidence of either a good relationship with a bank manager which enabled him to borrow the money with which to build the eight terraced houses on his land at the rear of The

Hat and Feather, though a gut feeling tells me that the money came from within the close Lee family circle. Bank Manager's do not have appeared to have had much influence on Fred's life, had he allowed one to have done so it might have prevented the ultimate disaster. The renting and future sales of the cottages would have provided either a steady income or large intermittent capital windfalls. The eventual sale of The Hat and Feather to Richard Watt involving a huge sum of money in 1895, further added to the family wealth and well being. There was talk of share dealings in which brother Robert, as a major shareholder with Taylors Eagle Brewery, advised Fred to invest in the company which was rapidly expanding. He would have benefited enormously when the Eagle Brewery eventually succumbed to the offer to buy by Marston's, the Burton-on-Trent brewers. This would happen some time after his arrival at The White Lion. He arrived there a comparatively wealthy man in his late thirties full of self confidence, with a small world at his feet. Little did he know that The White Lion and the events that took place there would quite literally be the death of him.

Let us examine or ponder over some of the events that contributed to the demise of this gentle and over generous yet foolish man, and indeed some of the people involved, sadly it must be said that some of these may have been members of the family. Too wealthy, too soon, the easy going Fred did not run a tight ship and the family crew would grow up lacking certain disciplines. Around the corner, his older, wiser brother Robert was working assiduously and methodically toward the development of his retail wine and spirit business. He was setting a blinding example of being able to work within strict financial confines, he knew where he was going but that it might take a little longer to get there. He was there also to offer his younger brother advice should he need it. The disciplines missing at The Hat and Feather were not replicated in Robert's homes, his girls were well educated, disciplined and well protected. In all probability, Robert's choice of wife had much to do with this. Fred's wife Jeannette was to succumb to the temptation to over luxuriate and eventually take to the bottle.

To revert to the theme of "too young, too much, too soon", everything in Fred's life had been arranged and planned for him. The Hat and Feather had been allocated to him from the outset. In his youth it had been developed, well managed and was ready for him to step into like a new set of clothes. He had a beautiful young wife, soon two young sons, a thriving business and property and all before he was thirty years old. It was all too easy and set the pattern for the indulgent lives that he and his family were to live from then on. The ultimate price that eventually was to be paid was to become too terrible to comprehend. Contributing to that end we must not forget the great number of new friends that he would acquire the moment he became a licensee, the "hangers on" that are the bane of the life of the landlord. Were they able to recognise this? The young and naive Lee family would fail to determine that among the back slapping, compliment paying clientele that they were acquiring in the early days at The Hat and Feather was the human baggage that they would take with them to The White Lion, and that would be partly responsible for his ultimately awful death in that inn's stable so many years later.

Let me not, in my cynicism, fail to acknowledge that life in those delightful formative years of marriage was enjoyed to the full. There was much love between man and wife. The two little boys, Tom and Oliver, were growing up and everything pointed to a happy and contented home. Then Fred succumbed to Richard Watt's pressure to sell the inn and move to The White Lion. Life then became much more complicated. The thirty year involvement with the Knutsford Council, the equally long service on the Royal May Day committee, the treasureship of the Odd Fellows branch, the Knutsford Flying Club, the Freeholders Association, the allotment, all this led to him taking his eye off the ball at home. There he appeared to take too many easy options, and either be unaware or ignore matters that could and would undermine him. It would also be appropriate to note that all his other interests and activities took him away from The White Lion for considerable lengths of time and while the cat was away, the mice most certainly came out to play.

A classic example of Fred's generosity, and there would literally be hundreds of them, was when his eldest son Tom was given a large sum of money with which to start life in the United States of America. Given the circumstances his father would hardly have expected him to make his fortune. More of this farce later. Tom duly returned to Knutsford, married and lived rent free in one of his father's Church View cottages for the rest of his mercifully short life. He was also allowed access to The White Lion bar where he developed his fatal taste for the hard stuff. My remark regarding his presence at the bar on the night that his mother was killed is evidence of this. He should have been at home with his family. The youngest son, Maurice Victor who, when after his mother died in 1910, and he, only nine years old, was lavished with such loving and generous attention, that it would eventually change his life, again with dire results.

Two smaller examples of Fred's kindness and affectionate nature were when his granddaughter Bessie, and Tom's eldest child, was gifted piano lessons and also dancing lessons held in the glorious ballroom at the famed Royal George Hotel, scene of many glittering county events through the centuries. An extremely pretty and vivacious little girl amongst all the Lee boys, mother was the apple of Fred's eye. To have met my mother Bessie was to realise the reason why she never became a ballerina, she was however to lead my father and many other people a right merry dance in the years to come.

What then of his immediate family's part in Fred's demise. His constant to-ing and fro-ing between the inn and his many other interests as mentioned, led to his absence from behind the bar, the very place where a landlord's presence is a necessity both in the management and hospitality sense. No wonder he never saw Jeannette imbibing to the epic proportion that she fatally did or son Tom consume the vast quantities of ale which were to lead to his dramatic end. Between them they would have made a huge hole in The White Lion's bar profits, it is also likely that quite a lot of drink was "on the house" to various favoured "hangers on". Many would be drinking from the inn's abundant trough. It is also probable that there were many fingers in the till, if there was a till at all. What fiscal amounts were not filched were asked for and given. Tom in a poorly paid job of work, was always hard up and had only to ask his father for money, for it to be given. The weakly young Maurice Victor had, after his mother's death, been cherished and spoilt with vast amounts of money lavished on him, which led to his inability to manage money. Sarah Margaretta Jones, known affectionately as "granny Henshall", was also hardly beyond reproach. An ever present at The White Lion, she and her prison warder husband enjoyed the inn's conviviality. She also obviously had the confidence of Fred and with it the opportunity to take from it. There was the famous occasion, in family terms that is, that on her death in 1917 in County Terrace, an obviously knowledgable member of the family went round to her house to recover the large amount of cash that certain members of the family knew she had stashed away in it, only to find that it had gone, and presumed taken by another knowing member of a growing family circle. This of course, begs the questions, how large an amount of money? And if 'large' where did she obtain it? It was obviously large enough to merit the attention of two sides of the family. She could have saved it from both her and her husband's earnings, but their joint income surely did not allow for this, anyway joint income it had not been since 1888 when she followed her daughter's good fortunes to Knutsford, a period of twenty nine years in which in theory, she had been dependent on John Henshall's salary. Anyway, what was wrong with banking a large amount of cash? Had she never heard of a bank? So how had she acquired it? Borrowed it from Fred in lieu of an IOU? Been given it by her daughter, and taken from the till or safe? Am I being hard on them and overly suspicious? Maybe, maybe not, but it is hard to get the faint smell of corruption out of my head.

What though of the IOU's? bearing the names of the not so good citizens of the town who had grown to know "en masse" that good old Fred Lee was a soft touch? I suspect these may have been largely small time clientele of The White Lion, with a fair number of bigger borrowers who he knew through council and May Day committee dealings, the supposedly more respectable borrowers. His brother George was a principle witness at the inquest and responding to the suggestions by the coroner that licensed premises had generally at that period been having a lean time, replied that his brother had told him that "things were very rough" and that "the house had not been doing as well as ought to do". Good heavens above, did Fred not realise that the moment he lent the money to the borrower he would not see that person again, because as with most borrowers of cash they largely never intend to repay it. These after all were mostly public house frequenting types, who would have then have spent the money in another of Knutsford's many licensed premises and would never for shame return to The White Lion, no wonder business was bad!

The house safe was large and apparently crammed with IOU's, it would have taken many hundreds of borrowers to cause him to take his own life, and out of these there would have had to have been a few quite substantial ones. Surely when the borrower of a larger amount of money came along, should Fred not, with whatever business acumen that he must have acquired during his working career, been entitled to ask that person to outline his reason for borrowing and his plans for repaying same. If it was supposedly for some business venture, was he not able to ask for an outline of the project and then ask for time to deliberate and then maybe advise on the matter, informing the borrower that this was his intention, that would certainly have put people off if it was their intention to be dishonest.

Perhaps I am elevating the level of borrowing on too higher a plain and that the volume of IOU's would suggest maximum loans of one hundred pounds, or fifty pounds, with the mass of them around the twenty, ten and five pound mark and that the approach was made in the inn's bar area.

What of Fred himself? Of course we can lay the blame for his suicide at the doors of the numerous scroungers and "hangers on" who bled him into oblivion, but how could a man so experienced in business, so involved in local politics and administration in many small forms, working on various committees with well intending fellow citizens of the town, apparently not comprehend that other men had their own agendas, and that they possibly did not match his own. The opportunists amongst them would have sized up Fred's affable, easygoing, generous and honest nature and considered him ripe and ready for picking. Why did the so trusting Fred not take a good hard look at the motivation and character of the people he dealt with and obviously on a frequent basis? How could his judgement be so bad and he so naïve? Every time he opened his safe, he would have been reminded of the situation that he was allowing himself to be dragged into. The names and dates on the IOU's should have warned him that he was heading for some form of financial difficulty, it was not to be. There appeared to be some awful need to be seen as a splendid fellow by all and sundry. As an amateur psycho-analyst I fail by many a country mile, a practising one would have a field day.

It is significant that George was not aware of Fred's financial plight, Fred had chosen not to ask his tough minded brother for advice, also we do not know for how long he had been lending money. His eldest brother the wise, successful and businesslike Robert, had died only three years previously, and it is likely that Fred had been lending money when he was alive. He could have asked Robert for advice about what to do to redress the situation. Pride though might have come into play, and Fred loathe to involve his brother in his affairs. What ever happened to the brotherly togetherness that had been the great strength of the Lee family for so many years? It had evaporated apparently with their advancing ages. Fred could also have sought the advice of his bank manager, the steady drain on his fiscal resources would surely have caught the attention of him, presuming of course that he banked all of his money and there is every indication that he did not do so, and that he kept large amounts of cash in The White Lion. Not only was this known to his greedy and wasteful family but to all and sundry in the town. The White Lion itself had become the friendly lending bank and charged neither interest on it's loans or sought repayment of same, you could not get better terms than that.

What of George Lee's feelings at the time? At the coroner's inquest when giving evidence, he went on to say that he had "seen his brother only the previous evening" and that "he (Fred) had seemed as bright as he had seen him for a long time" but that he "complained of a bad head", it is quite obvious that this cheerfulness indicated that Fred had come to terms with his plight, and made his mind up to end it all in the stable the following morning. He added that Fred had never ever "suggested that he was tired of his life" and that he had only recently learned that Fred had "financial trouble" but he, on opening his brothers safe and discovering the contents said "the IOU's I have come across are enough to break anyone's heart" and that he realised that "his brother was a man who could not refuse if anyone asked him to lend something", "he was too good and honest a man" but added that he now realised that his brother's suicide was "largely caused through him being a fool to himself by lending people money". George was seventy five years old at the time of seventy year old Fred's death. We know of George's violent nature, so did everybody in Knutsford at the time of the suicide. The borrower's knew him to be a shadow of his vicious old self, and that there was little to fear in the form of physical retribution from that direction. Had George been in any way younger, a little punishment might have been handed out in the form of a few good hidings from the former bare fist fighter, and where possible some small debts might have been recouped, if it only meant emptying a few trouser pockets.

The coroner in his summary said that "allied to bad trade his (Fred's) problems had been added to by his generous disposition in lending money to people, had he not done so he would have had no cause to worry about money matters". It was as bad as that. The total amount owing in the form of the IOU's would have, if they had been honoured, been sufficient to make Fred solvent once more. It beggars belief that this was the case, it was simply horrific. If the Knutsfordians involved were in any way sensitive and self examining, then their consciences should have provided them with a few sleepless nights. Many mouths would have remained firmly shut, and heads kept well beneath the parapet. These awful people actually contributed to my great grandfather's death.

Pursuing the subject of recovering debt in the form of IOU's, it begs the question as to what measures, if any did the family take to do this, if this was at all possible. The beneficiaries were the three sons, Tom, Oliver and Maurice Victor. My no good grandfather Tom was permanently short of money, and it would have been a serious blow to his funds when his father died, no subs, no free drink. My uncle, Maurice Victor, the youngest, was a spendthrift if there ever was. Both were spineless and would have little savvy about how to go about this, as well as not having the funds to afford a solicitor. Only Oliver had any real intelligence, but bringing up and educating his three boys and repaying a mortgage, meant that he too could little afford to get involved. What would have been the use of using the legal profession any way? They would have been chasing mostly small debts and people who had not the means of repaying what they owed. All in all it was a no win situation. They might have taken some initial legal advice, and been told of the hopelessness of the case, I have no knowledge of the legality of IOU's and strongly suspect that in a court of law, they would be a somewhat "iffish" issue.

To revert to the ineptitude of sons Tom and Maurice Victor, both, in Fred's lifetime, had caused him considerable grief, much heartache and total embarrassment. It was ongoing and rife at the time of his death. His patience with them could have been totally exhausted. Most responsible parents endeavour to make financial provision for their children if their resources permit this, Fred and Jeannette had misguidedly lavished much love and money on their boys in their formative years, now Fred was being repaid cruelly in his late and lonely life by their stupid antics. Could it be, that Fred was so disappointed and disgusted by their activities, that he never intended that they should be left any of his money? Knowing from experience that Tom would probably drink his way through it, and Maurice Victor spend it recklessly and foolishly, instead preferring to ill advisedly loan it to people who had convinced him that they needed his financial help. You will read later in detail exactly why he might have chosen not to leave his boys any money.

At the age of seventy Fred was the oldest licensee in the Knutsford area. Most men would have chosen to retire at the recognised age of sixty-five. Had he done so he might not have had to resort to such a tragic finale. There would have been ample funds with which to enjoy his last years. Robert and George had the foresight to retire and to invest in a house and home in which to bring up a family or in George's case, enjoy his wife's company at long last. Not so Fred. He obviously preferred a varied, involved, busy and active life to the very bitter end. He had the opportunity to move into one of the houses he owned in Church View, most likely the one I live in now, but he chose not to do so. Having lived a lot of my life in various public houses and restaurants, I can assure the reader that it is no way to lead a normal life, exhilarating from time to time maybe, but there is little privacy to be had and the negatives far outweigh the positives. My father Harry, an unwilling licensee if there ever was, never owned his own home and he lived and died in licensed premises. Most of my father's licensing contemporaries wisely chose to invest in a house. Poor, foolish, honest Fred Lee also died in his public house, unfortunately very publicly.

Between 1930 and 1935, Robert, George and Fred Lee had all died, John had passed anonymously away ten years earlier in 1924. The three major players in this production had played major parts in Knutsford's political and business affairs in an extremely visible, and you must agree, in an oft times controversial manner which stretched over almost fifty years during the reigns of Queen Victoria, Edward the seventh and George the fifth. However, there is little evidence of their presence in the town. As must be the case in all our lives, we all have possibly questionable family histories which are well worth delving into, perhaps I have been somewhat fortunate that the Lee family were just that and chose a high profile lifestyle which turned out to be vividly colourful. Why else would I want to talk and write about them?

The reader will remember that this book could be subtitled "only pubs and horses" with apologies to the television programme from which I borrow part of the title. The horse it will be observed, played a major part in the lives of Robert, George and Fred Lee. For Robert the horse was his passion, his hobby, a thing of great beauty, the subject of his expertise and knowledge, an animal to be admired, shown and judged. For George, it was a practical animal, to be considered for it's value on the horse market. It was his way of making an early living, preferring to be the judge of horseflesh as opposed to running a public house. The horse was also his chosen way of going to war, his cavalry mount, his charger. For Fred, the horse was his relaxation to enjoy, to ride in Tatton Park as the guest of the Egerton family. It was his symbolic badge of office as he rode as Marshal at the head of the Royal May Day procession for so many years. It was perhaps fitting, though somewhat ironic, that he chose to end his life in a stable, hung by the neck by a rope halter from his horses hay feed, with his last earthly companion, the old white horse that carried him about Knutsford for so many years, looking on.

I do not wish to end this chapter on too melancholy a note and prefer to do so with a smile, if a somewhat sad one, not though a laugh or even a horse laugh. George Lee's wife Isabella died in the December of the year that Fred took his life, among the many wreaths at her funeral was one, would you believe, from the "White Lion savings club" could you not just die?? Sorry! – the word "savings" is not one that one readily associates with The White Lion, they obviously had more in the kitty than poor Fred had in the bank. Fred could have asked them for a loan! Whose money were they saving anyway? Had the names of some of the club's members been on any of the IOU's in his safe? Were any of them in fact saving Fred's money? It's all food for funny thoughts! We must now turn our attention to the fortunes, or to be precise, the misfortunes of Fred's three young men, it gets worse.

CHAPTER SIX

Thomas Livingstone Lee

Fred's eldest son – not a bright boy – expelled from Grammar School
– exiled to America aged fifteen – The S.S. Oceanic – a large departing
sum of money – the New York good life – returns home with gifts for
all – low quality jobs – marries sweet Annie Duffy – the bonny Irish lass
– Bessie and Geoffrey born – the emerging drunken bully – a wartime
respite – the gallant refuse lorry driver – the Chester pub crawl – the
stumbling drunk – Tom's bad Good Friday – head versus door handle
– the handle of God?

~°~

So passed into posterity a generation of Lee men and with them their
spouses, two of the latter we know to have been ladies who contributed
much to the lives of their men folk, they being Robert's wife Margaret
and George's wife Isabella. Perhaps because of her later addiction to
alcohol, I do Fred's wife Jeannette an injustice. In the early days of their
marriage she lovingly brought up her little boys, only later did matters
go so badly wrong. For the next generation of Lee men were a vastly
different kettle of fish. They were of course the children of Fred and
Jeannette. Robert's children, the three girls, Nelsie, Flo Flo and Maggie
were all to prosper and live relatively sedate lives, perhaps in the case of
Nelsie and Flo Flo somewhat unfulfilled and eventually reclusive. The
poor unfortunate John and his wife Sarah had sadly lost their only boy

Harry when the lad was only seventeen. George's marriage we know was childless.

Fred's boys unfortunately were destined to give him the roughest of rides in life, with the notable exception of the middle child, Oliver. Tom, the eldest and Maurice Victor, the youngest, were to bring embarrassment and shame to the family. Perhaps circumstances were partly responsible for Maurice's behaviour, but Tom, the grandfather who I was never to remember, was a sad specimen if there ever was. He was an unmitigated disaster, born at The Hat and Feather in 1885 it was downhill all the way until his awful death in 1935. Being the first born boy to young, adoring and wealthy parents and living in the rarified atmosphere of a public house no doubt meant that he was spoilt to death from day one, all of which may have contributed to him becoming a stubborn, demanding and badly behaved youth and a veritable monster in later life. What would become abundantly clear very soon was that he was not particularly bright or intelligent. Education in the town had come on by leaps and bounds by the end of the 19th century. Baron Wilbraham Egerton had built the Egerton School for Boys and Girls which very many members of both Lee and Howard families were to later attend. A new Grammar school was built on Northwich Road in 1887, it was a boarding school principally but which Tom attended as a day boy, and which cost his father £5 per year for him to do so. It was to little avail, the lad was unfortunately not up to it. Not only was he academically bereft but it appears that he had become an extremely badly behaved youth and he left school under a very black cloud in 1900 at the age of fifteen, possibly expelled. So bad a lad was he that Fred deemed it absolutely necessary to dispatch him forthwith at that extremely early age, to the United States of America and for him from then on to make his own way in life as an American citizen. He was thus engaged by the master of the S.S Oceanic to work his passage as a very young seaman, and on the 13th November in 1900 that ship set sail from Liverpool for New York.

What in heaven's name had the boy done that made Fred take such dramatic and drastic action? To cast your teenage son adrift in the world at such a tender age was a monumentally severe course of punishment. Fred we know to have been of a kind, gentle and generous disposition and it would follow that he would be of a lenient nature, but no. What could have driven him to make a decision that was so foreign to his character? Let us try to guess. He was dispatched immediately he left Grammar school. Was he expelled for some act that was so awfully wrong that this was deemed necessary? If this was the case it must have been something truly terrible, shall we try theft, assault on a teacher, mutiny? I have subsequently heard of a fire that occurred there, could it be that Tom had tried to burn the school down? I realise that these are outrageous suggestions, but the latter gives fuel for thought!

It is quite obvious that whatever happened it was sufficient for Fred to take action. The good name of Lee in the town had been besmirched or was about to be, hence the severity of his decision. Alternatively, I could be a little kinder in my appraisal of what might have been the case and suggest that he had been a consistently naughty boy, both at home and at school, and that his scholastic record at the latter was abysmal. That both Fred and the headmaster felt that Tom would never ever be capable of attaining a good position in a respectable business as long as he lived, which would have been a pretty hard judgement to make given his tender age, and would certainly not merit depositing him on the Americans. Could not an attempt be made to start him as an apprentice in some local trade? His father had after all served his time with an Ironmongery and Smithing business. By this time many local youths were taking early morning trains in the Altrincham and Manchester direction to work in both heavy and light engineering companies in that area, what was wrong with that? Would he not even have been up to that? No, no, he had most certainly participated in some dreadful act at the Grammar School.

Fred, knowing him to be an ill-disciplined and rebellious numbskull, removed him to another continent bringing the ultimate meaning to the phrase "get out of my sight". He should have known though, and in all probability did, that Tom was a monster of his (Fred's) own making and apart from the obvious personality defects that he developed, he and his wife Jeannette had been responsible for Tom in his formative years, becoming a spoilt, demanding little brat. A family group photograph taken shortly before and because he was due to sail to America, shows Tom with a forbidding scowl on his face. However, Fred was going to be made to pay for his decision to deport his eldest and far from dearest son, and much sooner than he could ever have imagined. He did not dispatch Tom without the financial means to make some sort of start, money enough to buy food and lodgings for quite a decent period of time. Remembering that Fred then aged thirty-seven was a comparatively wealthy man, and well able to finance Tom until he found a job of work. Shall we guess at a figure that Fred could afford of somewhere between £500 and £1000 pounds, a lot of money at the turn of the century and enough to salve the generous Fred's conscience and avoid him being considered too hard, in judgemental Knutsford's eyes, in sending a fifteen year old boy abroad for good.

What does a spoilt, thick headed rebel of a son do in such circumstances? The answer is to behave in the manner in which he was brought up, namely to enjoy the opportunity to over indulge in comfort and near luxury. He promptly booked himself into the best hotel in New York, let us imagine this to be the celebrated "Algonquin" from whose luxurious apartments he departed on a daily basis for two whole weeks on a massive shopping spree and spending his evening's enjoying Broadway theatre life to the full. The fine shops on Madison Avenue and Fifth Avenue would have benefited from his indulgence, and Macey's department store's turnover for that fortnight would have shown a marked increase. That done, he promptly re-registered as a seaman on the same S.S Oceanic that brought him to New York and sailed home for England, arriving back in Liverpool on the 5th of December 1900 with a boatful of parcels containing glamorous gifts for the whole family, probably wishing everyone a very Happy Christmas at the same time. Maybe Tom was not gifted with brains but in this one instance in his whole life he showed great initiative and damned nerve, albeit in the most dreadfully wasteful way. If only he could have channelled this talent more usefully for the rest of his miserable existence, then all would have been well.

What could the family do about it? Absolutely nothing. Fred's finances, depleted as they were in funding Tom's New York adventure, would be further damaged by having to part fund him while he took on various jobs which were low paid and offered no future, including filling bottles at a local bottling plant. He would continue to be a parasite feeding off his father to the end of his life. As for Fred, it would have been sometime before he was able to scrape the egg off his face that Tom had deposited there. The inquisitive and traditionally gossipy Knutsfordians would have had a field day. Fred possibly had declared nobly, that he was sending his son to the New World for his own good, in the knowledge that those who had previously made the trip across the Atlantic, were forging new lives and making their fortunes, and that Tom would no doubt do well. Imagine the fun they had at Fred's expense when they learned that Tom had treated the whole episode as part Atlantic cruise and part luxury overseas holiday bringing presents for his father and family bought with his father's own money, my, my!

In 1905 Tom met one Annie Duffy which was good fortune for him and considerably unlucky for her, because he married her the following year. The Duffy's were Dubliners and a delightful Irish family who lived in Northwich. Her father Michael had emigrated to Cheshire and gained employment with Brunner Mond, later to become I.C.I at the turn of the century. Annie Duffy was one of two sisters, Margaret her other sister lived in Bowdon near Altrincham in Cheshire. Through Margaret's local contacts Annie was able to seek and gain employment in that area which was perhaps the wealthiest and most affluent in north Cheshire, being conveniently close to Manchester's booming economy. She was to work variously as a house servant, sometime housemaid, sometime kitchen maid, and sometime house cook. She was a happy, kind and humorous girl who would have discharged her duties with enthusiasm. I grew to know and love her as my nanna and she retained these qualities despite having been married to Tom Lee. That experience could have quite easily quashed all the Irish fun that was her nature, fortunately it did not, though she was saved ultimately by divine intervention.

Her first job of work was at "The Firs" in Bowdon and the home of Hans Richter and his family. Hans Richter is of course internationally remembered as the first conductor of the then newly formed Halle Orchestra, Manchester's great gift to the world of music. Then having met Tom, married him and moved to Knutsford, an equally wealthy area with ample work for a girl with good references. She would have been forced to seek work, due to the low level of pay that Tom was bringing home from his poorly paid jobs. The couple were then living in

Middle Walk in Knutsford's Crosstown. It would appear that Fred Lee was insisting his son was to make his own way in life at that time, give or take the odd loan. Fred was certainly not going to let the young couple occupy one of his Church View cottages. Annie's first employment in Knutsford was with the Hartley family, members of which were solicitors and partners with Sedgley Caldecutt and Company whose premises were in Marble Arch, off King Street, a cobbled and arched passageway of considerable charm and previously mentioned as leading to Fred Lee's allotment. 1907 brought a temporary cessation to Annie's working life for it was then that a baby girl was born to the young couple, christened Bessie, she was eventually to become my mother. Two years later a boy, Geoffrey was born.

It was possibly here that the first indication of the very worst side of Tom's nature was to become apparent. Having been born at an inn and having lived in one all of his young life, ale was always available, and with his indolent nature he was never very far from the beer pump, and could be seen hanging around the public bar most evenings, as was clearly evident the night of his mother's fatal accident in 1910. There is also sometimes in the Lee family genes, the tendency for the bully to emerge, as was the case with George Lee. It soon became apparent that it was to be the same with Tom, but this only after a large intake of alcohol.

It may very well have been that having had to leave the comfort of life at The White Lion and for the first time in his life confronted by the sudden responsibility of work, a house, a wife and two children, he could not cope. The fact that his father was being firm with him did not help. He was thus left to bring up a family on a labourers wage and this was clearly not good enough for him. Life was becoming too hard for him to bear, but as with many working men in those days, it did not keep them out of the pub. Tom would go out, drink heavily and return late, always in his cups and highly resentful of the way life was treating him. He would become ill tempered and extremely peevish and keen to vent his frustration and anger on somebody, that somebody of course was his gentle and good natured wife. Many people change their nature in drink, many temporarily released from their daily anxieties become relaxed and happy, some generous and outgoing, some morose and introspective, some unfortunately become violent and it was into this category that Tom fell.

He was seen during working and daylight hours, as an affable easy going young man if somewhat unintelligent. After a night's boozing, he was a demon, a drunken bullying monster and what was known to only his immediate neighbours, a despicable wife beater. He probably felt even more sorry for himself when his mother died in 1910 and he twenty-five years old. The two young children as they grew up were to witness his ill temper and were badly affected by it all. It was my mother Bessie who related these events to me. It was the advent of the first World War that brought a respite for Annie and her family, a War that was to bring so much death and tragedy to so many lives actually brought a short period of peace to Annie and the children, for Tom's country needed him and he was duly conscripted into the Army.

Fortunately for him, he did not join the infantry or any other fighting unit that would place him in any danger, and he did not serve in any combat zone. He joined the then Royal Army Service Corps known today as the Royal Corps of Transport and whose function then was mostly about the transportation of men and supplies. This proved to be a lucky move for him in a considerable way. The Army taught him to drive a motor vehicle and this one factor meant that after the war, and he returned to private life, had the means of making a living. Simply by having a driving licence he was able to elevate himself if only fractionally in the job availability sense as a driver. It is with true irony however that the motor vehicle would eventually bring about his destruction.

While he was away from home during the war, his father Fred, realising that with Tom gone, that his little family without their wage earning father, were in financial difficulties. With that he promptly moved them into 4 Church View, one of his terraced cottages. There they were able to live rent free, a gesture typical of the over generous Fred, and enjoy a peaceful war with the two children quickly becoming apples in the eye of their grandfather, particularly my mother who he adored and who received the benefits of the piano and dancing lessons.

This was too good to last, and with the end of the war, and the return of the unconquering hero, the drunken status quo was resumed.

A great difference had occurred with it, in that the age of the horse in transportation terms had come to an end, and the age of the motor vehicle was with us, and with it, Tom Lee as an experienced driver. His wealthy uncle Robert and his father were now well into their service as elected members of the Knutsford Urban District Council and Robert as Chairman for the "technical instruction committee" which decided the town would need one of the new refuse collecting vehicles. This would have been a far cry from today's highly sophisticated wagons, but at that time was "high tech". One was purchased and you will no doubt by now have guessed who was employed to drive it, non other than the gallant Tom. In the words of the song "my old man was a dustman", it most certainly was a better paid job than that of pre-war bottle filler. He was also asked to drive the new motorised fire engine, and who had also served the Knutsford Council, if only for a short time as superintendent of the Knutsford Fire Brigade? Yes, his uncle George. It all rather smacks of nepotism and the Lee's closing ranks around the more worthless members of the family.

On the lighter side of events at this period of time and with the two children now at school, Annie Lee was again able to take a part time position "in service" to a noted Knutsford family. There were very many distinguished ones living here at the time, shipping and cotton magnates, industrialists, manufacturers and brokers, and professional men of every description. Her excellent references, spirited good manners and experience enabled her to obtain work with the Miller family of "Millers Baking Powder" fame, who lived at the old Courthouse in Over Knutsford, this is still an ancient, historic and lovely black and white timbered building. Here she was employed as a house cook. In later years she used to reminisce about the mischievous antics of the young Miller twin boys, Tony and Richard, the latter eventually to be Sir Richard. Tony is fondly remembered in the town for his services to the local Conservative Party and the British Red Cross, also for his great charm and conviviality. Annie was to be either the victim of, or share in their schoolboy pranks. They would have appreciated her good humour, indeed Tony Miller remembered her when I spoke to him about her some years ago.

To revert back to the darker side of the story, back from his own quiet First World War service, and now secure in his improved job of work and with it more to spend if not a fortune, and with no rent to pay for his father's cottage, Tom returned to his nocturnal drinking habits and with it so did the drunken wife beatings. This is not to say that this was an every night occurrence. The two children were growing up, and fearful for their mother's safety, would have protested over their father's transgressions. In 1930 Bessie met and married Harry Howard the newly installed and very young landlord of the nearby White Bear inn. Strange is it not that the link with the licensing trade was maintained? My mother must have been a little apprehensive, at least she was spared the scenes of occasional domestic violence. I say occasional because Tom's son Geoffrey was still at home and growing into a strong and athletic youth. He, no doubt encouraged by his pugilistic uncle George, had taken up the game of boxing. This was practiced at the Y.M.C.A conveniently located on Manchester Road, just four doors away from George's house, allowing George to be heavily involved in it's running. Geoffrey, along with many other Knutsford boys, fought in local amateur competitions, all of whom were coached by an old sweat by the name of Charlie Lewis. Geoffrey was now physically able to protect his mother from his father's drunken bullying and did so on many occasions. It is interesting to note that when George Lee died, the former British Boxing Champion Jock McAvoy attended the funeral.

With the tragic suicide of his father in The White Lion stable in 1933, Tom developed a more morose and melancholy side to his nature. The fact that his father had died penniless would have hit him extremely hard, not only was there no White Lion bar to scrounge free drink from, there was no father to borrow money from. More to the point Fred had made sure there was no legacy for him to drink himself silly on. It is quite obvious that this was intended, not only had Fred run out of money, but he had run out of patience with his wayward son. Tom was thus extremely resentful and the final downward spiral began. The drinking bouts became even heavier if less violent, this due to Annie taking refuge with her daughter at The White Bear.

It all ended in a dramatic and tragic finale on Good Friday the 19th of April 1935 in Chester. Tom had decided to spend this, the most solemn of Christian celebratory days alone away from his wife who was no doubt grateful for his decision. He took the train from Knutsford to Chester Northgate Station and from the moment he arrived, proceeded to give the Chester public houses a fairly thorough examination of their stocks of ale. It was quite literally to become the pub crawl to end all pub crawls. His final port of call that evening was a public bar hewn out of the Roman wall, and virtually under the clock tower as you enter Foregate/Eastgate Street, known as Huxley's vaults. It is no longer a place of pilgrimage for the family, being long gone, and is now a building society, an institution that Tom would know very little about, he borrowed his money from you know where. As drunk then as the proverbial skunk that he was, he still knew the time of the last train home from Northgate Station. He then commenced his last unsteady journey which ended within seconds of his leaving Huxley's, and when his head came into contact with a passing motor vehicle, fracturing his skull and killing him. Some of the evidence given by witnesses to the event and given at the ensuing inquest I will borrow from, some I will take the liberty of re-interpreting.

George Dilly of Crane Street, Chester said that "he was walking along Foregate Street, when he saw a man hurrying across the road with his head down, a car came up and the front of it passed the man but the rear offside caught him and appeared to knock him off his feet". On being further questioned by a solicitor "appearing for the relatives", Mr Dilly then appears to alter his evidence to say that "the man appeared to be stumbling across the road, he could not say whether he was drunk, but he was not walking naturally". A Mr Wilfred Price of Saltbridge, Saltney said "Lee was thrown between the old tram tracks". The car driver, Mr William Davies of Ellesmere Port, says that "he saw the shadow of someone suddenly dive in front of his car, he applied both foot and handbrakes, swerved to the left and brought it to a standstill in it's own length". A Constable Davies said "the rear off side door handle of the vehicle was bent backwards". A Dr Thorn-McDonald, House Surgeon at Chester Royal Infirmary said that "Lee's skull was fractured and he had other minor injuries but death was due to a fractured skull".

From all this it can be deduced by this occasional cynic, that Tom was out of his mind with drink, his brain numbed by it, and was at the time what the Americans would call a "stumble bum" and virtually legless. The well used expression "blind drunk" also comes to mind. He lurched forward unseeingly in a falling head forward position. So much was he out of control that he failed to see William Davies's car, even when it had virtually passed him, and that he had head butted the moving door handle. You may imagine how low his head was when you consider how far a car door handle is to the floor. It was a very strange coming together of propelled head and speeding door handle. Tom certainly chose a spectacular way of ending his sad life, and a very good way of testing the strength and durability of car door handles.

How the news of Tom's death was received back home in Knutsford by the family one can only guess as being with mixed feelings. Did his death that evening prevent a further beating for his wife? If so that was to the good, in retrospect and from subsequent comments by family members in later years, it was apparent the he was not long mourned over. Tom was killed on Good Friday on his way to his last station, it was bad Friday for him but perhaps good for many long suffering others. He also died at the entrance to St Werburgh Street which is dominated at the top of the street by Chester's ancient and beautiful sandstone Cathedral, it was in full view of the Cathedral that he met his maker. Was this some form of divine intervention? If you will forgive my religious theme, but could it be said that such an ungodly man as Tom Lee in his last moments had received some form of blessing and forgiveness?

CHAPTER SEVEN

Maurice Victor Lee

Motherless aged nine – badly spoilt little boy – Royal May Day crown bearer – the young Draughtsman Engineer – victim to sexual predator – homosexuality – alone after his Father's death – goodbye Knutsford, hello the City life – wartime Birmingham – tried, convicted and imprisoned – the last return to Knutsford – death through malnutrition – like his Father, a penniless end.

~

The body count of Fred Lee's family by death from unnatural causes had risen to three, one suicide and two terrible deaths by accident brought about by alcohol abuse. Tom and his mother Jeannette had quite literally drank themselves to death. This left only two remaining members of Fred's immediate family alive, his sons Oliver and Maurice Victor. I am choosing to deal with another sad life, and that being the youngest son's, Maurice Victor's, preferring to keep that of Oliver to the last which would enable me to end the story of this generation of Lee men on a more cheerful and optimistic note.

Fred's trials and tribulations had not all been caused by his hard drinking and bullying son Tom, his youngest Maurice Victor was to cause him considerable embarrassment as he grew into manhood, which as you will discover, is a possible misnomer. Born in 1901 he was only nine years old when his mother met her death. He was the youngest son of a father who himself had been the youngest son, and he like his father was spoilt to death, only more so. The death of his mother meant that he was to be lavished with even greater attention and affection. A nanny was employed to provide him with the love that his now absent mother would have given him, her name was Sarah Hughes and she had a lot to answer for.

Maurice was thus adored to the point of ruination, he was idolised by this lady who rather over gilded the lily. Fred must have given his full blessing for her to do so, and being the much involved man about Knutsford that he was, was not aware that her methods were not going to provide the child with a sensible and balanced early upbringing, and that they might one day prove to be a contributory factor in his unfortunate later life. It is worth noting that Maurice was a late addition to the family, being born nine years after his brother Oliver and sixteen years after Tom the eldest. When his mother died, Oliver was eighteen, working for a living, and enjoying good company well away from matters central to The White Lion. Tom, then twenty-five, was married with children and living in his own home, little Maurice was thus the centre of attention and had the field to himself.

It was as if Sarah Hughes had suddenly had a child herself, for she began to treat the small boy, as if he were several years younger than his nine years, and very much arrested the normal growing up process. He was most often seen in either navy and white sailor suits or alternatively in red velvet ones. He could be seen frequently in a small carriage drawn by a little Shetland pony which was led by Sarah. In this manner he was paraded up and down Knutsford's main streets becoming a feature in the daily scene of the town. Most everybody was aware of the sad circumstances relating to his mother's death and he was fawned over and treated with the greatest sympathy by all and sundry, all of which was hardly helpful to the development of the little boy. In 1914 at the age of thirteen, he was chosen to be the crown bearer to the Royal May Queen at the annual Royal May Day festival. The crown bearer is the key boy player in the crowning ceremony and has much local exposure prior to, during and after the event, becoming a minor celebrity. All of this only served to draw attention to this attractive little boy. With his father and his uncle Robert on the Royal May Day Committee there was little chance of him not being elected crown bearer.

The huge amount of female attention and devotion that was heaped on Maurice appears to have had an adverse affect on his overall nature and bearing. At home he was of course, the absolute spoilt child, his ever over generous father continued to lavish large amounts of money on him and pandered to his very whim as he grew up. He became a rather limp and flaccid youth, with an extremely soft centre. A kind, gentle, loving, giving and imaginative soul, he was also weak and very vulnerable. He was the complete opposite to the outgoing macho Lee male type, and in no way fitted into the familiar family mould. His father chose a career for him as an engineering draughtsman, he had a fine hand, and was artistic and articulate. This meant that his work place was the drawing office, a male enclave if there ever was, and one that despite his drawing skills would have been foreign to him. He would easily have become the butt of laddish humour and worst, laddish perversity, and therein lay the probable early route to homosexuality. With his gentle effeminate manner, I believe he became the innocent victim of the homosexual predator, for a homosexual he became. I hope I am not offending any reader belonging to today's gay community, but I am talking the language of 1920s and 1930s Britain when this practice was despised and illegal and if practitioners were caught "en flagrante" it meant a court action and if convicted, imprisonment.

Maurice continued to live at The White Lion until 1933 and the death of his father. Now alone and at the age of thirty-two, he was forced to seek accommodation elsewhere. Now exposed to the vagaries of the wide world, he chose to take a rented apartment nearer his place of work in what is now called Greater Manchester, a far cry from the warmth and comfort of old Knutsford. There he developed his taste for shopping and the theatre. He was fond of the music of the shows of the day, particularly those of Ivor Novello and Noel Coward. He liked to wear black tie for dinner and to entertain his friends. There is a telling photograph of Maurice, dinner suited in a restaurant surrounded by three, rather smug plainly dressed men with their wives or sweethearts. There is no doubt who is going to pick up the bill, his generosity was abundant, despite the fact that his father's money was no longer available it did not prevent him spending his wages on lavish presents for his friends and family. He was particularly fond of antiques and my mother, his cousin, was the recipient of many superb antique gifts, shades this of his father's reckless generosity.

During the Second World War and still employed in the engineering trade, it was deemed necessary that his draughtsman's skills were needed nearer the heavy engineering heart of black country England, and he was moved to Aston in Birmingham. It was there that he was found in a public place with another male in an indecent sexual act, duly taken to court, tried, convicted and imprisoned for I do not know how long, as this act was committed long ago in dark war time England and fortunately for him well away from Knutsford's inquisitive gaze. Anyway, he was now little remembered in the town having left it some ten years earlier, returning from time to time to visit relatives, these being mainly his niece, my mother and her family, so the lid was kept quietly on his imprisonment and the reason for it. He returned to Greater Manchester, after the war, taking an apartment in Stretford.

His visits to his niece's various homes, The White Bear, Red Cow and Kings Coffee House, were fraught affairs. Poor, effete Maurice was a ditherer, and my mother known for her impatience and sharp tongue, would too easily be upset by his indecision, never the less despite his foolishness, she understood that the life he was living was an extremely sad, poor and lonely one. He would always join us for Christmas, and with quite a few children present for the holiday, party games were many and Maurice was always encouraged to take part. Without exception there was not one game played which he did not fail to bring to a chaotic end with his dithering, all of which used to bring howls of laughter from us all. It was not unkind laughter, we did not laugh at him but rather with him. He did not mind but was glad to have the warmth of the company of family around him.

On other occasions when visiting my mother and family, he would have his dinner with us prior to catching the last bus to Altrincham, and thence the train from there to Stretford. He would pick and scratch at his meal for hours, under the baleful glare of my watching mother who would incessantly remind him that if he did not hurry up he would miss his bus or train, he always missed it, despite my mother's fury at him for doing so. He was quite happy and content in the knowledge that at least for one more night he had good company and a warm bed. My father died from a brain tumour in 1970 and uncle Maurice came to stay with us for the funeral. We were then managers and tenants of the Kings Coffee House, known now as La Belle Epoque. This was the very site of the old Hat and Feather inn which his father had owned and where his two brothers were born. Within a few days of my father's death, Maurice collapsed and died, mostly through malnutrition, he had come to die in his old family home. We buried them both within the week, strangely many more members of the Lee family were to die on the site of the old inn. Tom's wife Annie died there of cancer, her son Geoffrey died there of a heart attack, and his sister, my mother Bessie, died peacefully there when in my care. It is so very strange, that all these Lee's came home to die on the site of the old inn, none of them actually lived there at the time of their deaths.

In an attempt to sort out Maurice's miniscule affairs, I took my mother to his Stretford flat. It was a bitterly sad moment for us both. A single bed in a small room, in a terraced house in a dingy street, a few books, some private papers. There was nothing for us to take away that we could remember him by. Most vividly I recollect an unpaid bill for a brown harris tweed overcoat from the 50 shilling tailors in Manchester, just like his father he had died penniless, just like his father his poverty was largely due to his reckless and foolish generosity.

CHAPTER EIGHT

Arthur Oliver Lee

Born in The Hat and Feather – aged eighteen when Jeannette was killed – courtship with Dorothy Jackson – the good Jackson influence – Dorothy the 1904 Royal May Queen – marriage in 1914 with War looming – enlists in the Army – from Veterinary Corps to Royal Artillery – cotton brokerage – three fine sons – the Post War bond between Uncle George and Oliver – recession – the move to Sale – George's confession – heart failure and death at only forty-seven.

~

As previously said, there is a much brighter story to be told about Oliver, the middle child among Fred's three sons, but even he failed to live long enough to enjoy the full fruits of life. Born in 1892 at the old Hat and Feather (Kings Coffee House/La Belle Epoque) he moved with the family to the ill fated White Lion circa 1895 when Richard Watt acquired the inn for the very purpose of building his Gaskell Memorial Tower and Kings Coffee House. I believe he was educated at Baron Wilbraham Egerton's new Church of England school, then winning a scholarship to Altrincham Grammar School. He was a much brighter and more intelligent youth than his two brothers, the dim witted Tom and the weakling Maurice. On leaving school he became apprenticed to a very fine Knutsford grocery business. Aged eighteen and living at home when his mother Jeannette had her fatal headlong fall down The White Lion staircase in 1910, he might just have been less traumatised by the event than the nine year old and very vulnerable Maurice.

During his teenage working years, he had the good fortune to meet Dorothy Jackson, one of several daughters born to Thomas Jackson a Knutsford solicitor. The Jackson girls were a breath of fresh air and were a happy, vivacious, outgoing, bevy of extremely pretty girls of which Dorothy was amongst the prettiest. She was pretty enough to have been chosen to be the Knutsford Royal May Queen in 1904. Their courtship enabled the Jackson family to exercise some influence on Oliver's crucial and developing young life. He was welcomed into a warm more vital and secure family environment than the rarified and volatile public life that existed in The White Lion. His brooding and moody elder brother Tom, though married was still an ever present at the pub's bar. Maurice was being ruinously brought up, and I suspect the atmosphere was somewhat too stifling for him in comparison to the well balanced Jackson home.

Oliver and Dorothy were married in 1914. Perhaps in the knowledge that with the increasing likelihood of a war with Germany, there was every chance that Oliver would be enlisted. I am unsure as to whether he volunteered or was later conscripted, but join the army he did. At first he served with the Royal Veterinary Corps, which belonging to a family with a huge interest in horse welfare and having lived in public houses all his life that stabled the animal and traded commercially in them, it would have suited him well. He was a very able rider, as of course were many men in those days. His uncle George would also have imparted his considerable equine knowledge at this time, perhaps enviously watching his young nephew prepare for a war that would, for a short time, be fought on horseback. A huge bond was forged between Oliver and George at this time, with Oliver playing the part of the son that George had never produced. There was of course plenty of work for the Royal Veterinary Corps in the early stages of the First World War. The army owed it's mobility to the horse, artillery guns were pulled by them, the cavalry were still mounted and the infantry still had to march. There was a desperate need for more horses, and what the army could not purchase, they requisitioned. Even the man in the street had to prove his need for his horse, if he could not, it was taken from him and he recompensed.

As the war progressed, in came mechanisation, and with it motorised transport, giving employment to his Royal Army Service Corps brother Tom. The Veterinary Corps was then able to release many of it's men to the fighting arms of the army, and Oliver was transferred to the Royal Artillery and served with a field gun regiment through to the end of the war, and beyond it when his unit stayed on in Germany as part of the British army of occupation of the Rhine.

After demobilisation he returned to Knutsford and his patient and loving wife Dorothy. At some stage he began work in the cotton industry, it is said brokering in that commodity. The cotton trade was flourishing once more, Knutsford being adjacent to the cotton capitals of Liverpool and Manchester, was home to many families whose livelihoods depended on the business. For a time Oliver prospered, buying and living in smart newer houses to the south west of the town in Cranford Avenue and St John's Avenue. In those houses he and Dorothy produced three fine sons, Kenneth, Neville and Brian, whose lives I will touch on shortly.

It is appropriate at this moment to refer again to the close relationship that existed between Oliver and his uncle George. The bond that had been forged between the two men prior to the First World War had been further strengthened during and after it. When Oliver finally dispensed with his battledress, he became the apple of George's eye. The antics of his other two nephews would hardly have impressed George, in his eyes Tom was a burgeoning wife beater, and drunkard, and young Maurice a spoilt and effeminate child, neither of them displaying any of the manly traits that he deemed vital.

Oliver was now an old soldier, so to speak, and able to relate his stories of what service life was like on the front lines of Belgium and France. George would have been mightily impressed with his tales of modern soldiering and warfare. The conversations that ensued would have been worth a king's ransom to him. He was now well into his sixties and the Boer War twenty years or so in the distant past. He was now obtaining military updating at first hand. It was during these conversations that George, determined not to be outdone on matters of war, regaled Oliver with his stories concerning his adventures with the Cheshire Yeomanry in the South African Boer War. More to the point he began to unburden himself about his much earlier life in Knutsford, as a horse trader, young Yeomanry trooper, licensee, committee man, fire brigade superintendent, pugilist, master of boxing ring ceremony et al. It was then that he at last revealed his part in the ghastly story of his brush with the unfortunate Irish horse dealer, and the poor man's subsequent manslaughter or murder, (which ever way you view it), in skeleton alley and the disposal of the body in the Knutsford Moor's quicksand. Oliver became the conduit for George's stories and these were relayed in turn to the next generation of Lee men. Mostly they were repeated by Oliver's eldest son Kenneth, who no doubt, being the wonderful story teller he was, was perhaps guilty of certain embellishments, if indeed these were necessary. The other two sons, Neville and Brian certainly chipped in and my mother Bessie also was aware via her Grandfather Fred, and added much that made sense of Fred Lee's tenure of The White Lion.

Oliver's career did eventually take a turn for the worst. The First World War was not only a catastrophe in terms of the tragically massive loss of human life and it's subsequent domestic and economic upheaval. The European economy was shattered, all of which eventually led to widespread recession and with it the massive unemployment of the time. Oliver's business was caught up in this and duly folded. The cotton industry had begun it's long decline. He was forced to seek employment where he could, and found work with Turner Newall, a giant company then manufacturing cement on the vast Trafford Park industrial estate in West Manchester. This unfortunately entailed moving his family away from his beloved Knutsford to Sale in Cheshire, where the cost of living was less excessive and he could be nearer to his new place of work. His three boys changed schools where necessary, Ken Lee being a pupil at Altrincham Grammar School and Brian at Sale Grammar School. Exceedingly well brought up by their parents, the boys would all do well in their careers. Oliver however did exercise a strict discipline, which the young Lee's, and Ken in particular found it hard to come to terms with. This fortunately failed to subdue their ebullient nature, their cheerfully optimistic and oft times flamboyant character shone through. The discipline though was deeply ingrained and would stand them in future good stead.

Misfortune and eventual tragedy however were still waiting in the wings. Ken Lee was finding his father's disciplinary attitude far too difficult to bear and was continuously at loggerheads with him. So much so he deemed it necessary to leave the family. He left not only that, but England itself, and sailed to India to join the Indian army. In 1935 with all the tales told by his great uncle George and his father of military daring, it was an absolute "must do" that Ken took up soldiering, and far afield at that. This was to affect Oliver to a considerable degree, coming as it did only one year after the death in 1934 of his great friend and mentor, his uncle George. This only one year after the dramatic death of his father in The White Lion stable in 1933, the very year Adolf Hitler came to power in Germany. These were bleak times for Oliver, bringing three boys up had not been easy, his financial resources had been limited. Life had been very difficult of late.

Oliver was only forty-seven years old when on the 14th of December 1939, only three months after the declaration of war with Hitler's Nazi Germany, he had a massive heart attack and died instantly leaving Dorothy and two sons at home, Ken now being very much at war in the Middle East by then. Oliver was brought home to Knutsford and buried next to his mother and father. There was to be a shaft of light in the family affairs. Uncle George had died leaving his estate to his nephew and Dorothy was able to return to Knutsford and enjoy the closer company of her own family, living peaceably in George and Isabella Lee's Manchester Road house, albeit in wartime conditions and worryingly with two of her sons, Ken and Neville, soldiering overseas.

CHAPTER NINE

Oliver's Sons – Kenneth Lee

Born in Knutsford – Altrincham Grammar School – joins Indian Army – Maharatta Rifles Major – the war in East and North Africa – Anglo American field intelligence – back to Far East by parachute – an Indian bride – divorce – an intellectual soul-mate – a Hampstead home – executive recruitment in Berkeley Square – two sons – Rotten Row riding in Hyde Park – death in the saddle.

~

The story of Oliver Lee's three charismatic sons for me has always been an uplifting one. It was as a callow youth, that I first came into contact with them. I have come to realise that I am something of a romantic by nature, and at that time, highly impressionable. Whatever, they have remained in my mind as almost heroic figures. We are talking mainly about the immediate post war period of the late 1940s extending through the 1950s and into the mid 1960s during which time they flitted in and out of the Knutsford scene before all marrying and going their respective ways which eventually took them permanently away from the town and their mother Dorothy. That is not to say that their visits to her and Knutsford were infrequent. The town had always meant a great deal to them, their great uncle George's lurid stories repeated and embellished by their father had given it an aura which verged on the mystical. A visit to Knutsford was a pilgrimage and as far apart as they then all lived, they would rendezvous here and descend on, among others, my mother at her various homes, The White Bear inn, The Red Cow inn and The Kings Coffee House/La Belle Epoque, the latter being the site of the old Hat and Feather, where their father was born and so many more Lees were to die. Out would come the whiskey bottle, all then was fun and laughter and all the Lee family stories would be retold over and over again. These three handsome, educated and beautifully spoken men were an absolute joy to behold and be with.

Kenneth (Ken) the eldest, by my book was a colossus. I first met him as a small boy when visiting his cousin Bessie, my mother, then at The White Bear. They were very fond of each other and shared the same huge sense of humour. Born in Knutsford, educated at primary school level, he won a scholarship to Altrincham Grammar School and not long after leaving school with his father's strict disciplines becoming ever harder to stomach, the independently minded Ken said enough was enough and fled the family home. It was very much in the Lee tradition that he chose to put on military uniform. Having listened to tales of daring do exchanged between his Yeomanry great uncle and his artilleryman father and duly impressed and influenced, and with the sense of adventure that was deeply ingrained in the Lee character, there was little other choice than an army career. His choice of army verged on the exotic, not the British army, where tradition was uppermost and a career with promotion a tediously slow process, but the Indian army. There had been since it's formation, a large British presence at officer level within the ranks of it's native regiments many long years before the Indian mutiny, and it was well understood that promotion and advancement was a good deal quicker.

He was commissioned into the Maharatta rifles circa 1935, though I would have some difficulty in confirming this with their records, and it was first thought that he had joined the Rajputana rifles. With the outbreak of the Second World War and with no immediate threat to it's own borders, India sent some very fine Indian army divisions to East Africa to deal with the problem of Mussolini's Italian armies that were threatening British colonial interest in the region following their subjugation of Abyssinia. These included the superb 4th Indian division which was an integral part of General Montgomery's famous 8th army which after many trials and tribulations finally defeated General Rommel's German-Italian armies at El-Alamein in Egypt in 1942 this being the battle regarded as the turning point in the war. As to whether Major Ken Lee was with the division or another division at that moment in time, I do not know, to ascertain that would be like looking for the proverbial needle in the haystack. At some time his talents were recognised by the higher command and he was seconded to an arm of military intelligence and it is conceivable that he might have sat behind a desk for a short while in Cairo, we do know that he was temporarily re-united there with his younger brother Neville, then serving with a unit of Royal Electrical and Mechanical Engineers (R.E.M.E) and part of the renowned 7th Armoured division, the original "Desert Rats'.

With the long delayed entry of the U.S.A into the War, forced as it was by events at Pearl Harbour, American forces were at last in action in Algeria and Tunisia. From this point on, Ken became part of a small joint Anglo-American battlefield observation and assessment team, swanning around with his American opposite number in a jeep and being fairly vulnerable in the process. Ken's wife Sheila told me that his American colleague came to live in London after the war and told her that he owed his life to the courage and experience of Ken, this after they had driven their jeep into a minefield. This joint exercise became ever more necessary as the Anglo-American armies landed first in Sicily and then on the Italian mainland at Salerno. They remained together as the allied armies fought their difficult way north through Italy and to the end of the war with Nazi Germany. I have a dog-earred photograph of a handsome, somewhat languid Ken, sat smilingly in his jeep with cigarette holder clenched between his teeth, this somewhere in Italy.

After the European war, Indian army units were then transferred back to the Far Eastern theatre of war against Japanese Imperialism, which after many long years, had at long last turned in favour of the allied armies. Indian divisions serving in the Mediterranean theatre of war were sent home and thence to Burma to join other Indian divisions which had been fighting a desperate war with General Bill Slim's 14th (forgotten) army in the jungles of Burma for many a long year. Ken, Indian army man that he was, went with them, being returned to his own regiment which I was still unable to determine, even though my attempts to do so were perhaps somewhat flimsy. I can only think that his spells of free wheeling within intelligence units outside the family of his regiment had put a spoke in the wheel of the regimental record of it's varying strengths. Through a further conversation with Ken's wife Sheila, she was able to recollect that he had confided in her that the most terrifying memory of his war had been when he was parachuted into the Burmese jungle. This after a very brief instruction in the dark art of parachuting. This was not the normal way to return to your regiment which makes me think that he was still probably further involved with military intelligence.

Ken returned to England after the atomic bomb had brought an end to the war in the Far East. He brought with him a most lovely high caste Indian wife named Sally, who appeared in Knutsford dressed in traditional Indian finery, causing immediate family and, to this then thirteen year old boy in particular, gasps of admiration and sheer wonderment. Knutsford had not seen the like before, the now demobilised Ken and his stunning wife then went to live in Sale. Whether the change of climate and culture from hot and exotic India and the early glamour and excitement of a relationship forged in immediate and triumphant war time conditions, had anything to do with it, but now in dull post war north east Cheshire and nearby grimy blitz hit Manchester, the marriage fell apart. Sally then embraced Catholicism in her anguish and chose a convent life in Lancashire. The marriage had also been a childless one. Ken subsequently met Sheila, a very beautiful, fair and highly intelligent actress, who became his intellectual soul-mate and a lady of considerable talent and someone determined and able to forge an individualistic career within the relationship, and at the same time provide a loving home in which to bring up a family that they both so very obviously wanted.

They moved to London, setting up home in Hampstead. Ken as ever at the cutting edge of affairs, formed one of the earliest executive recruitment companies in England, with offices in the exclusive Berkeley Square, an extremely prestigious address from which to do business, which soon prospered. Sheila studied for and soon became a highly reputable stress therapist working from her Hampstead house. Her reputation was soon sufficient to merit a double spread feature article in 'The Woman's Journal', a leading ladies magazine in 1983. The article reveals the high intellect with which she approached her work, she is now an equally well regarded osteopath. They lived their lives in considerable comfort, soon the two boys, Thomas and David were born. Tom of course being named after his great great grandfather, and founder of the Lee's little licensing empire in Knutsford.

In true tradition, Ken renewed his and the Lee family interest in horse riding, no stranger to horses, he would have ridden with his regiment in the pre war days of his service in India. Forever a man who lived his life with great dash and style and with some degree of Lee showmanship, he rode, along with the best of people in Hyde Park on Sunday morning's, after all London society had been riding in Rotten Row for hundreds of years, and Ken considered himself to be and certainly was among the very best. It was here on one sunny Sunday morning that the misfortune and tragedy that oft stalked the Lee family, struck once more with cruel and devastating affect. When in the saddle and in all his glory, Ken had a massive heart attack which killed him instantly. It was said that he was dead before he fell to the ground.

So died a man whose charm, eloquence and vivacity touched all who met him, and whose courage had been proven in time of war, and in the unquiet peace of post war England. With an equal amount of courage, Sheila continued in her chosen career, and at the same time bringing up and educating her two young boys, both of whom developed the same individualistic and independent frame of mind as their parents which would have delighted their father and made him extremely proud. Ken was only fifty years old at the time of his death and there was almost certainly a still more brilliant career ahead of this most original man. It will have been noted by the reader that Oliver, his father, had also died of a heart attack and that he was only forty-seven years old at the time. It may just have crossed the minds of Ken's two brothers, Neville and Brian, that there may have been a connection between these two early deaths, and that there might just be an inherent heart condition in this branch of the family, if so, they may be forgiven for that.

CHAPTER TEN

Oliver's Sons – Neville and Brian Lee

Neville Lee was born in 1922 and educated in Knutsford, living both there and later in Sale, after the family moved there. The Second World War came too soon for him to establish himself in any profession or job of work. He was soon recruited into the army, serving in the western desert with the redoubtable 8th army and then beyond Africa, possibly staying with it through the Italian campaign or if his R.E.M.E unit was attached to the 7th Armoured division, shipped home to England with them prior to their involvement in the Normandy landings and campaign in 1944. Never having talked to him, and being too young to do so, I am rather vague about his movements.

He returned to Knutsford after the war, and worked for Russell Frowde, a Knutsford bookmaker, who had a fine large house on Knutsford's prestigious Legh Road and offices in both Knutsford and in King Street, Manchester, the latter being the equivalent to London's Bond Street. For Russell Frowde was the gentleman's bookmaker and a man of some distinction. A former wartime Royal Airforce Wing Commander with Bomber Command, he was the recipient of the Distinguished Flying Cross (D.F.C) for his gallantry. His extremely beautiful wife had done her bit in the war, in the most entertaining way, enjoying a very sporty lifestyle which led to a quite lurid divorce. Gladys Frowde was one of the many colourful characters that my mother assembled around her at our White Bear inn during the war.

Either through the divorce which may have destabled the business, Neville left it, and then met Kay. They soon married and moved to Wakefield in Yorkshire. Neville was then a sales representative with a leading animal food producing company. His pretty and vivacious wife was highly involved with amateur dramatic society acting, in which she soon had Neville interested and subsequently involved. They were shortly engaged in assisting with the restoration of Wakefield's lovely old Victorian theatre. It was here after it's completion that the terrible jinx that was stalking the family, struck devastatingly once more, for during one evening performance at the theatre, Neville had a heart attack and died there and then. He was only sixty-one years old. The Neville that I remember was equally as handsome as his elder brother Ken. He too was charming, spirited, full of vitality and with a rare sense of mischievous humour which he coupled with the most infectious of laughs, he was great fun. Poor Kay was thus left alone to bring up their one child, a son, Simon, who if there was ever a chip off the same block as his father, it is Simon Lee who has all the outgoing characteristics of him.

If Neville had ever become concerned about the possibility that he too might suffer from heart disease and die prematurely like his father and elder brother, then Brian the youngest brother could very well have been forgiven for being exceedingly anxious for his own life. The signs were patently obvious, father aged forty-seven, Ken fifty, and now Neville sixty-one. I have little doubt that the possibility of an early demise might have crossed his mind, we know that there existed a very close bond between the boys, and the loss of his two older brothers would have been more than keenly felt.

Born in Knutsford, but moving to Sale with his family in 1932, Brian was educated at Sale Grammar School during the war when both Ken and Neville were soldiering in the Middle East. I am unsure of his early working life, but he did join Robert Lee and Partners, his brother Ken's Berkeley Square head hunting company. He was extremely attached to Ken and his time with him would have benefited him immensely. He was devastated when Ken died, and indeed it is said that he suffered a nervous breakdown because of it. It was most probable that he left his brother's business at this time moving north to Yorkshire and taking several jobs there as a salesman which would have placed him nearer his brother Neville and the rest of his family, including his mother in nearby Cheshire. At sometime he met and married Betty, and they moved to Chinnor in the south Oxfordshire Chiltern Hills, where he became managing director of his own substantial industrial cleaning company, which served mainly the hospital services. He later became a consultant to the south Oxfordshire National Health Authority. Again, in true Lee tradition, he found time to put on a soldiers uniform, and obtained a territorial commission with the Oxfordshire and Buckinghamshire Light Infantry/Green Jackets. He and Betty produced a son Jonathan, who lives in Wiltshire and works with the hospital services there.

Brian fortunately managed to survive the foreseen threat of any early death, but the possibility of it would have caused him great stress, which to all who knew him was not obvious. He retired from business and moved to North Wales, buying a lovely large old house in a quietly historic little village near Ruthin where his typically ebullient and generous nature made a huge impression on his fellow villagers. I know this first hand having subsequently talked to several of them who referred to his good humoured influence in the more serious of the village's affairs. It had to end, and end it did. I suppose sixty-seven is near enough to our allotted span of three score years and ten, but is still far too young to die, but die he did and of a heart condition. With his death ended a generation of Lee men, who I believe brought colour and warmth to all who had the good fortune to have met and known them. They belong to a breed of men who are increasingly difficult to meet this day and age. Though I was too young and perhaps at times too far away from them to know them more intimately, they influenced my life and thinking to a considerable degree.

Tom, Simon, David and Jonathan Lee are keenly aware of their family history and are quite rightly extremely proud of it. This is reflected in the names of their children, for there is now amongst others, a George and an Oliver. The young men and their families now all live a good distance away from their Knutsford roots, Hampshire, Middlesex and Wiltshire are a fair way away from Cheshire. There is increasingly less reason for them to visit, but I hope they do and that on occasions the young Lee's are brought here and shown the places where their forebears initially struggled and eventually succeeded in making their considerable presence fealt in this old town. Who knows, perhaps one day one of them might feel there is once again the opportunity to make their own mark in the Knutsford story.

Addendum

I have to confess to being guilty of literary licence in the chapter regarding my great uncle George Lee, particularly with regard to the matter of the alleged accidental killing of the Irish horse dealer. (See Chapter Four pages 29-50)

In an effort to make some sense of this affair I needed to conjure up a likely scenario with regard to the disposal of the unfortunate mans body. Knowing of the Lee mens close boyhood association with the Knutsford Moor I took it upon myself to imagine that the best place to dispose of it would have been in quicksand in the depth of the marsh. However by the late 1880's the moor was becoming a tamer animal, and anyway it would have been a long, cumbersome and somewhat horrific journey for the two Lee brothers, with their gruesome burden.

What also of the passage opposite the front door of the then Hat and Feather Inn being called by the Lees, Skeleton Alley? Which intimates rather emphatically that this was where the skeleton was found some forty years later. Because of this my interpretation of possible events was a constant source of irritation to yours truly. Unhappily I let my version of events stand. However by a happy coincidence I was let off the hook. In August 2010 the late Major Kenneth Lee's wife Sheila visited Knutsford with her son Tom and his young boys. We dined and in the course of the conversation which as ever dwelt on the family doings or ill-doings if preferred, Sheila disclosed that Kenneth Lee had told her that the skeleton was found entombed/embedded in or under a wall in one of the many old decrepit, disused, tumbledown and uninhabited sheds, cottages, workshops and outbuildings that occupied today's large moorside car park, and which were bounded by Malt Street, Cotton Shop Yard and Bakehouse Yard, all of which town boys of many generations including my own came to know as a playground, if a somewhat dangerous one. Thus I am able to rest my delicate case and ease my conscience.

Tinker, Tailor, Soldier, Restaurateur

Introduction

In the second part of his bi-part family history and memoir, the author introduces his father's family, the Howard's and tells of their smaller part in Knutsford's more immediate past than that played years earlier by the voracious and controversial Lee family. We meet his Grandfather Albert Howard who played a key role in the business affairs of Richard Harding Watt, the self made Architect who nearly but not quite, turned Knutsford into an Italian hill town. He then charmingly informs us of what it was like to live as a small boy in the town during the 1939-45 Second World War. He tells of life in his father's ancient hostelry, The White Bear Inn, of Lord Egerton's part in the lives of Knutsford boys, of his apprenticeship as a bespoke tailor in war torn central Manchester, and then humourously recalls his national service with an armoured cavalry regiment in Germany during the Cold War.

He goes on to tell of life as a menswear buyer with Harrods, his disenchantment with a subsequent takeover leading to resignation and his entry and long time love affair with the restaurant trade, which commenced with the immediate success of his first venture, "The Tavern", a Danish restaurant. He further relates his trials and tribulations in the business after the sad demise of his much loved father when taking on the head lease of the Richard Harding Watt built, Kings Coffee House, reflecting without melancholy on how the building, built as it is on the site of his Great Grandfather's old inn, The Hat and Feather, had subsequently been the scene of so many family deaths, many unexpected.

More joyfully he tells of his joint triumph with the former first manager of George Best, when the two of them turned the ailing KCH into La Belle Epoque French restaurant, a triumph sadly marked by the almost immediate tragic death of his partner in a road accident involving a drunken lorry driver.

His late adventures include his sojourns around the UK as an in-house consultant to the private restaurant business and a period as a high class tour guide with his own personalised travel company. Thrown into the mix for good measure is a thought provoking chapter on his great passion for cricket.

He ends his story with a piece on his five year spell as custodian of Arley Hall. The seat of the 11th Lord Ashbrook. It is a roller coaster tale and resume of a highly diversified life and one obviously thoroughly relished.

Contents

Contents

CHAPTER ONE

Tinker

The Howards – 18th century Georgian Manchester – St Ann's Parish – Bow Lane – Holy Moses and his tribe – the tinker tale – Albert Howard – the Peterloo affair – Howards to America – the leather trade – Richard Harding Watt.

~

Welcome to the second part of this book and to the Howard family, whose affairs in comparison to that of the rumbustious and controversially ambitious ones of the Lee family, certainly pale, but are not without merit, and I believe you will find of interest, as the family played it's part in the Knutsford story from the turn of the 19th century to today. I tell it as the last member of the family now living in Knutsford, this now covering a period of a hundred years.

The Howards arrived in Manchester, having departed Yorkshire in the early 18th century, settling in the heart of a then densely populated Georgian city and in the parish of St. Ann's. My own branch of the family lived in Bow Lane on the edge of the parish, and next to the parish of St Peter's, separated as it was by green fields. Bow Lane was a narrow, winding, bustling thoroughfare of small shops and houses, with tradesmen of every description working in lofts and attic rooms above both. My namesake, John Howard, is the earliest known member of the family. Born in 1716 he was a grocer who died in 1800. His tombstone is one of only half a dozen retained and placed against the back of St. Ann's church. My great great great grandfather was Moses Howard whose successive wives, Jane and Sarah, gave birth to a tribe of boys named, James, John, Thomas, Abraham, Jude, Moses, Aaron and Josiah, which leads me to believe he was the bible thumping variety of ancestor. We have gone steadily downhill since then, my great, great grandfather John and his wife Mary produced a further twelve children, amongst them my great grandfather, another Moses who, with his wife Mary Jane "Tinker", produced a further eleven children including my grandfather Albert. All is now revealed as to why part of this book includes a "tinker" in it's title. Non of the Howards, as far as I know, were ever members of that profession, I am just grateful that in marrying Mary Jane it allowed me the opportunity to attempt to be neat and clever with it.

My grandfather Albert was born in Bow Lane in 1867 and was one of seven brothers. At some stage the ever growing family, and there was a twenty three year span between the first and last child, moved to Blackley in north Manchester. The Victorians by then were winning their battle to demolish delightful but dilapidated Georgian Manchester and impose their grand but overweight architectural style on the city. Charming little Bow Lane was retained but now serves no greater purpose than providing goods access to the rear of the new and bigger premises at the front. At the entrance to the Lane there is a blue commemorative plaque attached to the wall, signalling the fact that Ernest Jones, a barrister at law and a Chartist leader, had practiced in Bow Lane between 1865 and 1869. It also notes the fact that Jones was born in 1819, the year of the Peterloo Massacre, which brings us back to a passage in the first part of this book where my great, great uncle Joseph Lee, the Knutsford blacksmith and farrier to "A" Tatton troop of the Cheshire Yeomanry had ridden with the Yeomanry to St. Peter's Fields, but along with the rest of his regiment, had not participated in the cavalry charge which cost so many innocent lives. Bow Lane was perhaps the last thoroughfare in the parish of St. Ann's and adjoined that of St. Peter's Church and it's fields. It is easy then to imagine many Howard's being among the 50,000 crowd that Saturday afternoon, being addressed by "Orator" Hunt the so called "popular agitator" for industrial reform. Surely Ernest

Jones's parents were also among the throng that day, and that their views subsequently influenced their son sufficiently enough for him to become a leading member of the Chartist movement, bringing with him his agile legal brain. So indirectly this was the first meeting between Lees and Howards, as for the Howards, interested as they probably were in industrial reform, they were also taking the afternoon off from further adding to their ever increasing family numbers.

Despite some little improvement in the lot of the working man towards the end of the 19th century, it was still sufficiently hard enough to prompt three of Moses's seven sons to pack their bags and emigrate. George and Herbert sailing off in the late 1890's to America to be followed later by Harold the youngest son, at the turn of the century. Fred Howard had a good position with Baxendales, a leading Manchester retail company and was moved to their Dublin branch, he and his family remaining in Ireland for good. John, Tom and Albert were less venturesome but Albert, the second oldest of the brothers, had long been influenced and to a great degree had been trained by his father in the ways of the leather working trade, Moses having for most of his life, worked as an artisan leather worker in his attic workshop and rooms in Bow Lane. Albert thus became a knowledgeable force in the Manchester leather industry and was able to command a good position in that trade. His considerable services were acquired circa 1895 by Richard Watt and Company, who had been developing what was a small but exclusive fine leather glove manufacturing business into a larger and more progressive limited company. Albert very soon became Richard Watt's head leather buyer and by far the most influential member of the company.

At this juncture it is appropriate to re-introduce Richard Harding Watt, for you will have already met him in the first part of this book, as the man that my maternal great grandfather Fred Lee sold his public house, the old Hat and Feather to in 1894/5, enabling Watt to build first his Elizabeth Gaskell Memorial Tower and then the Kings Coffee House in 1906-1909, this later to house the La Belle Epoque restaurant. Watt proved to be the catalyst in the affairs of both Howard and Lee families. We have already seen the carnage Fred Lee's move to The White Lion in 1895 ultimately brought on him and his family, so Watt was to influence the lives of the Howards, thank heavens it was considerably less dramatic and life threatening, never the less it was to affect us markedly and changed the direction of quite a few lives.

CHAPTER TWO

Richard Harding Watt and Albert Howard

South African gold mining – world travel – keen draughtsman – the leather glove manufacturer – enter Albert Howard – moves to Knutsford – builds "The Croft" – the Italian influence – Legh Road villas – an Islamic skyline – Art Nouveau – The Ruskin Rooms – the Howards to Knutsford – Cranford Gardens – The Gaskell Memorial and Kings Coffee House – Watt marries at sixty-four – Albert and Watt part – the Wilson sisters – Albert takes the White Bear – Watt killed by bolting Horse – a bee in my bonnet – Clough Williams Ellis and Portmeirion in the 1930s – "Richard Watt, I've never heard of him" – Watt built his villas thirty years before – Williams Ellis inspired by Watt?

~

Richard Harding Watt was born in 1842, possibly in South Africa and allegedly of Boer origins, with the Boers being Afrikaners of Dutch descent, the surname "Watt" does not support this, and I suspect his origins, though South African, were actually British. His father being an early English fortune hunter, searching for gold, might have married an Afrikaner woman. Watt was extremely wealthy at a young age due to his father striking it rich, dying early, leaving him with a substantial income from the South African gold mining industry. This sequence of events, is I think largely supposition on the part of previous researchers, and I apologise for us all being somewhat vague on the subject. An alternative

13

suggestion is that given his 1842 date of birth, the timescale could indicate that he himself was a young prospector who had successfully mined for the precious ore. It is more likely though that he was made wealthy by inheriting his father's wealth and that his father and mother before dying early, as they were alleged to have done, ensured that their son was given every opportunity to develop experience and character in the true Victorian tradition of taking the grand European tours, and also, having colonial backgrounds, encouraged him to travel ever further and around the world, embracing virtually every continent, recording much of what he saw by drawing. He worked variously, once taking a job in a surveyors office in Brisbane, Australia in 1864. Perhaps this was part of a grand personal plan evolved at such an early age, he was twenty two. He was an avid sketcher, and his sketch books reveal his passionate interest in architecture; no accident then to work briefly for a surveyor. Returning to England he then studied at an art college in London and four years later had qualified as an art teacher. Though he was never to teach, he had developed his artistic skills and was also an excellent draughtsman. All would stand him in future good stead.

However, Watt obviously had something to prove to himself and to the world at large. That was that he could succeed in business in any way that he chose to do, and that he was not a mere dilettante preparing to idle his way through life on the back of investment and profit. He chose to go into the leather goods manufacturing industry, whether this was from scratch I am not aware, it is more likely that he purchased a business, this was in nearby, to Knutsford that is, Manchester. This was a small exclusive leather glove making business to become known as Richard Watt and Company, a company which he developed extensively and extremely profitably with offices in Manchester and a factory in Stockport, at the same time choosing to settle in Cheshire, buying a house in affluent and leafy Bowdon. If Watt's business was to thrive, and it did, it needed skilled men at the helm. Enter then my grandfather, Albert Howard, who you know became his head leather buyer. Thrive it did, failure was not in the frame for this buccaneering business man. In the year 1895, he deemed it necessary to move house, leave Bowdon and settle in rural Knutsford just six miles away. He felt the need to own a larger and more individual house, but not the need to buy one. His creative nature was such that he had the urge to design and build one to his liking, and to suit his particular needs. His early flirtations with architecture so many years previously were at last beginning to come to the fore, along with his architect John Brooke, they created "The Croft", a house inspired by William Morris and the Arts and Craft movement. This was completed in 1895 on land on the west side of Legh Road, an exclusive thoroughfare with large prestigious Victorian houses on the east side overlooking a wild tract of land which fell steeply away into the marshy valley below where the little stream the "Lilybrook" rose and then meandered between Knutsford's two hillsides, creating the Knutsford moor in the process, before flowing gently into Tatton Mere and beyond. This marshy tract of land was known to Knutsfordians as "Molly Potts Moor". Richard Watt renamed it "Sanctuary Moor" which became it's official name.

Watt, at the time of purchasing the land on which to build "The Croft", took the opportunity either then or very soon after, to purchase much of this precipitous wilderness. Little did the luckless house owners on the east side of the road with views over Molly Potts Moor know what hell Watt had in store for them. This first flirtation with architecture and building triggered him to enter a phase in his life that in layman's language is hard to describe. For the next fifteen years 1895-1910 he became an almost demonical but inspirational amateur architect and builder, but with one colossal difference, that unlike his very English house "The Croft", everything that he undertook to design and build had an Italianate aspect. So in 1897 he commenced to build along the western edge of Legh Road what Sir Nikolaus Pevsner, the architectural critic and author of the series of books reviewing the architectural styles to be found in the English counties, described as "the maddest sequence of villas in all England".

Watt had visited Italy in 1883 as a wealthy Victorian and fallen in love with it. He was to make more visits and acquaintances over the years, including that of Prince Umbergo with whom he hunted. Back in Manchester the early Victorians had commenced in 1828 to dismantle the Georgian city, and had almost completed the job by the turn of the 19th century. Amongst the last buildings to be demolished, were the vast Manchester Royal Infirmary in Piccadilly Gardens where my great, great grandmother worked and dallied so frivolously, and near fatally, with Doctor James Livingstone in 1865, and St. Peter's Church in St. Peter's Square. From his offices in Piccadilly, Watt would have witnessed the demise of the classical infirmary and perhaps subconsciously, or indeed very consciously, made a mental note of what was happening to the huge piles of defunct stonework that the demolition men were storing away. He had more than likely earmarked many of the more prominent features of these buildings, the gatehouses, lodges, porticos, columns, doorways and the more exuberant protrusions. Eventually these were purchased from the demolition company catalogues. He then proceeded to construct the largest imaginable carts with wheels six feet in diameter and have these pulled to Knutsford by teams of heavy horses. This stonework was taken to Legh Road and dumped strategically on the land he had obtained to build his villas. Work commenced on these in 1897 where he variously employed the services of several noted architects, namely Harry Fairhurst, Walter Aston, and W. Longworth. All were taken at some stage by Watt to his beloved Italy to allow them to see and study at first hand what he had in mind.

It is sometimes forgotten, conveniently, by researchers or indeed overlooked by amateur historians, that the principle reason for travelling to Italy in the first instance was business. Watt had long known from his travels that some of the finest leather to be obtained in Europe, was to be had in Tuscany with Florence at it's heart. For some years he had been making the journey, but with my grandfather Albert Howard as his sole companion. This of course to allow Albert to study the Italian leather market and as head buyer to make the ultimate decisions as to what was needed in quantity and quality, with Watt obviously controlling the purse strings at source. It must never be forgotten that the profits from the successful leather glove making business were being used to finance Watt's flirtations with the building of his Italianate villas. This expense of course he would eventually recoup when the villas were completed and sold at great profit, so my grandfather played an important part in the Richard Watt story. Albert would continue to accompany his employer to Italy along with each successive architect that Watt engaged, increasingly being trusted to get on with the job as Watt became more and more obsessed with the architectural aspects of his journey. At the same time Watt was taking the opportunity to gather what treasures he could find along the way, which would serve to embellish and adorn his buildings. These included exotic ironwork, fountains, pediments, architraves, balusters et al, which were then shipped to England. The journeys though vital, did have their lighter moments. They would have enjoyed themselves to a high degree, sightseeing, wining and dining. My grandfather must have subsequently let it slip in a later conversation or been accidentally overheard by my father as a young man, that there had been a fair amount of "wenching" along the way.

Meanwhile, back home in Legh Road, work on the villas was being completed on a huge scale and at a frantic pace. Watt then back 'in situ' could be seen sat astride his horse, riding among the various building sites with his architect, clerk of works and various foremen, discussing, cajoling, and ordering all to a point of distraction, his drive and energy seemingly boundless. It must be remembered that he was not building Italian houses in dry and sunny Tuscany, but in wet, cold and often soggy Cheshire. There was the increasing likelihood that the houses being built as they were on a steep hillside might from time to time, slide down it, and they did. It must have been a hellish place to work and hectoring, driving, bullying Watt insufferable to work for and with. There was once a point when a site foreman threatened to take a gun to him, shades this of gold prospecting in South Africa where local labour was black and very much cheaper.

Not content with changing the Knutsford skyline on the south side of the town, Watt had also turned his attention to the north end of it and when John Long's tannery business went to the wall in 1898, he bought it. Beautifully situated on another steep slope and the last significant site immediately before entry to Tatton Park via the Knutsford gate, Watt had exotic plans for it. He was going to turn it into a model steam laundry. Good heavens above! What the Dickens is so special and different about a steam laundry? you might say, even though this one was to incorporate a row of cottages built for his workers down the side of the sloping Drury Lane. Not a lot I suppose, unless you were someone with a creative imagination who had travelled extensively to the far corners of the world and been hugely influenced by many of the varied architectural styles seen en route. Then perhaps you also might build a laundry which would echo your journeys, which is what Watt precisely did. He had obviously been to the Middle East, and so built a laundry that included an eight sided tower which was an exact replica of a tower he had drawn in Damascus. The laundry chimney combining feature with function, was enclosed in a minaret similar to the one he had sketched in Palestine. The round headed windows of the drying room were Byzantine in style and the domes of the boiler houses suggested Mosques. The resulting silhouette had a startling impact on the Knutsford skyline.

The cottages he built for his employees in Drury Lane had and still have verandas and balconies with overhanging eaves and with further disregard for uniformity and convention, one has a great gate within an archway and one with a round headed door that displays a wonderful swirl of art nouveau ironwork. Watt is regarded in some quarters as having designed in the art nouveau style before Charles Rennie Mackintosh was acknowledged to have done so in 1897. This would be explained by his visits to the many exhibitions being held in Brussels in the late 19th century and where Count Victor Horta first created the short lived movement in 1893. Some of Watt's earlier interest in the English Arts and Crafts movement manifested itself in his "English" house, "The Croft". The philosophy of the movement's high priest William Morris both moved and excited him. Concerned as it was with the squalor and suffering wrought upon the working classes by the industrial revolution, and with the need to seek ways of improving the lives of the poor. So Watt took up the cause of championing the underdog.

For several years he was elected to serve on the Knutsford Council as clerk of works. He discovered that with six hundred houses without running water, Knutsford despite it's genteel image, on close inspection was home to many of the very poorest. He would also discover who the various property owners were, and which of them might eventually accept an offer to buy. His keen eye would have taken into consideration the central position in Knutsford's main street, King Street, of the old Hat and Feather inn owned by my great grandfather, Fred Lee. Shrewd as he was he might also have suspected that here was a man quite amenable to a good offer, thus there evolved a plan in his mind for his ultimate triumph, that of the eventual building of the Elizabeth

Gaskell Memorial Tower and the accompanying Kings Coffee House, now housing the La Belle Epoque restaurant. From that fatal moment in 1895 when he courted Fred Lee, and my great grandfather accepted his offer, he kept his intentions quiet.

So Watt became the enlightened employer and good landlord. His workers enjoyed the pleasure and privilege of living in his quaint cottages. They and other occupants of the houses that he had either acquired or had built and then rented, were likely to be called on from time to time, and asked as to whether they were comfortable and also it might be added to ensure they were keeping his properties clean. Never the less his kindness and benevolence were always uppermost. In 1902 he took the care and needs of his small workforce to an even higher ideological level, when nearer the top of Drury Lane and beyond his laundry, he built the Ruskin Recreational Rooms. By now a believer in the social function of architecture, these rooms were designed not only as a means of improving living conditions but intended to influence the minds of his staff and their families. The second floor of these rooms was built as a library and a recreation room where reading, discussions and musical evenings could take place. This formula was to be repeated later in 1907/1908 with the opening of the Kings Coffee House, this time the good, and it might be added, the bad citizens of the town would be invited to enjoy similar pleasures, unfortunately with little success.

At the same time as this, living in Blackley in north Manchester, Albert Howard, his wife and three children, two of whom were very young, were beginning to suffer the purgatory brought about by the spread of heavy industry. The health of his son Harry and his sister Isa were being badly affected by the increasingly dense industrial smogs created by the chemical industries now located there. Watt then insisted that they moved to Knutsford, building a pair of Italianate cottages, one for them, the other for Entwhistle, his clerk of building works, on land he had purchased adjacent to the laundry and recreation rooms. Previously incorrectly researched information had led all to believe that the Howard cottage had been built to house Watt's foreman joiner, not so. This gesture of Watt's serves to underline two things, one that he was a caring and considerate employer, and two, that my grandfather played a major role in Watt's affairs.

Watt by now was using his third and final architect W. Longworth, which in truth was not the case, "using" Longworth is an accurate description, but as his architect he certainly did not. Having been on site variously in Legh Road and Drury Lane and working with Brooke, Fairhurst and Aston, the clever and determined Watt had by now developed a real passion for architecture and now after grasping the fundamentals of the trade, became keen to establish himself in the role, believing he could achieve his ambition if he built his houses entirely by himself with the minimum of professional assistance. Poor Longworth was reduced to being used as a draughtsman, model maker and foreman with little say in the design of the remaining houses that Watt was to build. In an article in the Architectural Review in 1940, it was suggested that Longworth was made to sign a guarantee that he would act only as an architects ghost, agreeing to suppress his name so that Watt could claim the credit and responsibility himself. Between 1904 and 1906 the last of the houses in Legh Road were completed. Watt could now turn his attention to his final and most celebrated architectural achievement, the Elizabeth Gaskell Memorial Tower and accompanying Kings Coffee House.

The deed of sale between Fred Lee and Watt for the old Hat and Feather inn had long been concluded circa 1895 and work was commenced in 1906 and was completed with the opening of both in 1907. In 1906 and at the age of sixty-four, Watt was at last able to marry his patient and long standing lady friend, Ethel Armitage, daughter of a lift manufacturing father, with a factory in Broadheath, near Altrincham. Her father had refused to let her marry Watt, because of Watt's infuriatingly dominant attitude. It is not difficult to imagine the constant friction between the two hard headed businessmen. Never the less it seems so grossly unfair that they were not permitted to do so, it makes one wonder as to whether they were ever able to enjoy any kind of life together at "The Croft" before their marriage. The thought seems manifestly intrusive given those late Victorian/early Edwardian times, maybe they did not, what of course is so very sad is that they were never able to have children, and that there would be no heir to the family glove making business. Albert Howard did go on record as saying that from the moment that Watt married, he became more irritable and difficult to work with. Could it be that my grandfather felt he was losing his place in the Watt order of things?

Not that the opening of the Gaskell Memorial Tower/Kings Coffee House was a hugely joyous occasion, friction had long been building up between the Knutsford Council and Watt, and by the time of the ceremony was fairly acrimonious. The Council, among them my great grandfather, Fred Lee and his wise and widely respected elder brother Robert, and who knows maybe even the other irascible brother George, who briefly served on it, were alleged to have stated that they did not realise that the slender needle tower, part built as it is of white Portland stone, was going to be so tall. This sounds particularly silly given that plans would have had to have been made available and ultimately approved. I think if that sort of comment had been made, it was made by councillors placed under pressure by the traditionally narrow minded Knutsford electorate, who had now for many years thought of Watt as quite mad. If there was ill feeling between he and a council which included the Lee brothers, then I have to declare on Watt's behalf, it would smack of gross hypocrisy if Fred in particular had voiced adverse opinion and comment, after all he had been only too pleased to accept Watt's money in exchange for The Hat and Feather. Maybe too much has been made of this.

Certainly from 1907 onwards, it is said that after the long and bitter arguments with an unsympathetic Knutsford Council, he was much troubled, and by now much older became a rather embittered man, and much harder in his dealings. The second phase of the Kings Coffee House was completed in 1908. The whole concept was as has been mentioned, very similar to that of the Ruskin Recreation Rooms. It's purpose was once again an exercise in the social function of architecture, but this time in a very public way. Here again above the coffee house itself, we find a library and reading room, both open in the evening as well as in the daytime, where the citizens of the town could call in and catch up with the news in the daily papers and magazines, enjoy a cigarette and a cup of coffee. Upstairs was the most splendid room, and one which would feature much in my own business affairs during my later tenancy of the property. In this room were held concerts, discussions and musical evenings.

The 1908 extension included a large room which doubled as a ballroom and art exhibition room with access via French windows to a large roof garden, where summer parties for Cheshire debutantes could be elegantly held. A balcony dominated by the huge columns rescued from St. Peter's Church in Manchester, overlooked a pretty Italianate cobbled courtyard, enclosed at it's far end by a magnificently roofed archway secured by huge ornate iron gates. The extension also included a further number of bedrooms which allowed some of the more privileged to stay. These included the author John Galsworthy, of Forsyte Saga fame and members of the Edwardian theatrical profession.

It was all very sophisticated and exactly as Watt intended. To ensure this he engaged two extremely enlightened young ladies to manage the establishment for him. Alice and Ethel Wilson were chosen not so much for their managerial skills, but rather for their artistic background and their modern and liberal viewpoints. Both were excellent artists and displayed their paintings in London, Manchester and Birmingham. Ethel's work is well recorded. Close friends of Emily Pankhurst the suffragette leader, Alice served a small spell in prison for her belief in the movement. They were totally at ease with the county people whose daughters had their 'coming out' parties there. Ethel Wilson was to marry John Hall, then a sub editor of the then renowned Manchester Guardian. All in all it was a glorious and glittering time which was to last very briefly, and brought to earth with the start of the first great War and the ensuing human carnage.

In the summer of 1910, Watt entertained Albert Howard and other senior members of his glove making business at The Kings Coffee House, they were all to go the following day on a coach trip to the Great Orme at Llandudno on the North Wales coast where the event was recorded by photographs. There is little photographic evidence to show Watt in his lighter moments, and Albert proudly framed those of himself with his employer. He did not allow for the destructive streak that was part of my mother Bessie's nature, she eventually burnt them when she found them in the stable loft at The White Bear inn during her tenure there in the 1930s, what of the White Bear then?

That very same year 1910, it became patently obvious to my grandfather Albert, that he had arrived at that moment in time when he had to make the most momentous decision of his life. He and Watt had been together for nearly twenty years, Watt was now a cantankerous sixty-eight years of age and with the completion of The Kings Coffee House, his rich vein of creativity had finally run dry. Watt's voracious appetite for his architectural endeavours had meant that his interest in his glove manufacturing business had declined and which was being neglected with inevitably disastrous results. Albert would have been struggling along with other senior members of the company in an effort to keep it afloat. The writing however, was on the wall and he felt he had no other choice than to part company with an employer with whom he had shared so many business adventures. One who had treated him so kindly, building his Knutsford home for him and his ailing family, it would have been a huge wrench for him.

There were few opportunities for a man of forty-three years, who had spent all his life in one type of business. The leather industry was in decline, and he would have expected a similarly important and well remunerated position, which if available, he would have had to travel to and perhaps even have to leave Knutsford which he came to love. He was too old a dog to be taught new tricks. He did what many men who had left jobs in mid life did, he took a public house. So the Howards thus entered the Knutsford licensing trade, a trade once dominated in the town by the Lee family. That however was a few years earlier, and only Fred Lee was still practicing in that business in 1910, and this at the ill fated White Lion. No warning bells would ring in Albert's head when he learnt that Fred Lee's wife had been killed there as a result of alcohol abuse. They ought to have done!

The decision all came about through Albert's Welsh wife Kathryn Williams. Her brother Edward Williams, like George Lee, had been a former trooper with the Imperial Cavalry Yeomanry in the second Boer War, and after the war, like hundreds of ex-soldiers, had joined the South African police forces. On retirement from that he had returned to England and taken the licence at The Rose and Crown inn in Knutsford, coincidently formally owned by the same George Lee, who having sold it, was now owned by Groves and Whitnall, a Salford brewery company. Edward would have taken The Rose and Crown to be near his sister and be fairly near his former home and relatives in Rhos-y-Medr near

Ruabon. Historic and pretty Knutsford would also have proved an attraction. When Albert was considering his future with Richard Watt, it was his brother-in-law that influenced his decision to take a public house, and when The White Bear in Canute Square became vacant, which was also owned by Groves and Whitnall, recommended Albert to his employers. It mattered not that Albert had no experience, Edward Williams would have certainly initiated him in the fundamentals of inn keeping, but Albert's background was impeccable, sensible, loyal, hardworking, well travelled, he was a model employee. So the Howards left Cranford Gardens and moved up the hill to The White Bear which was to become the Howard family home for nearly fifty years.

What then of Richard Watt? He retired in 1911, aged sixty-nine, the year after Albert's departure. I have had little time to discover what happened to his business, maybe he was able to sell his declining company. Perhaps it's only real value was the central position it occupied in the heart of Manchester, and it's assets in bricks and mortar and therefore substantial. He would have spent his retirement years somewhat discontentedly, these however were to prove to be short. In 1913 on his way to catch the mid-day train to Manchester, and standing upright like a charioteer, as he always did while driving his horse and trap from "The Croft" to enable him to proudly view his splendid Legh Road villas, his horse suddenly bolted, throwing him backwards out of the trap and onto his head, killing him. Thus died a rare breed of man, the like of which we rarely see today. He was never recognised for his achievements in his own lifetime and much abused by many who failed to realise his true qualities and values. Knutsford though will long remember him, his legacy is here to stay and for all to see. The tall white Gaskell Memorial Tower and accompanying Kings Coffee House, the Ruskin Recreational Rooms, the Legh Road villas still attract huge attention. Television and film companies are never far away. To arrive from Manchester by train to Knutsford with it's sudden sweeping panoramic view dominated by Watt's architecture, is for me, always an emotional moment. Richard Harding Watt has never been properly acknowledged, perhaps someday, someone will write the definitive biography on the man, certainly the fact he was creating Art Nouveau in Knutsford at the same time as Charles Rennie Mackintosh was creating his art nouveau Glasgow tea rooms has been overlooked. Watt had purchased the old Hat and Feather in 1895, for the precise purpose of creating his Coffee House/tea rooms, but could not complete the work before Mackintosh had done so in Glasgow. On the subject of the rightful acknowledgement of Watt and his Italianate architectural creations, I have long had a 'bee in my private bonnet' now for some years, and this is the opportunity to release it.

In the mid 1920s Clough Williams Ellis, an aristocratic and autocratic wealthy landowning Welsh gentleman of considerable ancient pedigree, bought a coastal property named Alberia from his uncle Sir Osmond Williams of Deudraeth Castle. The property was located near Porthmadog on the Mawdach estuary and overlooking Cardigan Bay. It was also just five miles from Williams Ellis's own historic home, Plas Brandanw. The area of land was comprised of miniature cliffs, pinnacles, plateaux, a small valley, a waterfall and a coastline of rocky headlands, caves and small sandy bays. The idyllic scenario presented to Williams Ellis, a practising and naturally gifted architect, though an unqualified one, but never the less a fellow of the Royal Institute of British Architects, the opportunity to build an Italianate village. This supposedly inspired by a chance visit to Portafino on the Ligurian coastline of the north western Italian Riviera, Portafino's beauty being long acknowledged worldwide. Like Richard Watt, Williams Ellis drew his architectural inspiration from visits to Italy, Watt though having made many more journeys there through his early youthful grand touring and his later business trips, the latter some thirty or more years earlier. There was just one building on the newly acquired Welsh property. This being a large old house situated at the water's edge. In 1926 he converted this into a hotel, not unlike you may deduce, Watt's Kings Coffee House and Hotel of 1907. It was not as well conceived and managed though as the Coffee House, proving in it's early days to be a somewhat disastrous venture until the intervention of James Wylie, an artist and a former Oxford hotel owner who turned things around. From then on Williams Ellis continued to develop the property, building his romantic and charming village which was completed in 1931. Renaming it Portmeirion, it could and would be said that it is now equally famous for it's beauty as Portofino itself and deservedly so. It has subsequently brought great pleasure to countless thousands of entranced visitors.

In the late 1960's, I had the privilege of being able to sublet a part of the Kings Coffee House by my father who held the head lease, from the owners, the Knutsford Council. In 1970 my father sadly and painfully died from cancer, and I was asked by the Council if I was interested in taking the head lease. This I accepted gleefully, such was my pleasure in becoming totally involved with such a beautiful, and by now, a famed building noted for it's Italianate architecture, that I resolved to visit Portmeirion, feeling to have something in common with that far more notable collection of Italian styled buildings. Full of almost childish enthusiasm I arrived there and almost immediately to my utter surprise, saw walking towards me, the legendary and easily identifiable figure of the great architect, Clough Williams Ellis himself. A beanpole of a man, then well into his eighties, very tall and gaunt, and as ever, clad in his almost regulation garb of brown tweed Norfolk jacket, brown breeches, long yellow stockings, yellow waistcoat, bowtie and with tweed hat set jauntily on his head. Unmissable!

I was almost overcome with awe at the sight of this imposing and celebrated figure, finding it hard not to genuflect due to my deeply held respect for the man. Never the less I quickly resolved to speak to him. I had little or no time to think what to say as he advanced on me, what I eventually spluttered out was something along the lines of "Mr Clough Williams Ellis, forgive my impertinence in approaching you, what a marvellous place Portmeirion is. I live in an Italian building in Knutsford built by a man called Richard Harding Watt". No more did I have time to say, he looked down at me, and I am 5ft 11ins tall but was shrinking by the second, and extremely coldly said five short words, which eventually became burnt into my thick skull and memory. "I've never heard of him" was his reply, and with that he brushed past me and was gone. I was left floundering like a fish out of water, I had been deservedly and most thoroughly put in my place. At the time the words "I've never heard of him" meant little to me other than a quick retort to dispense with my presence. I supposed he could have chatted for a few minutes to enquire exactly who Richard Watt was, but no, and I let the matter go. A few days later I began to recall my brief encounter and conclude that things did not quite add up. Here was a man of considerable knowledge and vast experience, sophisticated, well read, well connected, enormously well travelled, with public school education at Oundle, who studied science at Cambridge University without graduating, and whose career as an architect took him the length and breadth of the country, including work at Bolesworth Castle for the Barbour family here in Cheshire, the Castle not being that far from Knutsford. Portmeirion is anyway no more than eighty miles or so from the town as the crow flies. Chester lies just inside the Anglo-Welsh border and has been a trading destination for North Walians throughout the centuries. From there he would have undertaken the first class railway journey to Manchester, and not failed to have been impressed by the panoramic view of Watt's Italianate Knutsford skyline dominated to the north by the Ruskin Rooms and Drury Lane, to the south by Swinton and Coronation Squares, with the Gaskell Memorial Tower and Kings Coffee House proudly sat in the very centre of the town.

Williams Ellis, well read as he undoubtlessly was would have kept abreast with the latest information emanating from the architectural and building trade journals, magazines and periodicals available. The "Architectural Review" and "The Builder" were must have's for the working architect, he would have read with keen interest Sir Nikolaus Pevsner's comments about Watt's Legh Road houses, being "the maddest sequence of villas in all England". Long before Williams Ellis's interest in architecture "The Builder" had published the drawing of Watt's first house and home "The Croft", a drawing which had been exhibited at the Royal Academy in 1895. Though only a schoolboy then he would have picked up on this fact later in life. What he surely would have read would have been Marjorie Sykes's and Christopher Neve's four page article in the Country Life magazine of March 1976, which heaped huge praise on Watt's endeavours. This though after my visit to Portmeirion. Never the less it is now certain that Williams Ellis knew all about Richard Watt, but why on that day summarily dismiss him? I came to the conclusion that I pressed the wrong button and took him completely by surprise, totally off guard, his five word reply revealing hidden guilt. This man, who liked to be called "the father of fallen buildings" had suddenly been reminded of someone he knew had been collecting and collating architectural bric-a-brac and incorporating it into Italianate styled buildings in Knutsford nearly thirty years earlier. In fact if Watt had been able to have had his way, Knutsford too might have looked like an Italian hillside town. His 1898 drawing of a proposed post office illustrates this perfectly. He was also involved with the most impractical schemes for giving Knutsford a formal water front.

Several years later and after converting the dear old Kings Coffee House into the La Belle Epoque restaurant, I sat late one evening after the restaurant had closed, conversing with the secretary of the postal society of Great Britain, who was staying in the hotel. He was doing his homework with a view to using the La Belle Epoque as a venue for the society's annual dinner. I must have been enthusing over the history of The Kings Coffee House and about Richard Watt and his architectural ventures in particular, as a result he asked me if I would talk to the society after it's dinner and relate the Richard Watt story. I agreed and then realised how little I knew about Watt at that moment in time, and that if I was going to give value I could not rely on my enthusiasm alone, I was going to need some facts and figures to support me. This of course meant much time and effort to do so, and I waded in as best I could, knowing little then of the Watt story that I have related in the previous paragraphs. I was motivated and indeed frightened at the prospect of having to talk to such an illustrious audience. Up to that point I had only ever spoken to my local cricket club committee in a secretarial capacity, and anyway hated the idea of actually standing up and speaking to a large number of people. I needed facts and rather quickly. My research led me down many an odd avenue, one of which was to inadvertently come across the fact that at some stage Clough Williams Ellis of Portmeirion had bought, trees, shrubs and bushes for his project in North Wales, from Caldwell and Sons of Knutsford, a highly regarded garden nursery firm who celebrated their bi-centenary in 1980, and who were considered to be the most prestigious company in the north of England, with accounts all over the country, some of which were worth retaining by the Cheshire records office in Chester. Their garden nursery was situated on the Chelford Road in Knutsford which is no more than a hundred metres or so, again as the highly active crow flies, from Legh Road where Richard Harding Watt's array of Italianate villas had stood in celebratory style for nigh on thirty years. So much so then for Williams Ellis's five little words "I've never heard of him". This was an absolute fib made because I had inadvertently touched on the sorest of points and questioned his credentials with regard to originality, and that Portmeirion owed it's inspiration, not to a chance visit to Portafino but maybe to Richard Watt's Italianate ventures in Knutsford. Who knows? Maybe Williams Ellis even enjoyed lunch that day at The Kings Coffee House! Oh yes, my speech to the postal society of Great Britain by the way was a resounding flop.

*Cranford Gardens. Built by Richard Watt for his leather buyer,
Albert Howard and his family in 1904.*

*Albert Howard and family in
1917. They were then living at
The White Bear. Sidney, the young
man in military hospital uniform,
is set to return to active service in
Belgium, he was killed in action
serving with the Manchester
regiment at Passchendaele
months later.*

The last of the old Manchester Royal Infirmary. Much of the then defunct ornamental stonework such as gatehouses, porticos, columns and doorways was purchased by local architect and businessman Richard Harding Watt. It was then carted to Knutsford to adorn the Italianate villas and other buildings he was erecting in the town. He must not have had use for these last remains of the Georgian MRI.

The White Bear Inn circa 1910, the year Albert Howard took up the licence. The Howard's retained the licence for almost 50 years. The inn is almost certainly 17th century, and was a staging post for "The Aurora", a coach and four running daily between Liverpool and London.

Richard Watt's 1898 drawing of his proposed post office. Ignored, instead he built the second phase of the Kings Coffee House. Note how Watt's drawing continued to reflect his Italianate plans for the town.

The management and staff of the Kings Coffee House pictured on it's roof garden in the 1930's.

WINES OF FRANCE. CRICKET CLUB V .... C. CLUB

HOME CLUB .... INNINGS OF CLARET (RED BORDEAUX). PLAYED AT .... ON .... 19....

VISITORS

	BATSMEN	TIME IN/OUT	RUNS SCORED	HOW OUT	BOWLER	TOTAL
1	HAUT MEDOC					
2	CH. LYNCH MOUSSAS	1959	PADILLAC £1.85 £1.00	ST EMILLION		
3	CH. LANGOA BARTON	1962	ST JULIEN £1.50		1962 £1.80 £0.95	
4	CH. LA LAGUNE	1962	LUDON £1.80 £0.95	31. CH. LA CLOTTE GRAND CRU CLASSE		
5	CH. RAUZAN SEGLA	1964	MARGAUX (CH. BOTTLED) £1.80 -	32. CH. GRANGEY CRU BOURGEOIS	1962 £1.55 £0.85	
6	CH. CANTEMERLE	1964	MACALI (CH. BOTTLED) £1.80			
7	THE ABOVE LISTED WINES ARE ALL GRAND CRU WINES			MEDOC		
8				33. CH. LA FLEUR ST. BONNET CRU BOURGEOIS	1964 £1.25 £0.70	
9	GRAVES (RED)					
10	CH. MALARTIC LARGRAVIERE	1952	LEOGNAN GRAND CRU CLASSE £2.00 £1.05			
11	POMEROL CH. LA POINTE	1962	£1.75 £0.25			

RUNS AT THE FALL OF EACH WICKET AND NO. OF OUTGOING BATSMAN

EXTRAS — BYES, LEG BYES, WIDES, NO BALLS

TOTAL — FOR .... WKTS.

BOWLING ANALYSIS — OVERS, MD'NS, RUNS, WKTS, AV.

	BOWLERS			
1	WHITE BORDEAUX			
2	GRAVES			
3	CH. OLIVIER	1960 £1.20 £0.70	38. BARSAC	£1.20
4	SAUTERNES		39. CH. FILHOT SEC DRY SAUTERNES	1964 £1.60 £0.80
5	CH. RIEUSSEC	1960 £1.50 £0.90	39A. MANBAZILLAC	£1.15 £0.65
6	CH. D'ARCHE LA FAURIE	1962 £1.65		
7	LA FLORA BLANCHE	£1.50 £0.85		

RESULT — GAME STARTED — GAME FINISHED

The first wine list of The Tavern restaurant, hand written in a cricket score book, it underlines the owner's passion for the game and complimented the restaurant's cricketing theme. £1.80 for a bottle of Chateau bottled Claret in 1965 will not now buy a glass of plonk!

34

The author as secretary and Bernard Raffo as Chairman of Toft Cricket Club contemplate their clubs chances in 1972, the inaugural year of the National Village K.O. cup, Toft won the trophy in 1989 beating Hambledon C.C at Lords.

The Author's mother, formerly Bessie Lee, as Lady Mayoress with Lord Leverhulme at a scouting occasion.

Nick Smith conducts a wind ensemble comprised of members of the Royal Northern College of Music on the roof garden of the La Belle Epoque restaurant.

Courtesy of Cheshire Life Magazine

The author with Tim Hudson (left), the former controversial cricketing entrepreneur at Birtles Old Hall.

Clive Howard as Chief Drill and Musketry Instructor to the then Royal Hong Kong Police, escorting the Princess Royal, their honorary commander-in-chief as she inspects a guard of honour.

Clive Howard escorting the then Governor of Hong Kong, Chris Patten as he inspects another guard of honour.

The scene at Government House in 1997 as the Governor Chris Patten leaves his residence the day Britain handed the colony back to China. The Union flag is being lowered, and a bugler sounds the last post. The Governor is on the dias. Clive Howard can be seen in khaki uniform at the front commanding the ceremony.

CHAPTER THREE

The White Bear Inn

17th/18th century coaching inn – "The Aurora" stops daily Liverpool to London – heathside neighbours Elizabeth Gaskell and Edward Higgins Highwayman – Albert Howard arrives 1910 – Sidney killed in Belgium 1917 – the Manchester Regiment – Albert dies of cancer 1928 – another alcoholic landlady – son Harry takes the licence – marries Bessie Lee 1930.

~

The White Bear inn is the most prominent building that one sees if you approach Knutsford from the north and west, it is also the most attractive. It appears as you enter the town, to block the road which is the A50 and the former main road from Manchester, Liverpool, Warrington and all the major industrial towns of the north west of England. Until the 1930s all the traffic was forced by the position of the inn to turn left into narrow winding Princess Street and out again between the Church, the prison and Baron Wilbraham Egerton's Gothic old Town Hall and then continue south to the Potteries, the Black Country Midlands and eventually to London. In the same 1930s, to alleviate the congestion and havoc wrought by the increasing density of traffic to Princess Street, a short bypass was cut by the side of The White Bear which necessitates that all traffic approaching the inn from the north has to break hard and swing right to avoid it. As a boy my bedroom was the end one, and I could almost see eye to eye with approaching lorries and their drivers as they swerved to avoid it. Many could not and I would find them protruding out from my bedroom floor. With the advent of the M6, this is now a rare event.

The White Bear is an ancient hostelry dating back to the late 17th century, it is basically a low timber framed Cheshire brick building with a thatched roof. When it was eventually purchased by Groves and Whitnall, they in their infinite wisdom decided the building was insufficiently attractive and needed to be made to look old, would you believe? This they did by rendering the brickwork, whitewashing it, and then attaching to it the multitudinous mock black timbering that adorns it to this day. Though phoney, the building is still an eye catching one. Fortunately the ceilings of the interior are far too low to allow any further tasteless excesses. Though they are improving somewhat, there are fewer better exponents of tastelessness than brewers. The same Groves and Whitnall brewery decimated the meaderingly delightful mid 17th century Rose and Crown inn in King Street, shortly after my great uncle George Lee had sold it to them in the late 19th century. Before the by-pass, the inn was part of a row of buildings which was named Heathside, for the simple reason that it was opposite the famed Knutsford heath. The heath has figured prominently in local history terms, circa 1648 it was the scene of a skirmish between royalist and roundhead armies prior to the battle of Warrington in the English Civil War. In 1745 it was an encampment for Bonnie Prince Charles's rebellious army on it's way from Scotland to it's stuttering halt and disarray at Derby. From the middle of the 17th century it had been a racecourse, where the gentlemen of Cheshire wagered against each others horses and which ceased to exist in 1873 with the advent of the railway and the influx of what were termed 'low life punters'. In the Second World War it was turned into an American Ordnance camp. In peaceful times it has been for ever the scene of the Royal May Day Festival and crowning ceremony.

Further along Heathside is "Heathwaite, the former home of Elizabeth Gaskell, the town's own beloved authoress, whose presence here meant that Heathside would eventually be renamed "Gaskell Avenue". A few yards away was the home of a certain Edward Higgins, on the face of it a solid local citizen, who was later revealed to be a dangerous and murderous highwayman. The White Bear inn being only a couple of hundred yards away, would have served as his local inn. There he could have quietly considered the passengers and their luggage alighting from the "Aurora", the incoming stage coach from Liverpool which changed horses there and picked up travellers on their way to London, and of course on it's return journey which it performed on a daily basis. There are many legendary stories about Higgins, who was eventually unmasked, apprehended, tried and convicted for murder and hung in Carmarthen in 1767. Into this historic old inn in 1910 entered my grandfather Albert Howard with his family. Knowledgeable and experienced in general business matters, but only six years a resident of the town and still unversed in the way of country town living, he was about to be initiated into the volatile and unpredictable way of life of the public house landlord. The Howard family was to remain in The White Bear for almost fifty years.

Groves and Whitnalls proved to be exacting employers, rigid stock control was enforced by a team of stock takers, and I still remember as a small boy what ill-effect the impending visit of a Mr Johnson had on my father's nervous system, after he had succeeded his father as licensee. I have a letter from the brewery to my grandfather baldly stating that if the sale of a certain newly introduced bottled beer called 'C ale' did not improve, his position of landlord would be reviewed. The customers were not interested in this expensive small beer, much preferring their pints of mild or bitter, or even 'mixed'. On one occasion Albert unwittingly got on the wrong side of the law, which mortified him when he was summoned to court and charged with serving ale to a minor. Unknown to him a neighbour had sent his small daughter to the side door of the inn with a jug which the barmaid filled with the ale, this unfortunately was witnessed by the local police sergeant whose action brought the case to court, Albert was not convicted for this iniquitous crime.

It was a far more tragic event that was to despoil Albert's life at The White Bear. Sidney, his eldest son, a bright handsome young man with who it was generally agreed, had a great future in the Manchester insurance business, was called up to serve in the First World War in 1916. He joined the 12th battalion of the Manchester regiment, ordered to France and was invalided home from the trenches there. Later that year he rejoined his battalion in Belgium, only to be killed by shellfire in the Passchendaele mud in October 1917.

Earlier in 1915 Ernest Williams, the son of Edward Williams, the aforesaid landlord of The Rose and Crown inn, and cousin to Sidney Howard, had been killed by Turkish rifle fire on hill 60 when serving with the 6th battalion of the Manchester regiment in the disastrous Gallipolli campaign. Public houses should be places where people go to relax and to take their minds off the cares of the day. The two old timbered inns, The White Bear and The Rose and Crown would have been rather melancholy places to go to enjoy a beer during the First World War. The Howard and Williams families paid the heaviest of prices for their patriotism as of course did thousands of others. It could have been even worse for the Howards. Harold the youngest of Albert's brothers and the last of the three that had emigrated to America several years before the outbreak of the war, returned to fight for his native country. He also joined the Manchester regiment, he quickly made colour sergeant with the 16th battalion and was eventually badly wounded in the legs in France and invalided out of the army. These young men were fiercely loyal to their roots and the city of Manchester and it's famous regiment. Harold Howard returned to Florida where he prospered, cheekily adopting the rank of former captain to help him on his way and to impress the more gullible Americans. A tough, uncompromising man, who on the one occasion that I met him, frightened the life out of me with his strident and controversial points of view, emphasised by lashing about with his walking stick.

I have heard it said that considerable anxiety can be the cause of cancer, and Albert Howard had had more than his share of that, however it is a proven fact that smoking can kill. Albert, like a great many men in the early part of the 20th century, was a pipe smoker. There were few minutes of the day when there wasn't a pipe clenched between his teeth, lit or unlit. Whether it was the worry of his working day or the fact that he was a heavy smoker, it is not possible to say, but he developed a cancer of the mouth, which proved fatal and he died in 1928, aged sixty-one. The licence of The White Bear then passed to his fifty-eight year old wife, Kathryn Howard, formerly Williams. She, if she had not been drinking by then, and it was likely that she had, since Sidney, her son had been killed, certainly took to the bottle to help her through her immediate sorrow and loneliness. Unfortunately, conducting business in an alcoholic haze is no way to succeed. Living in the inn with her at the time of Albert's death were her twenty five year old son Harry and his older sister Isa. The problem was, how long would it be before a brewery so strictly controlled as Groves and Whitnall, would discover that The White Bear was not being managed in the manner that they would prefer? As sympathetic as they may have been at the time, they most certainly would have dismissed my grandmother in due course. To avoid this, her son Harry, had no other recourse other than to take on the licence himself, which was the very last thing that neither Albert or his son would have wished. Albert's time at The White Bear had been a tough and tragic one, he was not a career licensee, and would have preferred to stay in the leather industry. He had endeavoured to ensure that his two sons had respectable careers, Sidney in the insurance business and young Harry in engineering. Harry in 1928 was a draughtsman engineer with the Linotype Company in Broadheath, near Altrincham and was progressing well. Like his father, he had no real desire to be involved in the licensing trade, he had however a duty to keep a roof over both his mother's and his own head, so it came about, he became at the age of twenty five, a particularly young landlord, single, with the weight of the world suddenly on his shoulders.

In 1930 Harry married Bessie Lee of the inn owning Lee family whose interest in the trade in the town was reduced to just the one inn, The White Lion, and that for not much longer. He inherited a lay-about father-in-law, Tom Lee of drunken bullying celebrity, and a generous but self destructive pub keeping grand father-in-law, Fred Lee, neither of whom were destined to play much further part in life, departing this planet with the maximum amount of controversy surrounding them. If anyone should have been aware of the perils of pub owning, it was my father, but he was made of much sterner stuff, and needed to be to cope with the business and a wife as tempestuous and provocative as my very pretty and vivacious mother Bessie. She also had no real wish to be involved with the licensing trade, was it any wonder? She had witnessed at first hand the disastrous affect that drink had played in her life and the resultant physical and mental pain suffered by her mother, through her father's drinking. My mother had character in abundance, she was born and brought up in Middle Walk, just across the Knutsford Moor and opposite the main town. This is known locally as Cross Town. Cross Towner's by tradition were a quirky, awkward and individualistic lot, and my mother had many of their characteristics. She was strong, if somewhat bloody minded, pithy, outrageously straight to the point, with a dry humour which was oft times double edged which could be personal and very cutting. There was also an underlying shrewd country wisdom about her which she inherited from her gentle Irish mother, Annie (Duffy) Lee. Thus the Lees and the Howards, two inn keeping families, were joined and this is where I come into the picture.

CHAPTER FOUR

Boyhood Memories of Wartime Knutsford

1940 the earliest memory – Dunkirk survivors – the Blitz – the 'sluts' – the Parachute Regiment – Knutsford, the regiment's heart – paratroopers as family – Captain Turnbull's buttons – The White Bear as unofficial headquarters – the Americans arrive – General "blood and guts" Patton – a riotous mix of soldiery – roll out the barrel – the town air raid shelter – a sporting background – the burning White Bear.

~

I was born on the 22nd of March 1933. Roughly at that moment, Adolf Hitler was being voted into power in Potsdam, near Berlin. This murderous little Nazi's ambitions for Germany were soon to turn Europe into a bloodbath. It was also going to turn the peaceful British way of life on it's head and of course by late 1939, we were at War. In May 1940, I was seven years old. This is the first year that I have any recollection of. Perhaps the events in it were so vivid as to cause me to remember them so clearly. Of course the significance of what I saw was lost on a seven year old boy, but in later years, such an avid reader of books as myself, was able to put the events into context. It is of course a great pity that such childhood memories were of matters linked to War, but circumstances dictated the case, and the romantically inclined and impressionable little boy that I was then, later became absorbed

45

in matters military and in modern British history. My only toys as a boy were boxes of lead soldiers, which were forever scattered over my bedroom floor.

Knutsford, like many country towns in Britain at that time, soon became a centre of military activity, surrounded as it was by the parklands of the great country estates which were all very soon put to use as army camps. My end bedroom provided me with the most impressive views, with windows on one side overlooking the Knutsford heath, and on the front looking at the oncoming traffic and also into Canute Square, the town's main arena and the scene of so much activity in wartime Knutsford. I would sit for hours in my bedroom lookout, watching the world go by and events unfold. My very earliest wartime memory was of the hot early spring day in May 1940, when I watched my mother hand out cups of tea to a group of rather bedraggled and poorly dressed soldiers sitting around The White Bear courtyard. These turned out to be men rescued from the Dunkirk beaches, while outside the gates of the inn, a long line of private cars queued down the Manchester Road on their way to Knutsford Railway Station to meet the train loads of men still arriving, and who would then be taken to Tatton Park, to the brown bell tented camp which was to be their temporary home prior to rejoining what was left of their units and regiments. Knutsfordians as ever patriotically rallied to the call for help in those dark days, and I began my collection of army badges and my first jagged piece of shrapnel. The Dunkirk veterans became the first of a long line of soldiers that used The White Bear as their local inn.

Sometime not much later in that year during the Blitz of Liverpool and Manchester, my parents deemed it necessary to move my little sister Jeannette and myself to the depths of The White Bear's ancient beer cellars, in case, during the air raids, Knutsford was mistaken for Manchester. A stray bomb had earlier decimated a local house, killing ladies who, in the best Cranford tradition, were ignoring the bombers and having dinner as was usual. On most occasions we were both carried to the cellars in the arms of a band of jolly Royal artillerymen stationed at their base in nearby High Legh. This splendid bunch of chaps, who nicknamed themselves "the sluts", laughed and sang through the night as the Dornier and Heinkel bombers droned overhead on their journey of destruction. I suppose the close proximity of the numerous wooden barrels of ale helped cheer them. Not long after this another momentous occurrence took place. The Parachute Regiment was formed at Ringway Airport, now Manchester Airport, which is barely six miles away from Knutsford. In 1940/1941 from this then smallish aerodrome, converted twin engined Armstrong Whitley bombers took off, circled the town before dropping sticks of six volunteer paratroopers through a hole in the bottom of the aircraft intending that they landed in the dropping zone which was located in Tatton Park, and hoping that they avoided the waters of Tatton Mere. This earlier 'modus operendi' was fraught with danger, and oft times as small boys playing on the Knutsford heath, we would catch sight of paratroopers with their chutes caught up in the tail of the aircraft. Little did we know then that those men had no chance of survival, as the aircraft eventually had to land. Soon the Whitley bomber was replaced by the American Douglas Dakota, that splendid workhorse of an aircraft from which men could be dropped relatively safely from side door exits.

Knutsford was the heart and home of the Parachute Regiment. There were no convenient army barracks in this then rural area of Cheshire to house the men, so the town became one large barrack, and Knutsfordians were asked, perhaps detailed might be a more appropriate word, to billet the men in their homes. This they did most gladly. These volunteer paratroopers were largely seconded from infantry regiments and The White Bear became the temporary home for several of them, the first two were former privates in the Royal Sussex regiment, and still wore their regimental shoulder flashes and cap badges. The red beret had not yet been adopted. Jimmy Grey and Laurie White were very different types of men. Grey was a cheerful cockney and I suspect was made of the right stuff for a paratrooper. White was handsome but in the eyes of a small boy, did not look at all comfortable. We suspected that he had a dubious background. Many years later my mother told me that she suspected him of stealing her jewellery and of bringing venereal disease into our home. Breakfast time was reveille time and was very early at The White Bear. I would be up with everyone else watching with delight these serious goings on, the two men would sit ready in our lounge, which was only called 'the sitting room' perhaps due to it's use in stage coach days. Dressed in their camouflaged smocks, on their heads the flat padded mushroom shaped hats that fastened under the chin. I cannot remember them carrying the 'tommy' guns and hand grenades, that much to my joy I had found stored in the under stairs cupboard. Jimmy Grey always looked cool and relaxed. White I am afraid to say looked pale, sweaty and anxious. He could be forgiven I suppose because these were the dangerously experimental days of jumping out of baskets attached to barrage balloons and holes in Whitley bombers. Then back to my bedroom window to watch the men arriving in their droves, to form up in troops under the eyes of their sergeant majors, before being lorried off to Ringway. Canute Square was the barrack square in those days, all very exciting for a small boy.

Later we were to billet a lovely Irishman named Laurie Wightman and a Scottish officer, a certain Captain Turnbull, late of the Argyle and Sutherland Highlanders or was it the Seaforth Highlanders? He, if arriving back late from the officers mess or some social event, would not trouble us to let him in but preferred to climb in through his upstairs bedroom window. A wild Highlander was Captain Turnbull, I was later to be the object of his wrath. On one occasion, his glorious Highland officers best mess dress, recently pressed and ready for the officers mess dance he was due to attend that evening at the Royal George Hotel, was hung behind his bedroom door, it's buttons gleaming. Those buttons proved to be a too tempting proposition. I did not possess one in my growing collection of badges and buttons, which also was a currency in the small boys market for military badges, so I cut them all off, kept one and swopped the rest with school pal Jimmy Harrison for part of his collection. My appalled mother on being confronted by the extremely irate captain as to the whereabouts of his dress buttons, had to run through the town in the black out to Jimmy's to reclaim them, hoping that he had not had time to swop them. She then had to sew them all on again. I then had to suffer my mother's temper, which when challenged could be quite spiteful. She possibly inherited this from her father Tom Lee, and I was often the butt of it, possibly mostly deservedly. She was quite inventive too. On a couple of occasions I was dragged crying and screaming, very publicly, a quarter of a mile along the heathside to "Kilrie", the local orphans home, where I was delivered to the front door as a prospective client. That really did frighten me, for a while anyway. Knutsford is the spiritual home of the Parachute Regiment, many men married local girls, many family friendships forged. There are always red berets to be seen at the Remembrance Sunday parade through the town, though they grow less in numbers now. Knutsford regards them affectionately, these men that fought in North Africa, Normandy, The Rhine, and of course so tragically at Arnhem. Many books have been written about them, in one of them I was pleased to read that The White Bear was regarded as the unofficial headquarters of the regiment. Veterans used to meet in the old stable yard loft. That was until the brewery in their infinite wisdom knocked it down and turned it into a beer garden.

The wartime clientele at The White Bear were a rich and wonderful mix of servicemen, paratroopers, artillerymen, airmen from the night fighter airfield at nearby Byley and then in 1942/43 the first Americans who built camps on the Knutsford heath and on the Thorneyholme estate. Richard Watt's Ruskin Rooms became the officer's mess club, and Lord Egerton's Alfred Waterhouse designed Victorian Town Hall became the 'doughnut dugout' for other ranks. We children of the town were glad of this at Christmas when we queued to receive our boxes of American 'cookies' including the famous 'Hershey bar'. Later General George 'blood and guts' Patton, the dashing and controversial hero of the allied breakout from Normandy and his race into the heart of Germany. It was outside the Town Hall that he made his critical anti-communist speech. Patton had been allotted the splendid Over Peover Hall as the headquarters of a fictitious American army, supposedly based in East Anglia and used to dupe the Germans into thinking it was going to be used in the invasion of Europe via the Pas de Calais. The ruse worked and crucially Hitler retained divisions in northern France, while the allied armies landed successfully in Normandy. Later he took command of the American 3rd army.

The mix of British and American servicemen in the town, proved at times to be rather volatile. There were dozens of 'dust ups' many observed from my bedroom outpost. Nothing too serious, just good old fashioned 'punch ups' that were soon sorted out by the hell bent arrival of jeep loads of baton wielding, white steel helmeted military policemen who laid about them with indiscriminate ferocity, packing their semi conscious victims into the accompanying station wagon. Once in a more peaceful, quite jolly, but never the less unlawful occasion, a group of Americans from the Thorneyholme camp, found their way into The White Bear beer cellar and proceeded to lift and carry a wooden barrel of best bitter up the steps to a waiting truck. All the time singing "roll out the barrel", while two huge soldiers gently pinned my struggling lightweight father to the wall, his feet dangling. No trace of the missing barrel was ever found. By the time of the 1944 Normandy landings, Knutsford became a quieter place as the military departed leaving little to remind us of their presence.

One relic of the war did exist for a while. This was the huge air raid shelter situated on the waste ground directly behind The White Bear. This was designed to accommodate the whole of the residents living in the centre of town. As a small boy it held a considerable fascination for me, so much so that I had several accidents in it, once falling into it and getting a mouthful of jagged slate for my pains. This was justice as I had moments earlier persuaded my little sister Jeannette to part with her pocket money, and was hurrying past the steep entrance on my way to the shops to spend it on the latest Arthur Ransome book, when I slipped and fell. I avoided the good hiding that I deserved, the slate protruding from my bottom lip was sufficient to deter my mother. It did not save me on another occasion after Mr Godden, the choirmaster at the Parish Church, driven to distraction by the naughty antics of his choristers, of which I was one, chose to dispense with my services for a prank involving a pyramid of kneelers from the top of which I fell. I spent a miserable month not daring to tell my mother, which meant I had no other recourse but to leave home for choir practice and the Sunday services. Sundays were a nightmare, turning out twice a day to attend matins and evensong, but instead having to kick my heels for an hour at a time on the heath until I was eventually spotted and got my just desserts from my mother.

The air raid shelter was, I prefer to think a catalyst in my life, as educationally I was proving to be a huge disappointment. My later excuse for this was that while attending the local Silk Mill Street infants school, we spent half the day practicing evacuation from the school to the shelter. We were thus part time pupils due to the belief that Hitler and the Luftwaffe would eventually locate Knutsford and destroy it in one massive air raid. The next stage in a Knutsford child's education was the move to Lord Egerton's school, situated in Church Hill and directly opposite the parish church, scene of my choral debacle, and where both my father and his brother, the ill fated Sidney, studied far more successfully than I was to do. The school was intended to prime children for their eleven plus examination which if successful, meant transference to the Altrincham and Hale Grammar Schools for boys and girls. My uncle Ken Lee, the brilliant but so unfortunate Indian army major, and my much cleverer sister Jeannette both attended these schools. I failed with flying colours, instead moving to Bradbury Central School in Hale, a school for the less academic and whose most famous former and at the time fellow pupil, was private Bill Speakman of the Kings Own Scottish Borderers, who won the Victoria Cross in the Korean War. This 6ft 5 inch hero, when facing hordes of Chinese soldiers, threw beer bottles when he ran out of ammunition. Beer bottle throwing was not part of our school curriculum.

My sister and I caught the 8.20am train every morning to our respective schools, I to excel at subjects which were of little use to me, history, geography and French were no subjects on which to build a career. Though I must say that the French did become useful in later years, particularly as I was eventually to become a French restaurant owner. Like my father, I was a decent athlete. He was once on Northwich Victoria's book as an amateur footballer, and had trials with Grimsby Town and played cricket for both local clubs, Toft and Knutsford. The early death of his father Albert, scotched any notions of a football career, and he was stuck with The White Bear licence from the age of twenty five. I was in the school cricket team, and was captain of the school football team, I loved my football. All my games for the school were away games, necessitating Saturday morning train journeys to Hale. On the subject of school train journeys, on one occasion arriving home from school on the 4.20pm in Knutsford, a train which transported the early editions of the Manchester Evening Newspaper, I was greeted by a howling mob of newspaper delivery boys loudly baying "Yah Yah John Howard your house is on fire". Sure enough a pall of smoke could be seen from the station steps, and the lovely thatched roof of The White Bear was found to be burning furiously. What Hitler's bombers had failed to do, a faulty chimney flue did, and I was to sleep under a tarpaulin roof for the next three months while the pub was being re-thatched.

My scholastic career ended in 1948, a sporting year for me, if there ever was. Through the kindness of Lord Egerton, I was among a group of Knutsford boys allowed the use of his Mayfair home, while attending the London Olympic Games for which he had obtained tickets for. More of this kind and generous man later. Earlier that year I had gone to Wembley with my Manchester United loving father to watch them beat a Blackpool team that included the great Stanley Matthews, by four goals to two. Howards had supported United for nearly a century, and Albert Howard when they were known as 'Newton Heath Loco'. Jack Rowley and Allenby Chilton, both United International footballers, visited my mother when she was recovering from tuberculosis, so father must have had a good relationship with the club. United are still adored today by yours truly.

CHAPTER FIVE

Tailor Part I

A trade, a must – career decided over a game of snooker – a tailoring apprenticeship – back in St. Ann's Parish, Manchester – Jolley by name and nature – teenage life in The White Bear – a rich vein of characters – father as cricket captain – seeing the dawn in – country boys and country estates – Lord Egerton's Boys Club – footballing virgins – coach Eric Jones – a transformation – the Egyptian National Football coach – the Boy's Club abroad – National Service beckons at last.

~

At the school leaving age of fifteen, my father had not decided in what direction my working career and future lay. I had no choice in the matter and would have liked to have become a 'pup' journalist on the local paper, but my best friend Leslie Groves, had already secured the job and went on to eventually become an editor on a national newspaper. My father though, never asked me if I had any preference. We never ever discussed it, he probably had very little confidence in me, and I was vague and woolly about the whole business. Two things were very sure, one was that I should never ever be encouraged to become involved in the hotel and licensing trade. A trade that he thoroughly disliked and the one that he had been dragooned into, having had no alternative other than to become a licensee to protect his family. He had also grown up in an environment of some unhappiness. His father Albert also having been a non too willing member of the trade, and who had endured a fairly torrid time of it. My father had also witnessed the dreadful demise of his grandfather-in-law, Fred Lee at The White Lion.

The other absolute sure thing was that my father was deadly intent on my learning a trade. His father after all had been apprenticed to the leather industry, and become a hugely successful buyer for Richard Watt. He himself had been apprenticed, and because of his father's death was a thwarted engineer. His brother Sidney had been an articled insurance clerk with a great future, before the First World War's trench mud claimed his life. So it was odds on that I would serve an apprenticeship somewhere, but where? It all came about over a game of snooker, my father was a keen snooker player, so keen that on the night of his engagement to my mother, he took the train to Manchester to watch the World Champions Joe and Fred Davis play in a tournament! He played the game competitively at the Conservative Club and in a more leisurely manner at his gentleman's club, The Tatton Club. Amongst his friends there, was a certain James Trevor, who lived at Plumley, a village a couple of miles west of Knutsford. He was a thorough gentleman and a tailor by profession, not just a tailor, but a 'town and country' tailor of some high repute and with his own business in St. Ann's Square in Manchester. I can only guess at the likely scene of Messrs Howard and Trevor enjoying a game together;

James Trevor:	"How's that boy of yours doing Harry? Good shot old chap"
Harry Howard:	"Well James, come to mention it, not too well at all, just left school. I would like him to learn a trade really. Well played James."
James:	"Have you ever thought of tailoring as a possibility? Bad luck Harry, in off, four away"
Harry:	"As a matter a fact James, I hadn't, but what do you think, is there an opportunity here? Great shot!"

James   "Well Harry, I myself don't need another
(with some thought): apprentice at the moment, but leave it with
                          me, I'll make some enquiries. Bad luck Harry,
                          snookered I'm afraid".

So it came about. Instead of catching the 7 something am train to Altrincham and Broadheath, and working in a factory like a lot of my school friends, and coming home like an oil rag, I was to spend the next five years sitting cross legged on a work bench, getting fingers that looked like over used pin cushions.

A small bespoke tailoring firm by the name of Jolley and Ward did need an apprentice, and the services of a truculent and less than enthusiastic youth were obtained, my father paying a small amount for the privilege, I receiving a pittance in wages. The firm occupied part of the third floor of number 4 St. Ann's Square in the parish of St. Ann's, the very Manchester parish the Howard family had lived and worked in since the 18th century. I did not know then that I was retracing the footsteps of my ancestors and like some of them, I too was working in the clothing business. At the time I did not care a fig. The square was still the fashionable heart of the city, though with the War only being over four years earlier in 1945, central Manchester was still largely no more than a bomb site, the very proof that the German bombers that had droned over The White Bear in 1940 had hit their target. For a sixteen year old country boy, this was a very strange environment to be pitched into.

Len Ward was a dour unforthcoming Devonian. Bill Jolley was a north Mancunian from Crumpsall, near to the Jewish business district of Cheetham Hill. He had all the awareness and understanding of Jewish business practices and was a pretty sharp practitioner himself. He was the force behind this little business which employed only a handful of hand tailors and tailoresses. He was a small rotund, bespectacled man with thinning black hair, and a matching fine pencil thin moustache. He was also jolly by nature and a great joker and wag. I learnt more than tailoring from him, his cheerfulness and good humour was infectious. He was kindness itself to me. His humour could however be a little unkind at times. The premises overlooked St. Ann's Passage, an affluent thoroughfare which oft times was the area where some of Manchester's less fortunate begged for money from their better off fellow citizens who abounded in the St. Ann's area. Manchester has always had a fine reputation for it's appreciation of good music. Many of the poor devils who needed to beg, practised the art of violin playing and, of course, a few of them needed more practice than others. At times they performed directly under the windows of Messrs Jolley and Ward. The sound was often unbearable and to deter this, pennies were heated until white hot on the gas jets that heated the heavy irons used for pressing. These were then picked up by pliers and dropped from the window at the feet of the aspiring musician, while Bill Jolley waited smilingly for the resultant scream of pain.

My apprenticeship lasted for five years, taking the usual additional forms of brewing up and running errands, the latter mainly to outlying under privileged parts of the city, taking the bundles of carefully cut trouser lengths and their trimmings to the trouser makers. A rare breed of man is the trouser maker, quirky, eccentric types, invariably tucked away in some run down back street attic, conscious of their lowly ranking in the tailoring order of things, unlike the precious jacket and topcoat tailors, who were at the heart of events, and at least saw their customers. They invariably vented their spleen on the visiting apprentices, one fellow used to hurl whatever was to hand at me the moment I put my head around his door. After five years this country youth could make a decent hand made suit in whatever style was decreed. The clothes that I stood up in, I had certainly made, and I felt quite cocky at this. My apprenticeship was over and completed by the early part of 1954 and at the age of twenty one, having had a reserved occupation, was now eligible for the call up to serve as a National serviceman. All my close friends had been recruited at the age of eighteen, all had completed their various tours of duty and were now well established in their respective chosen careers. National service was now to take the same two year chunk out of my life, as it did do for everyone who was male, fit and able. My military endeavours I will leave until later. What though of life in the post war White Bear? Up to the end of the war and during my school days, it had provided me with much excitement. I wished maybe that I had a been a little older at the time, and therefore able to understand the significance of events as they occurred. The many reverses and disasters that the Nation had endured during the early part of the war, Dunkirk, the Blitz, defeat in the north African desert, in the Far East at Singapore, all now had to be put into context by much later reading and study. At the time though I was not conscious of any aura of gloom and despondency settling over the bustling inn, life just seemed to go on as it must have done throughout the Nation. Now in my maturing teenage years, I was becoming more aware of what was happening around me in my now peacetime home. Little did I know how much life in the late 1940s and early 1950s was going to influence my later years. The White Bear was to serve as that oft times referred to 'university of life'.

Life in a public house is all about the people who frequent it and the type of people are often determined by the character and personality of the management. My mother and father were widely diverse individuals, my quiet, sporting and gentlemanly father attracted men of similar ilk to his bar. My handsome vivacious mother was a magnet for a rainbow raft of sometimes dubious personalities. Of course, my earliest recollections were of war time people, a host of military uniforms past by endlessly and all too quickly to remember in detail, I was much too young. My mother's friends were particularly striking. The Savage family managed 'The Bells of Peover', George Savage was a Freeman of the City of York, Vicki his wife was elegant and commanding. They were typical of a genteel breed of people who ran the more beautiful and better known inns and hotels of the country well before the brewery conglomerates imposed the succession of generally colourless and temporary individuals that largely prevail today, there are of course some notable exceptions. The Savages had four daughters all of whom were attractive, sophisticated and well educated, two were to marry extremely rich husbands, the other two, Joan and Pheobe, were very precious and lived their lives mostly in London. Like the Mrs Worthington referred to in the song, Mrs Savage didn't heed the warning and put them on the London stage, both being dancers in C.B Cochrane's 'Bevy of Young Ladies' that adorned the capital's pre war stage. Waspish and fay they flitted in and out of The White Bear on a daily basis having removed themselves from the dangers of the London Blitz. Phoebe, it was said, was romantically involved with a prominent army general of the day. Very Noel Cowardish.

Shortly after the war and at the beginning of my apprenticeship, the 1948 conquering Australian Cricket team, captained by the peerless Don Bradman, were touring the country. Hardly to be mentioned in the same breath, my father was a captain of Knutsford Cricket Club. The White Bear might just have been named 'The Cricketers Arms' judging by the number of cricket bags that were piled up at the back door on Saturday and Sunday afternoons, before my father departed with his troops, who returned with him to enjoy his hospitality until midnight. Knutsford C.C were a fine club in those days, numbering amongst it's players N.M.Ford an MCC cricketer who hit the longest straight sixes ever, and "Snowy" Nuttall, to whom scoring centuries was like shelling peas. The club, and myself as a junior member, were coached by Jack Tipping, a former Lancashire wicket keeper, who had the thankless job of understudying for the great Lancashire and England wicket keeper, George Duckworth.

The Old Trafford test match was attended for many years by members of the Cricket Society of Scotland who wisely chose to stay in Knutsford. A well heeled and jocular body of fairly prominent Scottish business and professional men looking to watch the match and have as good a time as is ever possible along the way, which is the duty of all such touring parties. They were led by Jimmy Fleming, a journalist and authoritarian cricket buff and included doctors, dentists, border mill owners, landowners and a Glasgow departmental store owner. They soon discovered that the most convivial place to obtain a 'wee dram' in the early hours was The White Bear managed as it was by a cricketing landlord. This spirited body of individuals knew no bounds when the opportunity for fun presented itself. On one occasion, a stone cobble was removed from a Knutsford street, it then became the 'Stone of Scone' that we English had pilfered from the throne of Scotland centuries ago. This was then reverently paraded with great ceremony at all functions that they attended. This damnedly ugly great stone looked particularly weird when placed in the centre of the dining table, whether it ever made it's way back to Scotland is anyone's guess. This well respected society of course had numerous contacts at the highest level of the game. This meant that they were often accompanied by members of the English Test team, amongst them Godfrey Evans, the hard drinking and ebullient wicket keeper, Bill Edrich, a particular hero of mine and a wartime bomber pilot with a D.F.C and Freddie Brown, the England captain no less, who was to return time and time again to the inn. It was here I suppose that my great affection for the game of cricket was spawned and nurtured, though my father did take me to watch the 1946 Indian team. More cricket later.

My mother's friends however were another cup of tea, or glass of Guinness to be precise. Her own coterie of ladies were various local shop owners, spoiled and bored housewives, who when my mother was in her cups, or should I say glasses of White Label Worthington, of which she was particularly fond, would verbally attack with great venom, describing aspects of their lives with which she did not agree. Being guests and rather obligated to my mother, they had to take the stick that she wielded. This was known to the family as my mother's "hymn of hate". When her liver had recovered the following day, she was all sweetness and light, and would not remember the episode anyway. The male members of my mother's late night parties, included amongst others, a dentist, a BOAC air pilot, the Town Mayor and the local police sergeant, the White Bear was never going to be the target of a police raid. Drinking and driving laws were then a thing of the distant future. There was anyway less traffic on the road in those days, especially so at three am in the morning. The only danger was driving into a ditch, and not involving anyone other than their silly selves. These late nightly sessions were not to my father's liking and he went to bed as early as business allowed, leaving the ship in my mother's irresponsible hands.

Before leaving Egerton Boys School, I had formed a relationship with a couple of boys which was to last some ten or so years and at least until we were all married and in our early twenties. Two factors determined that this close friendship continued. One was that we were essentially small country lads with a natural feel for our rustic environment. Knutsford is surrounded by historic and beautiful country estates, all of which had stately houses which were then still occupied by their distinguished families. Lord Egerton was at home in Tatton Hall, Colonel Leycester-Warren at Tabley House and the Leycester-Roxbys at Toft Hall. Our principal recreation was called 'going across the fields', if you remained on the appropriate footpaths and lanes it was possible to avoid these estates. It was though much more fun to trespass and take the risk of being caught by the various gamekeepers. This was a veritable wonderland over which to roam, we were not destructive hooligans, in fact we were all boy scouts who knew and obeyed the country code. That is to say though that we did not fish, snare rabbits, climb trees and take birds eggs for our respective little collections, we rode the occasional cart horse, borrowed the odd potatoes which we cooked in their jackets over the embers of the small fires we carefully lit in our country dens. We would quietly enter Tatton Park, swim across the Mere and back stark naked in the darkness of night, returning to enjoy our jacket potatoes. It was a frightening experience to be spotted by Ted Hart, the Tabley gamekeeper, who, despite the fact that he only had one good leg, never stopped coming after us until we were off the estate. Once when on the lead roof of the boathouse on the old Tabley Mere, we innocently carved our names into that then valuable, soft metal. Shortly afterwards a humorous thief stole the whole roof, carefully leaving the small portion of it where we had left our autographs. The local constabulary took this as clear evidence as to who the thieves were, and interrogated us individually to gain our confessions. Then the penny dropped and P.C Plod understood the joke.

The other major factor in our young lives was that with the war now over, the American army had vacated Lord Egerton's magnificent Victorian Town Hall, they having used it as their 'Doughnut Dugout'. Lord Egerton, dear Maurice, like his predecessor before him had the interest of the children of the town very close to his heart. Baron Wilbraham having built Egerton School in 1897 next door to the Town Hall, the latter being famously designed by Alfred Waterhouse of British Natural History Museum fame in 1871-2. The two buildings juxta positioned as they are, form an imposing sight at the head and centre of the town. Lord Egerton then generously had his Town Hall converted into what became known as the Egerton Boys Club, which I and my friends, along with the rest of the boys of the town, then joined. What a boy's club this proved to be. It had echoes of a public school, managed by a carefully chosen and extremely enlightened gentleman by the name of Peter Mathews. It's aim was to provide recreational and sporting activities, and how! Recreationally it had a philatelic club, a photographic club, chess club, theatre group and perhaps more. On the sporting front, indoors we were offered table tennis, snooker, badminton, basketball, boxing et al. Outdoors, athletics reigned supreme, followed by cricket and football. Here I was in my element, as a Knutsford junior cricketer I was in and out of my father's team, subject to the availability of senior members, now there was a youth club team to play in. My football career, such as it was, would not have prospered had it not been for the boys club, there would not have been a team in the town to play for. After playing with the school XI on Saturday mornings, I would hurry home to play again in the afternoon, where I was slotted into the variously age determined youth club teams, sometimes at under fourteen level, sometimes as the youngest member of the senior under eighteen XI.

Knutsford boys in the late 1940's and early 1950's were, until the advent of the youth club, a fairly uncompetitive lot. We were certainly not as competitive as our more suburban cousins, particularly those living in the Altrincham area, where post school football had been organised into youth leagues, with teams made up from boys that had left schools that had played fiercely contested schoolboy soccer, Bradbury Central being a case in point. I had had the advantage of this experience and was a more aware player because of it. The Egerton Boys Club thus entered these leagues and because of their rustic experience, were like lambs to the slaughter. I very well remember a junior XI match in which we were beaten 13/0. Now Lord Egerton had granted us the right to wear on our shirts the ancient heraldic device of the Egerton family. I realise I am risking the wrath of the Royal College of Arms or whatever when I describe it as a red lion rampant, grasping a black arrow in it's claws. His Lordship on Saturday afternoons, would drive onto the magnificent sports fields he had provided and park his sleek custom built Bristol sports car with it's famous M1 number plate alongside the touchline of the match in progress. He would then proceed to cinefilm the game, or should I say the carnage that was being wrought on his Egerton teams. This of course was quite unpalatable to him, he did not enjoy his lion emblazoned shirted teams being reduced to pulp.

Suddenly there was an edition to the youth club staff. A certain Eric Jones's services were engaged as football coach. A flaxen haired cockney of slight build with all the incessant verbosity of the inner Londoner, he had played on the left wing for Wolverhampton Wanderers and Crewe Alexandra. In the vast gymnasium hall of the club we were coached in the arts of trapping, heading, dribbling and passing a football. The talent that was apparent among many of the boys was quickly developed and we were very rapidly welded into an extremely good football team, with a team spirit that came with almost immediate success, and with the necessary zest for super fitness. We were virtually unbeatable. I well remember the day when we clinched our first league title, fittingly it was on our ground and against a very good side that if they had beaten us, would have overtaken us as champions. We won 4/3 and Lord Egerton was there in his Bristol sports car, recording our victory on his cinecamera, surely with a smile of contented satisfaction on his countenance, for he said not a word. If there is any better single example of Maurice Egerton doing the very best for the boys of Knutsford, I am not aware of it. I know I speak for the hundreds of young, and now old, men of the town, when I say that we owed him the greatest debt imaginable. He influenced our young lives more than we ever knew at the time and there was not a boy who didn't adore him. Of that particular youth club team, ten played in the final Cheshire trial match, several won County youth caps, and five were given trials by football league clubs. As for our brilliant coach Eric Jones, the job done, he left the services of Lord Egerton, and to prove his exceptional coaching ability, what was his next job? No less than be coach to the Egyptian National Football Team. From village youth team to National coach in one, is some feat.

Further examples of Lord Egerton's kindness, enabled us to take subsidised holidays in the Lake District, where I remember running up Scafell Pike, Skiddaw, Helvellyn and the old man of Coniston in shorts and pumps, carrying a packed lunch during the very hot cloudless fortnight we were there, much to the horror of booted and back packed regular fell walkers. We enjoyed two weeks in Paris, being far too young to enjoy it's nightly pleasures. As forementioned we spent a fortnight in his Lordship's luxury Mayfair flat in Curzon Street when being privileged spectators at the 1948 London Olympic Games, the athletic events being staged at Wembley Stadium. A most memorable holiday was taken in Holland, where we shared a country hostel at Lunteren near Ede, with a Dutch football team named "Xerxes", who were greatly kind to us. We played them at football and gave a good account of ourselves. On our arrival we witnessed the desperate exit of a terrified German youth, who was being smuggled out of the hostel in case he was discovered by the footballers, who it was thought certain would have extracted some form of retribution from him for the suffering that Holland had undergone when occupied by the Nazis, particularly during the winter of 1944-45 when the population had endured near starvation. The war of course, had not long been over then. This fact was further brought home to us when we visited the British military cemetery at Osterbeck near Arnhem, where thousands of paratroopers lay buried as a result of the desperate attempt to take and hold the Arnhem Bridge over the Rhine in September 1944. This visit by we Knutsford boys was particularly poignant, for many of us had shared our homes with these brave men when the Parachute Regiment was formed in Knutsford in 1940/41. Were captain Turnbull and private's Grey, White and Whiteman here?

At the age of eighteen, one left the warm family atmosphere of the Egerton Boys Club, not only leaving the club, young men were also leaving the jobs of work that they had barely settled to and were joining Her Majesty's forces as National servicemen. My own apprenticeship meant that I lingered on for a further couple of years. The highlights of which were weekends spent with my close friends, all of whom were now servicemen and who came home on weekend passes, all having obtained cushy home postings which allowed us to go dancing, drinking and chasing the young ladies of Alderley Edge, Bramhall, Macclesfield and Wilmslow, an exhausting process! How quickly my Olympian ideals became a thing of the past.

CHAPTER SIX

Soldier

To Catterick camp – another trooper – no tank troop glamour – the 68th training regiment – big Jim Edmonds – to Germany – the 4th Queens Own Hussars – Hohne and the 7th Armoured Brigade – Belsen Concentration Camp – a famous Colonel-in-Chief – the regimental typist – the troopers guide to German brothels – the Cold War – Colonel "Loopy" Kennard – life on the Luneberg Heath – Elizabeth Heidt – Lutheran family hospitality – military exercises – beautiful Baltic Travemunde – not so top secret tank – tested and failed – Sir Winston Churchill visits his regiment – demobilised.

~

As the prospect of National service grew ever nearer, equally so did the prospect for Knutsford and Cheshire boys being ordered to serve their basic training at Catterick Camp on the North Yorkshire Moors, which had the reputation of being a military hell hole. This was due to the town having long been associated with the Cheshire Cavalry Yeomanry and indeed then still having the "A" squadron camp at Shawheath as part of the territorial army set up. Former National servicemen would never be far away from recall for re-training, exercises and camps as T.A soldiers. Catterick of course, being a major tank training camp. So it came about that like my great, great, great uncle Joseph Lee and my great uncle the controversial George Lee, I became a cavalry trooper. Inevitably I had to report to Catterick in May 1954 to undergo basic training with the 68th training regiment of the Royal Armoured Corps. Here we were taught basic marching drills for endless hours, learnt how to fire the Lee Enfield rifle and the Sten machine gun, perform ceremonial pistol drills, the pistol being the standard fire arm for cavalry and tank regiments when on parade. After basic training, one was allocated a trade. Not for me the glamour of becoming a tank driver, a tank gunner or a wireless operator, no, I was destined to drive a typewriter and attended the necessary course which made me a regimental clerk. For the rest of my life, I was never to be far away from a typewriter.

The next step was to be allocated to the strength of a regiment, and it was ordained that I became a member of the 4th Queens own Hussars, who at that time were stationed in Germany with the British Army of the Rhine, or B A O R as it was and probably still is commonly known. The 4th Hussars at that time were up to full regimental strength and therefore had no immediate need for my questionable services until of course, one of their National service clerks was demobilised, and I would then be called to fill the vacancy. This did not occur until much later, and for several months I was on the strength of the 68th training regiment, doing very little of importance as part clerk/part store man to "B" squadron, obtaining weekend passes home was my principal objective. If these could not be obtained, like many others I would skip camp on Saturday morning, catch the bus to Manchester and train to Knutsford, enjoy Saturday night out with my friends and catch the midnight bus back from Manchester's Piccadilly along with hundreds of other bleary eyed 'squaddies'.

Many times this was not possible due to regimental duties, invariably these were all form of guard duties. Once I had to don the ceremonial dress of a 6th Inniskilling dragoon guardsman, adorned with a bearskin helmet and sword I stood at ease throughout a dinner held by officers of the regiment celebrating the Battle of Balaclava. Their cavorting was sufficient to keep me amused with the mess silver much to be admired as I sweated the night away under the weight of my ceremonial garb. Gradually one grew extremely attached to the North Yorkshire Moors. Leyburn, Middleham, Bedale and Richmond were little jewels of villages and towns, unfortunately there were only occasional glimpses of these. Life for a while was quiet, I was almost a forgotten soldier, which was perfect. It was the National serviceman's creed that he spent his two years as quickly and as undramatically as possible. I shared a two man billet with a huge hulk of a man from Market Harborough, who's passion like mine, was cricket. Whenever possible he played with a cricket ball, practicing his grip on the seam, his hands being so big as to almost make the ball disappear. We spent a happy time that autumn and winter tuning into the early morning radio broadcasts from Australia that brought the cheering news that Frank Tyson, and his fellow fast bowlers, were winning the Ashes series for England 'down under'. As with many men of great size, big Jim Edmonds had a heart to match and was as gentle as a baby.

The army took his considerable size into consideration when forming the regimental boxing team, in their eyes here was a heavyweight boxer in the making. So mild mannered gentle Jim was thrust into the ring against some pretty good fighters who gave the slow moving store man a fairly torrid time, until he, in angry response to the torment being inflicted, struck the one fatal blow with that huge right fist that brought the contest to a sudden end. When we were eventually posted to our units, he joined the 1st Royal Tank regiment in Egypt, and played cricket there for the British Middle Eastern Command Team. My last memory of him was in the summer of 1956 after we had both left the army. There was a knock on the door of the Red Cow inn which my father then had the licence for. There he stood hesitantly on the doorstep as my uncle quipped "blocking the daylight out", announcing the fact that he had been selected to play for Northamptonshire 2nd XI against Lancashire at Old Trafford the following day. I went along to spectate at a sparsely attended game, sitting at deep fine leg both to watch and chat with him at the end of his overs. I never saw or heard from him again after that. I hope fate and fortune favoured this lovable giant of a man.

Our idyllic existence at Catterick came to an end in the December of 1954 when the 7th Royal Tank regiment returned from duty in Hong Kong to take over the role of a training regiment. This coincided with a clerical vacancy over in Germany with the 4th Hussars, I was at last to join my regiment. We were moved out of our comfortable billet to holding hutments used only for this purpose until movement orders and travel documentation was finalised. These huts were on the edge of camp and were barely habitable, as no one ever spent more than a few days in them. There was no door in ours and most of the windows were broken. Unfortunately, being in late December, the weather took a turn for the worst, and North Yorkshire was hit by heavy snow storms. It was so cold that when we woke in the morning we found several of the more astute local sheep huddled round the stove for warmth. Like their human counterparts, these Yorkshire sheep were no fools. We were very soon Harwich bound and from there by boat to the Hook of Holland. From there we took the aptly named "military blue train" taking it's thousands of very glum looking servicemen to their various German destinations. My own destination being Hohne Camp, near Bergen on the Luneberg Heath not far from a less cozy little place called Belsen, known during the War as one of Adolf Hitler's bestial concentration camps, not exactly a health resort in 1955. I arrived in snow which did not melt until March, only then did I get my first glimpse of the local flora.

The 4th Queens Own Hussars were part of the 7th Armoured brigade which again was part of the famous 7th Armoured division who earned great fame fighting Rommel's Africa corps in the North African desert during the 2nd World War. We wore the famous 'Desert Rat' insignia on our sleeves and felt quite unworthy of this honour. The so called 'Cold War' was still being waged between the Warsaw pact countries and the North Atlantic Treaty countries of the west. Hohne camp and the brigade were only 30 miles from the border between west and east Germany beyond which were poised the mighty armies of the Russian led Eastern Bloc. We and the rest of the NATO forces were supposedly always at the ready to repulse their long awaited invasion, which of course never came. All both sides did was exercise and parade their strengths, flex their muscles, bare their teeth and eyeball each other across the manned barbed wire and land mined strip that the Russians had erected to prevent unhappy east Germans joining their only slightly then better off relations in the west.

The regiment was comfortably housed in the large barrack blocks vacated by the wartime German Garrison. The barracks were centrally heated, a luxury that British soldiers had rarely, if ever, enjoyed and we slept two or three to a room, at least we did in the 'fancy pants' headquarters squadron to which I had been allocated to. The 4th Queens Own Hussars were a flashy cavalry outfit with a long and illustrious pedigree. Formed in 1685 by order of King Charles the second at the time of the Monmouth Rebellion, it served with John Churchill, Duke of Marlborough in Spain, won it's first battle honour at Dettingen in the war of the Austrian succession, served throughout the Spanish Peninsula campaign with the Duke of Wellington, gaining battle honours at Talavera, Albuhera and Salamanca. Most famously in the Crimean War, it won it's most famous battle honour when it was one of the five cavalry regiments that made up the 'gallant 600' men that were the light brigade that mistakenly and suicidedly charged the main line of Russian artillery at Balaclava, an episode made more famous by Lord Alfred Tennyson's poem. This action was celebrated on the 25th of October every year. In recent years the regiment has been amalgamated so many times, it probably doesn't know what to celebrate. In 1955-56 it's honorary colonel was no less a person than that greatest of Englishmen, Sir Winston Churchill, who had joined the regiment in India as a Subaltern in 1895. Coincidently, his nephew Julian Sandys, son of Duncan Sandys the Tory cabinet minister, was serving with the regiment, also a Subaltern. Tradition dies hard particularly when it is remembered that the 4th Hussars fought under John Churchill in Spain.

From the great to the 'gor blimey'. I took up my exalted position as regimental part one order clerk. This was to type and reprint regimental standing orders from on high, from the war office via the colonel, not the honorary colonel I hastily add. I listed postings in and out of the regiment of its various personnel and had at my disposal a catalogue of standing orders that were to be repeated from time to time, mostly monthly. The completed orders were then issued to the other tank squadrons and pinned to their squadron office notice boards for the attention of every soldier who took little or no notice of what was decreed on them. That is I believe with the exception of the monthly occasion when I had to list all the out of bounds brothels in Bremen, Hamburg, Hanover and other towns in which these dubious pleasure palaces existed. Instead of heeding this warning about the dangers to their health, it is quite likely that some men waited with sharpened pencils at the ready for the names and addresses that I and the regiment were kindly providing.

I was also the regimental typist to the adjutant, captain T.W 'Tommy' Tilbrook, an owlish, whimsical man of quiet charm and high intellect, and of course to any other H.Q squadron officers that required my two fingered typing talents. The 4th Hussars had not long returned from Malaya where they had been active in helping to defeat the communist Guerrilla insurgency. Not long after my arrival at Hohne, the regiment acquired a new colonel, by name G.A.F Kennard a very tall, craggy, handsome, charismatic man affectionately and widely known by the nickname of "Loopy". He had served with the regiment in Libya and Egypt in the Second World War and had been captured in the ill fated expedition to Greece where it had suffered 90% casualties. He proved to be a popular and much loved leader, original in thought, carefree in spirit, he adored the 4th Hussars and was devastated when the regiment was amalgamated with the 8th Kings Royal Irish Hussars in 1958, the regiment then becoming the Queens Royal Irish Hussars with the command going to an 8th Hussar officer. That was a thing of the future and National servicemen never looked further than their two year duration of service. While the 4th Hussars were still an active unit, their Honorary Colonel Sir Winston Churchill died. The Nation mourned as one, and for a then former Hussar it was particularly poignant to watch the television that day and to see his coffin borne on the shoulders of the non commissioned officers of his old regiment.

In late 1999 colonel "Loopy" Kennard's death was announced in the Daily Telegraph along with a fitting obituary. How many National servicemen that served in the tank squadrons of the regiment got to know him I do not know, I suspect very few. We of headquarters squadron working along side his office possibly understood a little more. It was much later, after reading his autobiography, that I came nearer to understanding the nature of this gallant gentleman, who could imbue a heavy armoured regiment with the spirit of a mounted cavalry one. In the February of 2000, a memorial service was held to celebrate the life of Lieutenant Colonel Sir George Kennard Baronet. It was held fittingly in the Chapel of the Royal Hospital in Chelsea, and I was determined to attend. I had little idea of what to expect. As a former bespoke tailor,

I am rather fussy about the cut of my suits, preferring if possible to have them cut in hacking jacket style. I wore my navy pin striped job, the brown trilby I always wear in the winter months to keep a balding head warm and always keep what is left of my hair longish, I was of course wearing my regimental tie. Quite unbelievably when hurrying through Sloane Square, I bumped into my old 4th Hussar colleague and close friend of forty-five years, John Anderson, who with his usual acerbic wit, described me as a cross between a horse racing trainer and a city bookmaker, which in a way I suppose was appropriate since I was attending the memorial service of a cavalry officer.

On entering the Chapel, I found myself in the company of dozens of gentlemen similarly attired, give or take the odd bowler hat. I must have passed visual muster on that parade. I discovered the following day from the "In Memoriam" column of the Telegraph that these included two Field Marshals, three Generals and five Major Generals, not to mention three Dukes, two Marquess's and three Lords of the Realm, mostly accompanied by their ladies. Many of course were the former captains and majors in the 4th Hussars of my day, and were now retired officers of senior rank and presently languishing in the Shires. I was shown to a front row pew seat by Cheshire's own soldierly Duke of Westminster, an all round good egg, fondly regarded in his native county. I found myself between two former officers of I know not what rank, for not a word was exchanged, which of course was expected. In a very short time I began to develop the mother of all inferiority complexes. Maybe I was sat between two Generals, either of whom might ask this former lance corporal of his military pedigree. I grew even hotter under the collar until finally all were seated. The last to take their seats were the honourable Sir Angus Ogilvy followed by the Duke of Edinburgh, deputy C in C of the now Queen's Royal Hussars.

There followed the most beautiful memorial service that one could possibly imagine, at times sad, but most times stirring, as the distinguished life of Lieutenant Colonel Kennard was fondly recalled. It was a most humbling and unforgettable occasion. I would have had time, before catching my train home, to have enjoyed a cup of tea or glass of champagne that was being offered in the marquee on the hospital lawn, but could not bring myself to do so. I felt this to be a family occasion, the army family. It was as if the cavalry club had been moved across London, and I had only ever been a very temporary member of the cavalry. I most certainly would have been the only National Service N.C.O in attendance and virtually an interloper. There again I do not do justice to a breed of professional men who I found during my short time with the regiment to be without exception, humane and decent and who I would have gladly followed. Had I ventured into that marquee and spoken to someone, I think they might have been more than generous in accommodating me, my courage however deserted me, and I left with the thought that maybe that day I represented the hundreds of National Servicemen that had passed through the 4th Hussars during Sir George Kennard's colonelcy and had been briefly touched by his brave and dashing demeanour.

A social existence in the regiment was just that, an existence. The Hohne camp was remote, with only the village of Bergen – Belsen, some short mile away. Home leave was out of the question, weekend leave available on occasion. We were however too poorly paid to tour a country that had been devastated by war and whose population was sorely deprived of the most basic commodities like soap, coffee and cigarettes. Talking of the latter, whether you required them or not, you were issued a ration of cigarettes, and like many others I did not. The regimental mafia mainly made up of scouses, cockneys and Glaswegians, were very soon aware of who did not smoke, and purchased that soldier's ration. There was of course a flourishing black market and the poor Germans were held to ransom by it. We were thus able to enjoy the occasional 'steak and kartoffeln' at the local gasthof with our added riches, averting our eyes as to what was going on outside the camp. The greatest of treats was a visit to the lovely, old black and white timbered town of Celle, which the War had managed to by pass. Once in the town's beautiful opera house, I wallowed in the luxury of a performance of La Traviata, given no less than by the touring company of the La Scala Milan Opera, riches indeed.

On winter Saturday afternoons, I played left full back for the regiment. We had two or three former football league players, two from Notts County and one from Alloa Athletic, who were the backbone of the team, who enjoyed moderate success against other regimental teams.

That was until one day in the Black Forest on a pitch that was a sheet of packed frozen snow, we played the Kings Dragoon Guards. We were without Scobie, our Scottish star and I was moved to centre half as cover for him, a position I had never had to fill before. We were opposed by a forward line composed of small Scottish second division players of the Ally McCoist, Kenny Dalglish variety, who had a low centre of gravity. These little nimble footed jocks literally skated through us to the tune of 10/0, it was a massacre. Shortly after this at a training session, a clumsy team mate put a stud through the top of my canvas training shoe and tore the nail off my big toe. This then turned septic and I was admitted to the British Military Hospital at Hanover, where the army doctors made a pigs ear of small operation which was never right until I was further operated on in Civvy Street. The one good thing emanating from this episode was that I was excused boots for the duration of my army service. A real blessing.

Sundays in the army are a sorry affair for the lower ranks, tradition has it that they lie on their beds reading the 'Beano', this after having slipped into the cook house for a breakfast of cold greasy fried eggs and bacon. If I did lie in my bed it was to listen to jazz broadcasts on either the British or American forces networks, not to forget family favourites and wallow in nostalgia for lost days at home. Very often we would take a Sunday afternoon walk, always gravitating to the isolated and melancholy piece of moor land that was the site of the former Nazi concentration camp of Belsen. The ghastly images shown on old film were still very much in our minds, these of course being of the poor creatures that had been either starved or gassed to death here not ten years before. Here could still be seen the large shallow pits and equally large mounds of earth that needed very little imagination to know what they represented. Here and there carved in small granite monuments were the simple ghastly facts that "here lie the bodies of 85,000 Jews, slain by the hands of the murderous Nazi's", and so forth, repeated again and again. It was a pretty morbid and miserable way to spend your Sunday leisure hours. It was possible then to dig the toes of your shoes into a patch of earth and to find rotting prison clothing and German military cap badges. I visited the site with my family a dozen years later to find a smart little museum that recorded the horrific events that occurred here in war, this for the benefit of anyone who was interested, not many were that day. There was still no evidence of fauna inhabiting the area, it was a well acknowledged fact that no birds ever flew over this grim piece of countryside. They most certainly did not.

On a more cheerful note, it was well known in the regiment that working as secretary for the major acting as president of the regimental institute was the prettiest of all German girls. Being engaged to be married after leaving the army, and not having seen a young lady for many a month, I decided to make her acquaintance. Her name was Elizabeth Heidt and she was as intelligent as she was pretty. She spoke fluent English and she too was engaged to be married, so we had plenty in common to talk about. It started a friendship which has lasted until now, albeit largely in the form of exchanging Christmas cards. We got on well enough for her to ask me round for dinner and to meet her mother and her fiancée, a splendid chap named George Schultz. Come to think of it, it was quite a step in the dark for them, after all I was a soldier in what was in those days, in the mid-fifties, a British army of occupation, it is quite possible that they could have been called collaboraters by their fellow villagers. Imagine Germany winning the War and occupying Knutsford, the locals would have frowned if my family had entertained a German soldier.

The thrill and expectation of meeting a German family in their home was something that I was not prepared to forego. Borrowing the orderly room sergeants bicycle, off I rode across the Luneberg Heath to Hermannsburg just some eight or nine miles away and deep in the forest. Frau Elizabeth Heidt was a grand matriarch of the Hanoverian Lutheran old order, plain and severe, at the same time warm and welcoming. George Shultz was equally formal, upright and correct, but extremely kind considering he was probably unsure what his fiancée was going to drag over the threshold. We ate a good solid country meal, and afterwards George serenaded us on his violin, with amongst other pieces, Mozart's Eine Kleine Nacht Musik. It was certainly the most beautiful day I spent in Germany. I visited the Heidts many years later in the mid to late sixties along with my wife and son. Then I was able to take gifts in return for their previous hospitality. We stayed in the Lutheran Missionary School that George was the Principal of. Not long after the now married couple left Hermannsburg to take charge of a missionary station in Northern Natal, South Africa, where they brought up a large family of their own as well as attending to the needs of their impoverished parishioners. Solid gold are Elizabeth and George Shultz, their children are also a great credit to them all becoming professional people living variously in South Africa, America and Germany.

The orderly room personnel rarely joined their comrades in the tank squadrons when the regiment went out on exercises across the Luneberg Heath, only twice to be precise and we were then like fish out of water, goodness knows what would have happened if it had been the real thing and the Russians had attacked. We, along with the members of the despised and pampered regimental band, when it was not playing in Nice and Monte Carlo, performed mundane duties which included mounting the guard. On one celebrated occasion I was detailed to superintend ablutionary duty, a position which it is difficult to describe. I had to take up my position in a room above the garrison guard room, and there hand out swab kits to returning soldiers who had been availing themselves of the pleasures of the flesh in the north German out of bound brothels. The great irony being that by reading and noting the addresses of these whore houses published by yours truly on regimental part one orders, I was probably the very chap responsible for their neurosis about contracting the clap. It was difficult for me to look them in the eye.

Headquarters squadron did manage to go out on exercise on one memorable occasion, it was called a 'wireless exercise' and was miraculously performed without the aid of a single wireless set. I suspect this was instigated by colonel "Loopy", who with the morale of his minor merry men close to his humorous heart, decreed that we needed to be rid of barrack room life, if only for a weekend. Where were we to be despatched? Into the heart of the Luneberg Heath for a weekend in the country seemed to be the logical destination, but no, certainly not. In truly stylish cavalry fashion, we instead made our way north to the Baltic Sea to the exclusive yachting and bathing resorts of Travemunde and Timmendorfer Strand. Here we mixed with the few Germans who had a bob or two in their pockets, probably as a result of their black market activities. We night clubbed Friday and Saturday nights away, and never went to bed at all, usually seeing the dawn in at the end of a jetty where we dangled our sore feet into the gently lapping Baltic Sea, before collapsing into beach chairs for the rest of the day. We danced with weekend partying frauleins without any sexual ambition, just to dance was sufficient, perhaps the famous bromide laced tea won the day. The poor girl who I had the last waltz with got a slap across the head by an unknown hand for her participation as we stood to attention during the playing of Deutschland uber alles. Never mind, the colonel would have been proud of us that weekend for upholding the regimental tradition for dash and initiative. It may not go down in the annals of the 4th Hussars as a battle honour to rival Balaclava, but we few could lay claim to Travemunde as a noteworthy social skirmish. As for our officers, I am sure they must have enjoyed the sailing, which I suspect was the object of the exercise in the first place.

The Christmas of 1955 will be long remembered with gratitude by the British army of the Rhine. The powers that be decided that we should nearly all spend Christmas at home with our families and friends, and this was my one and only home leave from Germany. We descended like locusts on Dusseldorf Airport and were transported by Douglas Dakota aircraft to Blackbushe military air base in Hampshire and then bussed by open top lorries to all parts of the United Kingdom. My decreed destination was Litherland Camp at Liverpool as the nearest depot for Cheshire and Lancashire soldiers. I managed to jump ship at Chester and hitch hiked the rest of the way home. Who says the army doesn't care about it's men? It damned well does and always will.

There were at times a reasonably serious side to life in the regimental headquarters orderly room. One such episode was with regard to the Conqueror tank. This was the very latest tank and designed to be potentially a war winning armoured fighting vehicle built to deal with every battleground situation and condition. The huge tank could fire huge shells from it's huge gun, rather like the navy's super battleships of the Second World War, nothing would be able to withstand the impact of it's fire power, and as it's range far exceeded the distance that the Russian tanks could fire, the fighting would be over before it started, so to speak, piece of cake! Very secretly back in the UK production of the Conqueror had already started. However, before going into full production the tank had to undergo testing and trials with an active unit of the British army. The most likely place that these tanks would go into action would be in the event of a cross border Russian thrust across the Luneberg Heath with the 7th Armoured Brigade directly in the line of it's advance. What better place to test the mighty Conqueror than on the same Luneberg Heath which was ideally suited to mechanised warfare. The regiment chosen to test these tanks was of course non other than the famous fighting Fourth Hussars. A troop of four Conqueror tanks was dispatched very secretly across the North Sea to Hamburg, where it had been arranged that the regiment's armoured recovery vehicles would meet the ship at the Hamburg dockside, load them up and bring them to Hohne, all very hush, hush. Unfortunately, the ship docked twenty four hours earlier than was planned. The Conquerors were unloaded onto the Hamburg dockside, and when the 4th Hussars tank transporters arrived as designated on the following day, they found half the young hooligans of Hamburg playing soldiers in them, so much for secrecy.

Major Davies, the Regimental Technical Adjutant was allotted the task of testing the Conquerors rigorously under simulated battle conditions. A quite brilliant tank technician, Major Davies was well up to the task and this is where I come into the picture. As the regimental typist, I was allotted to the Major and given the task of typing up his hand written reports which were accompanied by complicated pencilled technical drawings which, with considerable difficulty, I had to transcribe onto stencils which were then duplicated. The object of the exercise being to get these reports to the war office asap. I therefore had to lock myself in a small office and work through the night and have them ready for Major Davies to read and sign later in the morning. They were then given to a waiting motor cycle dispatch rider who like the pony express, would whisk them to Whitehall. As the first person, other than of course the colonel and adjutant, to see and read the reports, I was well ahead of the war office in ascertaining that all was not going too well with the testing of the Conqueror. It is now too many long years ago for me to remember the precise details, anyway, that would be far too boring to relate. There were very many problems with the juggernaut but two outstanding defects were the cause of it's demise. One was it's sheer size and overall weight displacement, which made it extremely slow on the one hand, and on the other hand, despite good firm going on the sandy blasted heath, if there was any moisture about it was prone to sink up to it's hull and become nothing more than another defensive artillery piece. It would have been perfect if any action could have been conducted along an autobahn. The other main defect was the size of it's weapon, which was far too big, not usually regarded as a defect this, but in this instance all too true. The very large gun mounted on it's huge turret obviously needed to fire very large shells, unfortunately whoever designed this aspect of the tank, had not been able to come up with an adequate solution for transferring these very large shells to the breech of the very large gun, so the job was left in the very small hands of the poor bloody gunner. He, in action conditions, might very well have been able to load say four shells before collapsing in a heap, thereby becoming the first casualty, and this not as a result of enemy involvement. On reading this I too was near to collapse but with merriment. The official wording in military terminology was 'loader fatigue'.

So the 4th Hussars were probably instrumental in ending the career of some erstwhile tank designer, for on the damning evidence of Major Davies' reports, the Conqueror was a "lulu" and withdrawn from active service. It makes one wonder if, when it is deemed necessary to design an armoured vehicle of any description, the services of regimental technical adjutants might be considered useful at the drawing board stage. If they are not they should be, if what happened to the once mighty Conqueror is anything to go by, it would certainly save the tax payer a lot of money, millions of pounds and with only four very large heaps of rusting metal to show for it.

With the excitement of Christmas leave over, the year 1956 dawned. For me demobilisation loomed large on the horizon. In the nearer future, for the regiment, it was a time of great excitement. It had long been known that the Honorary Colonel-in-Chief of the 4th Queen's Own Hussars, this being no less a person than Sir Winston Churchill, was going to honour his old regiment with a visit in the spring of the year, so the 4th Hussars began to prepare. The regiment with it's long history and with famous battle honours to it's name, was very proud of itself and rightly so, we had a lot of tradition to live up to. The barracks were spring cleaned, fresh paint was everywhere, the battle squadron tanks and armoured cars, greased and polished, along with everything else that moved. The squadrons were never off the parade ground square, we were drilled and drilled until we were punch drunk. We marched and countermarched, uniforms pressed, boots gleaming, webbing blancoed, badges gleaming above the left eye, all this under the predatory gaze of Regimental Sergeant Major "Jesse" James, the smartest man in the regiment and a first class example of that very special British army breed, the RSM, the man who breathed life into every military unit. My office was next door to that of RSM James, he came from Warrington, just twelve miles up the road from Knutsford, and had enjoyed a few pints of bitter in The White Bear in his time. He was a fervent supporter of Warrington Rugby League club, a club that I had watched occasionally, so we could converse about the talents of such Warrington stars as Gerry Helme, Harry Bath and Brian Bevan.

Now there were over 500 men on parade when the regiment turned out, and the RSM couldn't possibly know the names, if any, of it's troopers and lance corporals. By jingo he knew my name and didn't he darn well use it. Perhaps it made it easy for him that I was easily identifiable by the fact that I was excused boots and therefore gaiters, and that my trouser legs flapped offensively in the wind. On the subject of not knowing or remembering names, there is a lovely story told against himself by colonel Kennard in his autobiography. He could never remember the names of his junior officers and preferred to give them nicknames instead, even the adjutant in the next office, captain Tilbrook, was nicknamed "Ticker Tom". On the day of Sir Winston's visit Colonel "Loopy" says he introduced no less than five officers as "Tom Williams", all of whom loyally did not bat an eyelid. The great day did arrive, the regiment presented itself proudly to the greatest ever Englishman, raised it's berets and gave him three rousing cheers. I would love to have been able to have done so, but unfortunately I was demobbed a few weeks earlier!! "C'est la vie"

I never disliked doing my National service, it was just the fact that it was an inconvenience to us all. It took two years out of our young lives when we would have preferred to be otherwise engaged, pursuing careers that had to be put on hold, being denied the opportunity to further educate ourselves, losing touch with family and friends, our social lives disrupted and so forth. On the other hand, looking back, there are a great many of us, myself included, that would not have missed it for the world. Initially we were subjected to the severest disciplines imaginable and it was hard to take, however, life in the armed forces soon kicked in, and we were afforded opportunities and experiences that in retrospect we were pleased to have taken part in. We had travelled and learned to mix with a variety of young men of widely differing backgrounds. If we had shaped up to it individually we would have learnt a considerable amount about life in general, and developed a greater number of human values and a more philosophical attitude to it. The disciplines that the military imposed on us, I believe, gave us a greater understanding of ourselves and others. No bad thing when one is constantly reminded almost daily, that there is much lack of self discipline, or lack of discipline in general amongst a large section of today's youth, that a spell of enforced military training would go a long way putting to rights. I am sure you will have heard this old chestnut before, never the less.

CHAPTER SEVEN

Tailor (Part II)

Jolley and Ward gone – Bill Jolley as Kendal Milne head cutter and tailor – a job for the boy – from White Bear to Red Cow – Chester's lunatic broth – father to Kings Coffee House – salesman to assistant buyer – a Harrod's man – assistant buyer to buyer – fashion shows – pantomimes with Bruce Forsyth and Norman Wisdom – London and Kitzbuhel buying – the House of Fraser loom large – central buying not a prospect – departure.

~

As it happens National service did not necessarily interfere too much in my life. I was at a career crossroads, but was not too badly upset about the situation and had not given it a thought during my time with the 4th Hussars. I certainly did not want to continue with a career in tailoring, not having then the imagination to realise there certainly was a future in that profession if one studied cutting and design. As luck would have it, that would have been a difficult thing to do, as Messrs Jolley and Ward, as fine a tailoring business that it had been, had ceased to exist. I never ever enquired about the circumstances involved, had the partners fallen out with each other? Was the business in decline due to the huge advances in the quality of ready made men's clothing? My initial feelings were of sorrow particularly for Bill Jolley, a man who had been very kind and patient with me during my apprenticeship. As it transpired, this shrewd little man had obtained the first class position of head tailor and cutter to the men's tailoring department of Kendal Milne and Company of Deansgate, Manchester who were then importantly part of the highly regarded and prestigious Harrods Group.

Bill Jolley, very kindly, knowing of my pending demob, had on my unknown behalf, spoken to and recommended me to the men's wear buyer at Kendal Milne as a possible future employee and, subject to interview, the job was mine. At the same time he had advised my father of his intention to take this course of action. He liked the idea being only too glad to see his vacillating offspring in some kind of work, at the same time he knew that subject to my compliance, I could hardly have had better employers. My father and mother had by this time left the old White Bear in Canute Square. It must have been a huge wrench for him, with it having been his family home for almost fifty years, however, he did not let the old inn out of his sight, moving just a hundred yards away to the Red Cow Hotel, which was larger and had a number of guest bedrooms with which he could increase his income by letting.

The only downside to this move was that his employers were now Chester's Brewery, who's beers had a reputation for having a volatile nature and being of a somewhat chemically engineered composition, which earned them the nickname's of Chester's "fighting ale" and Chester's "lunatic broth" which should have served as a fair warning to him. Having served Groves and Whitnall's innocuous and gentle ales for so many years, it took him many months to get the measure of their volcanic nature, if he ever did. This involved the use of a substance that looked like decorators wall paper paste, which was fish based and smelt dreadfully. This was poured through a funnel into the top of the oak barrels, and being an extremely thick mixture it spread itself, in theory that is, across the top of the beer and slowly sank through it dragging all the impurities to the bottom of the barrel, it was well named "lunatic broth" for it nearly drove my father mad. This mixture was called "finings" which must have been the foreshortening of the word "refining". What affect this beer would have had on it's customers in an unrefined condition heaven only knows, even refined it's affect was sometimes disastrous. It was the favourite brew of the great number of really likeable Irishmen that worked on the local farms, included among them were a pair of brothers named Michael and Joe, whose Donegal accent was so thick, you could cut it with a knife. They would stand together wordlessly sinking pint after pint until approximately 10.30pm and closing time, without any provocation, one would smack the other in the teeth and all hell would break out with all the other Irish lads joining in a scene reminiscent of the brawl shown in the old John Wayne movie "The Quiet Man". My father would vainly try to intervene but the local constabulary usually had the last word. All this used to drive him to despair, my father had a fine reputation in the town as a gentleman landlord and was well regarded. Such was his reputation that he was approached by the Knutsford Urban District Council to take on the lease of the council owned and magnificent Richard Watt built "Kings Coffee House", known now as the "La Belle Epoque". He accepted with alacrity and in no time at all he moved from serving chemically engineered beer and fighting Irishmen to serving tea, coffee and cakes to genteel Knutsford ladies. This in a building appropriately dedicated to Elizabeth Gaskell, the very champion of the gentle way of life in an English country town. At the same time, he was bringing my mother back to the site where the former Hat and Feather inn had stood, and where her father, the ignoble Tom Lee was born.

My interview was successful and I commenced work as a junior salesman in Kendal Milne's men's tailoring department in the summer of 1956. Selling is something I am not particularly good at, and again something I would not normally have chosen to do. I have little self confidence and am not forceful enough, yet here I was working with a bunch of tough older wartime ex servicemen who could sell snow to Eskimos. If and when as the junior salesman, I was allowed a look in, the same snow usually melted. However I had one considerable attribute that no one else had. Technically I was miles ahead of every one, except Bill Jolley, when it came to fitting a suit and knowing a fabric. My five year apprenticeship had not been in vain after all. Youth was also on my side, and I was surprisingly earmarked for a future in the men's clothing departments of the Harrods Group. Very soon I was attending courses and lectures about Harrods, their history, traditions, trading techniques and so forth, in short I became a "Harrodian" and unknowingly becoming an elitist, and from then on in my life something of a working snob in all I attempted, "attempted" being the key word.

It was not long before my immediate boss and menswear buyer, Colin Bailey, was given senior management status. His position was filled by his assistant buyer, Len Firby, a former Royal Navy man, I was then promoted in his place as his assistant buyer. I was up and running, running being an accurate description of my job of work, as this coincided with the most highly successful trading period that the men's tailoring department had ever known. Len Firby was proving to be a shrewd customer, cooking up wonderful deals with his suppliers, his turnover was enormous, and was largely based on the supreme quality of the ready made clothing that was being produced in Crewe under the label of Chester Barrie, an American company that traded in the States as Simon Ackerman. Such was the quality of this beautifully crafted, ready to wear clothing that it simply walked out of Kendal Milne, even at the higher prices that they were commanding at that time, we just could not get enough, and the suit and topcoat department just grew and grew, becoming a huge handful for Len Firby to manage. So it was decided to split the merchandise and create a new department called the Men's Leisure Wear. It was the country cousin to a renowned department of the London Harrods store trading as "The Way In". I was the lucky chap to be given a free hand with the buying, basically it was men's sports jackets which were largely bought and sold under the Daks Piccadilly label and which were not too far a cry from the quality of the Chester Barrie jackets. I also bought sheepskins and leather jackets and topcoats, shades here of my grandfather, Albert Howard's leather buying activities in the same Manchester Parish of St. Ann's sixty years earlier! For good measure I also bought for the upstairs ski wear department buying mostly ski jackets, ski pants, plus ski accessories.

The men's clothing departments even ran their own fashion shows, the brain child of Colin Bailey. These were a grand affair superbly organised and presented in the form of a public house or inn, which was named "The Whistle and Flute" cockney rhyming of course for "suit". Numerous invitations were sent out to selected customers from landlord Colin Bailey, asking them to join him for drinks at his pseudo pub which the display department had cleverly mocked up. Large quantities of alcohol were consumed by the invited guests to get them into a jocular mood and we were up and running. The male sales staff from the whole men's department were used to model the merchandise including yours truly, along with good friend and colleague, Sam Knowles. We two were considered pretty enough to be Kendal Milne's regular in-house male models, or "big girls blouses" as our colleagues aptly named us. Girls blouses or not, this occasionally meant swanning off to make television appearances which in those dark, still experimental days, were in black and white, which meant that fashion shows on television were a pointless exercise, nobody could see what colour the clothes were. To catch a fleeting glimpse of us on tiny TV sets meant sitting through either Andy Pandy or Bill and Ben the Flower Pot Men. Thank heavens most men were still at work at this time of day! Our biggest moments were appropriately during the pantomime season when our advertising manager thought it a good idea to precede the season's productions at Manchester's mighty Palace Theatre with a fashion show displaying ladies fashions modelled by gorgeous professional models. We two stooges were dressed appropriately to escort the girls on and off the stage. This procedure proved successful and lasted a couple of years, during which Bruce Forsyth and Norman Wisdom made us the butt of a barrage of smutty stag jokes. They both welcomed the opportunity to ad lib, Norman Wisdom naturally aped our modelling stances and reduced the whole show to a shambles.

The actual business of buying for Kendal Milne was of little hardship. I would spend perhaps a couple of months of the year away from the department, much of it was spent in London, and always weeks at a time in the pent house showroom of Simpson's of Piccadilly, selecting the coming season's sportscoat patterns, the finished article would eventually display the joint Daks/Kendal Milne label. The days work over I then had London to myself and I did not miss out the opportunity to enjoy the City, the London theatres were my preferred choice of entertainment. I also satisfied my appetite for jazz at Ronnie Scott's club, and visited as many of the City's most historic, not notorious I may add, public houses, but I was not "here for the beer" as the saying goes, I simply have always had a love for this country's more celebrated watering holes, with my family involvement in the inn trade for over a century, this will hardly come as a surprise.

The best buying trip of all was the one to Kitzbuhel in the Austrian Tyrol to buy the season's ski wear, I really ought to have paid Kendal Milne for the privilege of this swan. The store employed it's own in-house ski adviser, a delightful lady named Ronny Berko. To see her was to then understand the origin of her Christian name. Her hair was grey and close cropped, her features craggy and her skin brown and like a walnut. Aggressively fit and hyper active, she was a former Austrian Olympic downhill ski racer. It was at her magnificent chalet that I stayed, I say her chalet but I rather think that it may have part belonged to Rosemary Charrington, a member of the celebrated brewing family, who was very pretty and a little more feminine and shared the chalet with the more masculine Ronny. Rosemary bred King Charles spaniels as a hobby, all totally absorbing to me. Kitzbuhel of course is well recognised as one of Europe's richest and ritzier ski resorts, and offered many visual pleasures, not least from the top of the famous Hahnenkamm ski run. With work done, the evenings were spent rubbing shoulders with the world's wealthiest in their plushest restaurants.

This lotus eating period in my life was very soon to come to an end. A dark cloud appeared on the distant horizon in the form of a rumoured takeover by the House of Fraser, the dreaded Glasgow drapers. If true this meant rationalisation and the awful words "central buying" were soon on every buyer's lips. The eventful sight of a brigade of severe looking jocks in pinstriped suits and bowler hats marching in step through the store confirmed our worst fears. Our privileged little jaunts around the globe were soon to be a thing of the past. What to do? I was a member of a group of like minded young men who were all good friends. Virtually to a man we were convinced that the future was indeed very bleak, and that it would be better if we sought employment elsewhere. Four of us did just that. However of the four, I was the only one who had not obtained a first class job of work. I left with only a headful of half baked ideas. I should mention here that I had married my fiancé Iris and had produced a son, Clive. Iris had a good job of work as a secretary to the general manager of the new motorway service station on the M6 at Knutsford, which in those innocent days had, unlike today's operation, some semblance of style, which included an airport sounding first class lounge for first class customers. Something of a giggle this, when one can hardly bear to stop at a service station, except to use the loos. For a while then it was going to be my wife's wage that we would have to rely on, that is until I could get some form of act together.

CHAPTER EIGHT

Restaurateur – Part I

What to do? – father's offer – open a restaurant? – the Tavern – a Danish restaurant – without capital – Bass Charrington loan – another family licensee – the cricket theme – a slow start – the staff desert – quick success – The Good Food Guide – sporting and theatrical clientele – father's serious illness – head lease of the Kings Coffee House

~

I was in my early thirties when I left Kendal Milne in 1965. Little did we realise just how good life was in those days, until of course it was too late and the swinging sixties gave way to the savage and severe seventies. We owned a semi-detached house in Knutsford, purchased for £1800, which we eventually sold for a sixties fortune of £4000 and lived to rue that day as you can now add £300,000 to that figure. My wage at the time of leaving the Harrods Group was the princely figure of £1000 per annum or £20 per week, a figure which everyone regarded as being the amount you needed to earn to be able to regard yourself as having "arrived".

Apart from the small sum withdrawn from the Kendal Milne pension fund, we had no other capital, and yet I had aspirations to owning my own business. I contemplated opening a sports shop, where and with what I do not know. I dithered, and then I obtained another lucky break.

My father had by this time made his move from the eruptive Red Cow hotel to the calm of the Kings Coffee House, and was rightfully being asked for a rent increase for that privilege, by the owners, the Knutsford Urban District Council, who incidently once used the building as the council's offices, this after Mrs Richard Watt had gifted it to them in the 1920s. He had sublet a rather splendid upstairs room to the local de Tabley Masonic Lodge, and was passing on to them a very small increase in rent, all quite normal. This was the sixties and the rent increase was proportionally low, I think £1 per week. My reading, however basic, of the freemasonry movement, is that it is made up of men who are not short of a shilling or two. However, this amount proved to be beyond their means, so they refused to pay this enormous sum, packed their bags and moved to the vacant local electricity showroom.

My father then kindly offered the room to me at the same rent. I accepted not yet having any idea what to do with it. After considerable deliberation and as the rest of the building was a catering establishment, I thought a food orientated operation was appropriate. My wife and I decided to open a small restaurant, and one which would not compromise my father's business below, which would have been the unkindest of cuts. My wife of course, was working for the Top Rank Hovis Company who owned the Knutsford M6 service station, so she had one foot in the food industry. I knew nothing, but we did have this empty superbly classy upstairs room with a huge potential. What we needed was ease of operation, nothing as yet too ambitious, a small business in small premises needing a small staff. Before leaving Kendal Milne I had dined endlessly on cold buffet food in the buyers dining room and had enjoyed it. What could be easier than preparing food in your own good time, placing it on a table for people to help themselves? Simple! A little too simple, but hardly original, practically everybody had eaten at some time from a buffet table. It is here that the old Harrod's trading principals kicked in. Originality is the byword, how then to make something special and very different from the accepted cold buffet format? Where did the best and most well known cold food come from? Scandinavia of course, well known in Scandinavia but not yet presented in it's true form to the British dining out brigade. We decided to present food from Denmark, in "koldtbord" or cold table style along with Danish open sandwiches or "smorrebrod". I could at the time, locate only two or three restaurants in Britain that served Danish food, the Old Howgate inn, south of Edinburgh, a favourite of author William Boyd, and the Ebury wine bar in Ebury Street, London. Both however concentrated on "smorrebrod". We visited both and found the field open for our enterprise, but knew a visit to Copenhagen might benefit us more.

Ideas are one thing, having the capital to finance them is another. Other than the relatively small pension sum in hand, we hadn't a brass farthing, but wondered if a brewery might back us if assured that in return we would back them by stocking their beers, spirits and wines. We decided to approach Bass Charrington who duly and very kindly obliged, who's thinking may have been that though we might never achieve a huge turnover at least their goods would be on sale in a reputable little business in a characterful old Cheshire town, and one in which their merchandise was not that well represented, precisely why we chose them, anyway the amount of cash we needed was peanuts to them.

The room was gorgeous with a rich panelled Japanese pitched pine ceiling, huge windows and an entrance to the Elizabeth Gaskell Memorial Tower. There was also much evidence of Richard Watt's love of art nouveau via door and window fittings in brass and copper, the room just glowed. To function as a restaurant, we needed to fit a kitchen in a very small space, toilets, and an equally small bar which would sit in the entrance to the Tower, carpets and curtains, but most of all we needed furniture in the form of tables and chairs. The height of the room was such that at normal table height we felt that people were dwarfed and dominated by the extremely beautiful ceiling, and that it might be better if we raised them up a little to enable them to appreciate it. We designed our own furniture and had it hand made locally. It consisted of long high tables with tall stools, the latter proving to be a challenge to older customers who were prone to fall off them after a few drinks. There was also another particularly distinguishing feature, the table legs were specially made oversized cricket bats! Don't go away.

I decided that even with the natural charm of the room, it needed further added interest and though I despise the themed restaurant concept, the room still needed a story, but one that was not at all gimmicky. I confess to being a cricket enthusiast, lunatic might have been a more accurate description in those days. I was extremely involved with the game at local level through my village team, Toft Cricket Club, being long serving secretary, part time skipper, and coach to a large junior section. Hence the cricket bat table legs, to which were added framed cricket ties, antique cricket prints, a menu in the form of a large cricket ball, and a wine list in the shape of a cricket bat, both of course, in card form. It ended there and was done with some subtlety, however I had contrived to make the room look part restaurant and part cricket pavilion. The business needed a name and one that would easily spring to mind, I chose "The Tavern", the fact that the public bar at Lords cricket ground is known as "The Tavern" had nothing to do with it, I kid you, of course it did! The restaurant sign announcing this over the door was a huge wooden cricket bat. My later involvement with the game of cricket will be imposed on you in the following chapter. So there we have it, I suppose it could be said, a curious mix of Danish food, cricket theme, art nouveau interior all in an Italianate building administered to by two would be restaurateurs, but it was to work splendidly. Another rather significant thing occurred at the time, I applied for and obtained from a cricket loving Chairman of the local magistrates bench, a licence to sell liquor. I was a licensee, the very thing that my father had not wished me to become, and because he and his father, my grandfather Albert, had either unwittingly or reluctantly entered a business that they had an aversion to, and which had oft times treated them unkindly. This unlike my mother's side of the family, the licensing Lees who's chosen profession it was, mayhem or no mayhem.

The restaurant was opened in May 1965 by Manchester's Danish Consul, Mr Edward Bacon, or Danish Bacon if you prefer, a most charming man and future good customer. My wife trained an honest homely and capable female cook and administered to the kitchen in general. In true Harrod's tradition with merchandise knowledge essential, I applied myself to learning the wine trade, my public house upbringing had taught me enough about spirits and beer. The wine business was naturally a sheer joy to be involved with, I introduced myself to it through Raymond Postgate, and his little red book "The Plain Man's Guide to Wine", he became my mentor and was also responsible for the publication of every serious restaurant frequenter's bible "The Good

Food Guide" to which all aspiring restaurateurs endeavoured to be proficient enough to gain entry to.

The emphasis in the 1960s was heavily weighted towards French and German wines. The Australian, New Zealand and Chilean wines had still to appear over the horizon. The business was all about Bordeaux, Burgundy, Loire, Alsace and Rhone wines from France and the Rheinhessian and Rheingau wines from Germany. We were aiming to attract an upmarket, well heeled and fairly enlightened clientele who were likely to know their onions or wines to be precise. I simply had to know at least as much about the subject as they did, preferably more. We were very soon to visit all the French wine growing regions, it was easy to be enthusiastic, and if you are that, you are home and dry. I will never understand restaurateurs who make no effort to learn about the wines they are buying and selling and instead leave it to the wine merchant. It could mean buying the wines he wants to sell for his own good reasons, anyway he would really prefer to talk about his wines to someone who appreciates his skill.

When my wife left Top Rank Hovis, she brought with her, waiting-on staff from the Knutsford M6 service station. They were mature ladies of the "hello luv what would you like" variety. These we dressed in our chosen brown and beige uniforms and unleashed them, but to whom? I did not believe in advertising, so no one knew we existed. We were not at street level and therefore had no shop frontage, we were upstairs and really needed some finding. Our cricket bat sign was all that could be seen over the door at the top of a small staircase. I simply believed that if you are good enough you will do the business, and word of mouth was the way forward and the best form of advertising, the trick was to get the first punters up the staircase. We had two on Monday the first night and none then until the Saturday when we had six. This was all too much for the waitresses, so used to motorway bustle, they packed their bags and left. From then on, we employed young housewives who we knew mainly as friends and were charming, and a young Danish girl to add credence to our venture, it all worked like a dream. After three months we were doing two sittings on Saturday nights and were pretty full during the week. We had however to alter our cold food only format by adding a hot food menu to our Danish "koldbordt", we just could not envisage our customers eating cold food on cold wet Cheshire winter nights. After six months we had earned an entry into Raymond Postgate's "Good Food Guide". Hallelujah!

Our clientele we got to know, and on a fairly personal basis too. Being up front is essential in a small business, and I was always to be seen, I simply had to be to handle all the wine and liquor orders as well as customer's bills. We had a big sporting following, and naturally they were mostly cricketers, included amongst whom were the West Indian Test players, Clive Lloyd and Lance Gibbs, the England and Warwickshire fast bowler Bob Willis and other county players. We were also almost the unofficial headquarters of Cheshire County Cricket Club, who were dining here on one occasion when news arrived that a good result in Devon meant that Cheshire were the Minor Counties champions. This was the beginning of a long relationship with the Cheshire club. Actors Richard Todd and George C. Scott were occasional diners where as Omar Sharif did so on numerous occasions. A fervid bridge player, he had a regular rendezvous with a Mr Morley, a Knutsford man and frequent customer of the restaurant, who played to a similarly high standard.

In 1968 after only three years trading, we were going along at a great rate of knots, when two things occurred which changed the whole picture. My marriage got into difficulties, a situation for which I was largely responsible for. Even worse our landlord, my kind and patient father, after several unsuccessful operations, was in a life threatening condition and unable to conduct his own coffee house and hotel business, The Tavern of course being only part of the hotel and catering complex that the Kings Coffee House was. The whole business needed to be made secure, my father needed to step down, but my hard working, volatile and vulnerable mother was not the person to take over the administrative responsibilities of the business. Both she and my father believed it to be in the best interest of all parties if it were possible for me to take on the head lease, and at the same time the management of the hotel and coffee house, it seemed the obvious answer. The Knutsford Town Council, via their excellent town clerk Edward Morley, not the bridge player, instinctively knew that this was the best solution, so it came about. The business was made secure, my father could be nursed, my mother made safe and I was the sympathetic landlord to my wife and The Tavern.

CHAPTER NINE

Cricket

Fathers influence – Toft Cricket Club – Lords 1989 – Toft's history – twice evicted – Booths Park – Toft at low ebb – the junior section – invitation XI's and competitions, umpiring and touring – the Maxi Hudson Hollywood XI – Lord Tim in America – Botham versus Boycott – the Birtles Super Bowl – Tim as Botham's agent – a cricket revolution? – Ian as Hollywood star – Cheshire County C.C – sponsorship and publicity – alfresco broadcaster breakfasts – Blofeld's book launch – cricket in the Far East – the Hong Kong sixes – cricket in the blood.

~

I find it difficult to explain my love and enthusiasm for cricket. I suppose my involvement with the game was triggered by my sporting father's part in the game within the town. Whatever, it could be said that someone who opens a Danish restaurant in an Italianate building and then decorates the interior with cricketing bric-a-brac including antique cricket prints, frames cricket club ties, cricket ball and cricket bat menus and wine lists, has table legs made in the shape of cricket bats, and then names it "The Tavern" in honour of the famous "Tavern" at Lords Cricket ground, could be considered a cricketing maniac. All my distinguished customers were left with no doubt about my passion for the game. My father's earliest known participation in the game was as a young man of twenty four in 1928 when he joined the new Toft Cricket Club, the club which I eventually became so totally involved with from 1957 and remained actively involved with from then until the late 1970s, a period of over twenty years. These mainly were the years that the then ailing club re-invented itself from a lowly village club to one which has progressed into a Cheshire premier league club going on to win many championship and cup winning honours including winning the National Village Knockout cup played at Lords in 1989. To win the cup, we needed to beat Hambledon Cricket Club, the very club where the noble game was reputedly first played. The National press soon picked up on the fact that for Hambledon, this was a indeed a historic occasion and there was a great story in the making. The pre-match hype was intense, our opponents were interviewed by both the daily newspapers and television, their players achieving almost heroic status, "cricket was coming home" was one heading and the general theme for the whole of the media. There just had to be one winner and that had to be Hambledon, the perfect story with the perfect ending. Long and triumphal stories with stirring headlines were written in advance of the match and in anticipation of a highly emotional win for the oldest cricket club in England, after all they were only playing some village team from Cheshire called Toft. Toft of course, had very different ideas about how the match would be decided and won a rain affected game quite convincingly, much to the chagrin of the National media who hurriedly had to re-write their copy for Monday's sports pages. These were so miniscule they were hard to locate, Toft Cricket Club had become one of cricket's all time party poopers.

It had never been all roses for Toft, far from it. The club was formed sometime before the turn of the 20th century, the late 1880s is very likely, as no records were kept. They played their cricket on a field belonging to the ancient family estate of the Leycesters, an estate dating back to the Norman Conquest of Cheshire. The Leycesters were fighting squires and one Ralph Leycester so distinguished himself at Flodden during the reign of King Henry the VIII that the King rewarded him with the gift of a valuable stained glass window which recorded this fact. This mysteriously disappeared when the grand old house was converted to office accommodation. Perhaps one day the undeserving thief will return it to Knutsford. The commencement of the 1914-1918 World War meant that the team was disbanded as the men joined the colours. When they returned they found a new tenant farmer had ploughed the ground and refused to allow the club permission to play there again. No cricket was played until the farmer relented, was made a member and the new Toft Cricket Club was formed in 1928. My father joined them at this time, and his girlfriend Bessie Lee, soon to be my mother, helped with the cricketer's teas, prepared as they were in the old Toft schoolroom which adjoined the pitch and served as tearoom, committee room and changing room. My father's involvement with the club was brought to an early end by the previously related circumstances involving his father's death and his widowed mother's inability to remain sober enough to manage the old White Bear, with the result that he had no other choice than to take on the licence, marry Bessie Lee and be temporarily lost to cricket. Not long after he had settled to life as a licensee, he renewed his involvement with the game by joining Knutsford Cricket Club, the town club and one which was nearer and handier for his business. In those days the Knutsford club had a more prestigious fixture list and attracted better known players than Toft, those players though were not necessarily Knutsford men. The Toft side was less sophisticated and was always made up of local men, traditionally they were farmers, agricultural workers, plus gardeners and chauffeurs from the Toft estate, with a fair sprinkling of the slightly eccentric men from Crosstown.

Toft Cricket club had still to endure traumatic times. In 1938, ten years after obtaining it's cricket ground from the tenant farmer, the same gentleman again gave the club notice to quit. This contrary farmer doing his very damnedest to alienate himself in a club who's membership was largely made up of members of the farming community, very strange goings on indeed particularly as when asked for his reason for doing so, refused point blank to give one. The crisis was resolved in the most splendid fashion. The Cowburn family the then owners of the nearby Norbury Booths Country Estate, and of Booths Hall itself, another of the very fine and historic country estates which surround Knutsford, generously offered the club the use of a stretch of beautiful parkland within view of the hall, even going as far as building a pavilion for the club. Toft are thus the occupants of one of the prettiest cricket grounds in Cheshire, if not in England, and have never looked back, this despite the fact that though the ground is only half a mile from the old ground, it is now actually situated in Norbury Booths.

My father settled in comfortably with his new club mates at Knutsford and soon became Captain of one of it's teams. I was encouraged to join the club by him, becoming a junior member in 1946, the year that a very good Indian team was touring England, and which I was taken to Old Trafford to see. I was one of several youngsters lucky enough to be coached, as already mentioned, by Jack Tipping, the club's professional coach, and who had been the wicket keeping understudy to the great Lancashire and England wicket keeper George Duckworth. I played several times with my father's team but only when they were a man short. After leaving school and playing in a non too clever school 1st XI, all of whom being much more adept at soccer, I played with the Knutsford Youth Club XI. Cricket culture of course simply oozed out of the White Bear, my father's team mates were ever present, at times mingling with England Test Match players, such as Bill Edrich, Godfrey Evans and their seemingly ever present Captain Freddie Brown. Toss in the members of the Cricket Society of Scotland to further liven things up, it was all to often a rich mix and a stimulating and intoxicating place to be in, intoxicating being the more apt description as these gatherings took place mostly after hours and frequently until dawn. It was after National Service that I really became interested in cricket once again. There was little cricket to be had in Germany, where what games were played were on matting wickets, I seemed to lose touch with the game and drifted out of it for several years, paying the penalty in terms of experience and competitiveness. On demobilisation I found that most of my friends and youth club team mates had joined Toft Cricket Club and it made sense to join them. Little did I envisage the part that Toft would play in my life, sporting or otherwise.

In 1957 Toft were playing their cricket in the Cheshire Association, an erroneously titled body if there ever was, as most of it's clubs played their cricket in Greater Manchester and on not too well appointed grounds at that. We headed into murky Manchester to play our away games, our opponents thoroughly enjoying their visits to the glorious Toft ground. It was also an extremely competitive league, Toft at this time in playing terms were in the cricketing doldrums. The five all conquering teams of the late 1940's and early 1950's had passed into local legend. A fairly lax committee was much more interested in the quality of the beer being served in the newly installed, but rather primitive bar, we were more a drinking club than a cricket club. The playing standards were falling, there was little or no club discipline, and there was little to choose between first and second elevens. The 2nd XI enjoyed it's cricket, and was both a carefree and careless team, which everyone clamoured to play with, which is a sad sign in any cricket club. For whatever reason, I was voted onto the Toft Club Committee in the early sixties and was without any ambition within it. In an effort to promote the non existent social side of the club, a social committee was formed in which I and my great friend Bill Burgess, being overly socially inclined, were the mainstays. Lack of support from the main body of the club served to underline the fact that we were a cricket club going nowhere. Subscriptions were not being paid, attitudes were rebellious, behaviour often loutish, with Captains often having to go to the local pub to drag players away from their poker games.

In 1963 Bernard Raffo, a local hotel landlord and former cricketer with the Timperley and Knutsford Clubs who had played in my father's Knutsford team, was elected club Chairman, and was to remain so for twenty or more years, before becoming club President. At the same time I was elected club Secretary. We both shared the same ambitions for the club, our backgrounds were not dissimilar, and we soon forged a sound relationship and an understanding based on the premise that we had to arrest the downward spiral that the club was in and if possible take it to a new and higher level. The first job was to unload our freeloading and barely interested members. This was easily done by involving a newly introduced club rule which stated that if club members had not paid their subscriptions by the specified date, they were no longer considered to be members. In one full swoop the dead wood was cut away. This of course drastically reduced the playing membership to the bare minimum and something had to be done immediately to make up the short fall. We had though made provision to deal with the situation.

We decided that the future of the club would be best served by an injection of new and much younger blood. This we did by forming a junior section and appointing a professional cricketer to coach the boys. In 1963 I wrote to the local High School, asking them to place a notice on the school notice board to this effect. Enrolment day was Saturday morning and there had been little to indicate what the response would be prior to the day. I drove up to the ground and in so doing passed scores of boys heading in the same direction. Over a hundred boys of all ages turned up, with a very large contingent of characterful lads of school leaving age who would soon be drafted into our teams. The exercise proved conclusively that there always has been and always will be a natural interest in the game of cricket for young boys. It is up to schools and clubs to encourage and sustain this interest by seriously providing coaching and first class facilities to accommodate them. Our junior section proved to be a catalyst and an example of what could be done to encourage boys to play the game, and at the same time assure other cricket clubs across the county, that to survive and indeed flourish, they needed a coached junior membership. Most clubs in Cheshire followed suit and because of this cricket in the county is flourishing today.

Time however was needed for the boys to mature, never the less our teams were liberally laced with inexperienced youngsters, which meant that we enjoyed only mixed success. To avoid any dissolutionment in their ranks, we resigned out of the overly competitive Cheshire Association and joined the Cheshire Conference of Cricket Clubs, an organisation, bless it, dedicated to the principle of ensuring that cricket in Cheshire could and should be played by clubs intent on enjoying the game. There could be no greater axiom than that. Within that delightful context the boys came on in leaps and bounds, the standard rose and we started to win most of our matches, this in turn attracted many more mature cricketers to the club and Toft's little bandwagon really started to roll, success is, as we all know, prone to breed further success, and it was not long before the club was needing a greater challenge.

I have to confess to hating committee work particularly committee meetings, where I could barely articulate and became terribly self conscious. I found myself more of a listener, who considered the remarks and suggestions made by fellow committee members, often without any forethought but sometimes that offered a gem of an idea which could be developed. It was usually after and between meetings that Bernard

Raffo and I would get down to the nitty gritty of deciding the direction the club was to take. There were many skilfully disguised omissions and additions to the club minutes. What I did discover about myself was that I had an aptitude for detailed organisation and fairly ambitious planning, but needed to be left well alone to realise these talents and bring them to fruition. The Chairman of course was party to these ideas and was responsible for presenting them enthusiastically to the committee. These ideas are of course at domestic club level and were designed to first and foremost help promote healthy club and team spirit. We experimented with a single wicket competition, but decided that the "trios" or "three a side" form of cricket was the most attractive prospect. It was played on Sundays at senior level and involved every playing member of the club, it was a huge amount of fun, but keenly fought, and club spirit was never higher. We then staged the junior trios which was equally enjoyable and again a good exercise in getting the boys to mix and develop a sense of identity. This identity was furthered when I was able to persuade Mr Leycester-Roxby of Toft Hall, to allow the club to use part of the family's heraldic device. The Leycester "red buck", thus became the club's emblem and is proudly worn. Such was the success of the trio's format that it encouraged us to hold an "invitation" trios. The response was terrific, and teams from Derbyshire County Cricket Club, Cheshire County Cricket Club, the North Staffordshire league and the Lancashire league all accepted our invitation and sent strong teams all of which included professional cricketers. The Derbyshire side included future England wicket keeper Bob Taylor and fast bowler Bob Jackson. Invitation XI's came and went on Sundays, one side contained no less than four minor county captains, though I will have to confess that owning a cricket orientated restaurant was proving to be more than useful in providing contacts within the cricketing fraternity. It was also useful in another way, previously if the club needed permission to make any changes, as secretary I had to go cap in hand to the home of the owner of the ground and surrounding park, Mr David Cowburn, who was the President of the club. He was a very fair gentleman but exceedingly tough to deal with and I used to dread the visit. He then discovered The Tavern, became an excellent customer, and from then on we shared extremely amicable dry martinis on Sunday mornings, and he was very amenable. The club as had been said, owed it's very existence to the Cowburn family.

All too soon a keen competitive edge returned to our club game, we were now able to turn out particularly strong teams that needed much sterner tests than were being provided by the delightful Cheshire Conference of Cricket Clubs. We felt obliged to resign and subsequently joined the Cheshire Cricket league, a much tougher competition in which we were champions twice in our first four years within it. Thus the club began a cricketing journey which has seen it rise and rise, with it reaching it's pinnacle in 1989 when it defeated Hambledon Cricket Club in the final of the National Village Knockout Competition at Lords. Also over the years, cricket in the county has been re-structured and because of this, playing standards have become much higher. The club are presently members of the Cheshire County Cricket league, and play in it's Premier Division, a very select and an extremely tough competition in which most clubs now feel the need to employ overseas players to survive in it. We have enjoyed considerable success within it and are constantly striving for further honours. Junior cricket too is well organised throughout the county, so there is plenty of it for our young members to enjoy it at almost every age level, from nine to nineteen.

It was with much regret that I had necessarily, due to my increasingly involved business interests, to play a lesser part in the clubs affairs. I had had to stop playing cricket in 1965 due to my commitment to The Tavern restaurant and in 1970 due to the deterioration in my father's health, I had taken control of the Kings Coffee House. By 1974 the dear old Kings Coffee House had become La Belle Epoque restaurant, I had partners to consider in what was an extremely prestigious venture and simply had to be more committed to it, more of this later. It was in that year that I finally felt obliged to resign the secretaryship of Toft Cricket Club and it was a considerable wrench to do so. My commitment to the La Belle Epoque restaurant ended in the later 1970s with the sale of my share of the business. This allowed me once more to renew my acquaintanceship with the game. In 1978 the "new" Toft Cricket Club, the one reformed in 1928 after once more losing it's ground to the plough, celebrated it's fiftieth birthday. The highlight of a weeks festivities was a match between Geoff Pullar's invitation XI and the Toft 1st XI. Geoff

Pullar, once the renowned Lancashire and England opening batsman had retired from the game due to a leg injury and was now a resident in the town and a good friend of the club. He brought along a side which included seven International cricketers with the rest of the team being county players. I was made responsible for much of the organisation of the match and also did the match commentary. The game attracted a sizable crowd who were well entertained. The occasion also demanded that a short history of the Toft Club be written and included in the substantial match programme. Having been involved with some of the players from the early days of the club during my secretarial years, it was much easier for me to write this history, so it came about.

More freedom from the chores of the restaurant business in the early 1980s for a short time allowed me to travel with the 1st XI as umpire. It was in that role that I joined a touring team that went to South Africa at that time. The party included players from Toft, the Cheshire County team and Scottish County cricketers many of whom had been capped for Scotland. We were a fairly strong touring party who were faced by some very capable opposing sides, including the "Kingsmead Mynahs" who we played at the world famous Kingsmead International Stadium in Durban. It was in Durban that we were invited to a dinner at the magnificent Town Hall. The dinner was followed by a staged "This is your Life" programme which was virtually an occasion when the whole of a very great South African test team was paraded before us. Strangely included in the celebrity line up was the famous South African pioneer heart surgeon, Dr Christian Barnard. Perhaps this was because of the possibility of heart failure caused by the sight of so many cricketing heros. Another memorable occasion was the invitation to attend the final of South Africa's Premier Inter-state Cup Competition, the "Currie Cup" on Johannesburg's renowned "Wanderers" ground. It was during the tour that I learnt to my chagrin that my umpiring left a lot to be desired and that it was a far cry from performing in Cheshire league games. Again I was asked to write the accompanying tour brochure. This was fun to do, particularly with regard to the pen pictures of the players, the jocular insult being the pre-ordained method, nobody sued!

Little did I realise that these occasional involvements with local cricket were somehow coming to the attention of various cricketing bodies and peripheral individuals. With regard to the latter by far the strangest, was the invitation to join a small private organisation by the name of "The Maxi Hudson Hollywood XI", apparently I had been recommended by a cricketing friend. With considerable apprehension, I accepted the invitation to join a committee formed to assist the Hollywood XI fulfil it's cricketing ambitions. It did not take me long to establish that the object of the exercise was a publicity seeking one and my role was to be that of publicity officer. Maxi Hudson did indeed exist and turned out to be the wealthy American wife of Tim Hudson, a local boy from Prestbury near Macclesfield and the son of a reasonably wealthy Manchester cotton merchant. Public school educated at Strathallan College in Scotland, he was in his youth a fair cricketer and apparently good enough to keep wicket for Lancashire's 2nd XI and Surrey's 2nd XI on occasion as an amateur in the late fifties. Tim's story then becomes a little sketchy. Like many impressionable young men of similar backgrounds in the sixties, he became besotted with the music of that swinging decade and the music groups that proliferated during it. Tim was certainly not going to follow in his father's footsteps, spending much time in London, he briefly became the manager of The Moody Blues. A liaison of some sort with actor James Coburn led him to the conclusion that there were more opportunities to be had in the music business if he crossed the Atlantic Ocean to Canada and America.

According to Tim he somehow contrived to obtain a seat on the same aeroplane that took the Liverpool 'wunderkind' the Beatles no less, to the U.S.A. Quite how he achieved this is a matter of debate, however, his persuasive powers are now well recorded. Arriving eventually in Canada, he soon had his own radio show in Montreal before moving to California and joining K.F.W.B radio in Los Angeles, with whom as a disc jockey known as "Lord Tim" he dispensed public school Englishness over the airwaves for three hours every night, easily adapting to the role of English aristocrat he would have charmed both his audience and who so ever he met. Tall, dark and good looking, he eventually married the daughter of a highly successful Hollywood film producer. The marriage produced a daughter who they named "River", say no more! With his interest in the music business now at a low ebb and he far better off, his wife an interior designer, persuaded him to become involved with the property renovating business. At the heart of this was the purchase and renovation of fourteen old beach houses which he rented to pop stars Linda Ronstadt, "The Byrds" and The Eagles and others. Eventually divorced he met and married Maxi Gordon, with whom, after buying a property back in Cheshire, they commuted between Santa Monica and England on a regular basis, which would allow him to renew his interest in cricket, and how! Maxi was going to be introduced to the good life that many people live in this fair county and this was going to be achieved via Tim's passion for cricket, this through the formation of the Maxi Hudson Hollywood XI. The committee that was formed was comprised of various old friends and acquaintances from Tim's earlier days, a jolly nice crowd of decent people who were all equally passionate about cricket and who all had succumbed to his charm and enthusiasm.

Tim Hudson learnt the art of self publicity many years earlier. In addition to his persuasive powers, he made himself easily identifiable by wearing his long black hair in a ponytail and wore an Errol Flynn moustache, a battered Stetson sat on top of his head, his clothes consisted of a cricket sweater displaying the Hollywood XI colours with an old brown leather army waistcoat over, a long white silk scarf dangled casually from his neck. He presented a colourful and easily recognisable figure to the sporting world, which had heads turning and tongues wagging. He and Maxi were to be seen at major sporting events up and down the country, Test Cricket, Rugby Union Internationals and major horse racing meetings were always favourites and he very soon made contact with the people that mattered and who might be useful in the future.

Meanwhile back in Macclesfield, his loyal hardworking committee were beavering away. My role was to sell Tim and his ideas to the National press, and very soon we were holding press conferences at his new home, Birtles Old Hall, a grand old house, very soon garishly painted in the Hollywood XI colours of red, black, gold and green (for peace, love and understanding) which were a throwback to his hippy Californian period (he claimed to have invented the phrase "flower power"). Conveniently next to the hall and grounds, was the tiny Birtles Cricket Ground, home of the local village team. This he immediately purchased for £18,000 including the rustic wooden pavilion. The purchase was to be the key to his success of his whole scheme, no fool he. The initial and vital thrust of his ideas was the proposed staging of what he called "The world heavyweight cricket championship" pretentious of course, but headline grabbing. This was actually a cricket match between the two "heavyweight" cricketers of the day in England, the fact that there were some fairly decent protagonists of the game scattered around the cricketing world was of little matter, audacity was the operative word. The heavyweights were Geoffrey Boycott and Ian Botham. The reality was a cricket match between Boycott's Yorkshire and Botham's Somerset, they were to be attracted by prize money amounting to £10,000, an amount far in excess of what first class cricketers normally earned, maybe even in a season. Pre-match cocktail parties gave lie to the supposition that Geoff Boycott was charmless, in fact he was graciousness in itself and was well aware of the responsibility that he owed Tim for his generosity. Ian Botham we had little contact with until match day.

With preparations for the game well underway, Tim had obviously been well aware that the facilities at the Little Birtles ground were far from adequate and more to the point non existent. The cricket square was diabolical and without proper preparation was downright dangerous. To put this to right the services of a former Lancashire County Cricket Club groundsman were acquired, a man well used to bringing the Old Trafford square up to Test Match standard. The very finest caterers were to be hired for the occasion and would have been approached via a trip to Henley Regatta or Ascot. Their marquees would prove to be opulent and our distinguished guests suitably impressed. There was little provision for large numbers of spectators, but money taken at the gate was immaterial. This was to be a showpiece party that would have thousands of pounds thrown at it, £30,000 to be precise. Later when Tim's cricketing ambitions were being further advanced, a huge earth moving scheme was implemented which banked the ground allowing him to boast that it was a smaller version of "The Hill" on Sydney Cricket Ground. The Little Birtles Ground was then re-christened "The Birtles Super Bowl" and was entered through newly erected gates which echoed those at Lords Cricket Ground. Up to the day of the game I had been busy keeping the now extremely interested National press up to date with events, at the same time assuaging Tim's terrible thirst for publicity.

Came the day of the match and my allocated task was to meet and greet, guide and nurse the cricketers through the preliminaries including introductions to Tim and Maxi. The coach containing Ian Botham and the rest of the Somerset team arrived. Garbed in my publicity officers outfit of dark suit and brown trilby hat and looking like a poor man's racing commentator, I stepped forward to meet the team. The first man off the coach was Botham himself and before I could utter a word was greeted by the sporting colossus with the immortal words "who the f*** are you? I am truly not the most confident of people and was utterly flattened by this, but duly stuttered my introductions. Had I had the presence of mind and the wit I would love to have said "the man who is going to introduce you to the chap who is going to put a lot of money your way", had I been gifted with foresight I could have added "and one in who's company you will be seen in a non too favourable light". This was the moment that Tim met Ian. It was take-off time, from then on the Hudsons were flying, Ian Botham warmly embraced them and their wealth, and who wouldn't if you were a non too well paid cricketer that is. Their liaison would prove to be a highly controversial one, and one that would provoke much adverse comment in the media and most of all would shake the cricketing establishment to it's very core. Not long after, the services of the Maxi Hudson Hollywood XI committee were not much required. As for myself, having dealt with the press for some time, I had detected a change in their stance which was less favourable and more critical of the Hudsons and which I wanted no part of. I decided to opt out, thus protecting whatever local reputation I had, which was important to me as Tim was making a lot of local enemies. His well heeled and influential neighbours had cause to complain bitterly at his over exuberance and perceived un-neighbourly conduct. Local government too was keeping a watchful eye on any contravention of local laws. I also had the foresight to acknowledge that my role in Tim's affairs might very well come under scrutiny and that I would soon be adjudged as not being up to events at the now much higher publicity levels. I duly left leaving the gate open for the more famed and experienced commentators on the game to enter through, this they did thinking much of the rich pickings to be had. Tim's affairs were then something for me to keep abreast with in the National press and other media. They are fairly well known, but for the cricket orientated reader's interest I will briefly trace the route taken by Tim and Ian during their liaison, relying heavily on articles in the Sunday Times in October 1985 and in "You" magazine at approximately the same time.

It is not too difficult to visualise the impact that the extroverted and eccentric Tim Hudson had on Ian Botham, a man not unknown for his own extroversion and rebellious nature. Here was a man the more traditional and formal cricketing world had never seen before. There are a number of wealthy cricket loving country landowners with a cricket ground on their estate, who enjoy hosting "country house" cricket, it is a joyous form of the game and a delight to be part of. Ian Botham would not have been a stranger to it. That day though at Birtles Old Hall, I am sure was quite different. The garishly dressed, exuberant, fast talking Tim was a very different animal to the more reserved and gentlemanly cricket host, not that he was not the perfect gentleman, for he was. It was the flamboyant Hollywood razzamatazz approach that was different and that would have impressed. The infectious enthusiasm with which he soon expounded his multitudinous, original and highly optimistic points of view, at the same time hinting at the plans that he had in mind for both cricket in general and for Ian himself. Underpinning all of this was the inference that large amounts of money were available.

Barely a year later Hudson became Botham's agent, largely brought about by his Palm Springs offer to help provide legal assistance for Ian for what eventually turned out to be a minor drugs affair. Botham was still also at the time, embroiled in unresolved libel actions brought against the "Mail on Sunday" and the "Daily Express" over alleged incidents during England's 1983-84 tour of New Zealand. Very soon Hudson was negotiating with Somerset County Cricket Club over a salary increase for his illustrious client then earning £13,000 a year. The result being the infamous occasion in which the Somerset Club, anxious not to lose their Super Star, indicated their willingness to negotiate. Hudson then seized the initiative by refusing to travel to Taunton to discuss Ian's new contract, at the same time making noises about taking Botham up the road to Warwickshire County Cricket Club. He then insisted that Somerset came north to deal at Birtles Old Hall. They swallowed their pride and a deputation led by the loyal and long serving Brian Langford duly arrived at the hall only to be kept waiting for several minutes at "the tradesman's entrance", this "humiliation" Hudson duly reported to the press! The outcome was an increase in his clients salary to £15,500, making Botham the highest paid county player exceeding by £500 the £15,000 Essex County Cricket Club were paying former Australian skipper Alan Border, this of course to massage Tim's ego. However, Botham was paid no bonuses not available to other Somerset players. The Somerset club, despite being strapped for cash like all county clubs, were not too badly affected financially, being re-imbursed by the Test and County Cricket Board for Ian's appearances for England in Test and one day International matches. Shortly after this his Somerset team mate, the brilliant West Indian Test Match batsman, Viv Richards, became Hudson's second client.

Very soon, with the wind in his sails, Hudson was issuing loud proclamations about what he felt about the way the game was being administered and how he thought it could be re-structured. As one would expect, well at least by myself who with some little knowledge of Tim's thinking, expected it was going to be a case of light the blue touch paper and stand well back. Controversial pronouncement followed controversial pronouncement. He had extremely broad views and ideas about the game and how it should be played and presented. Unfortunately, as ever these ideas were wildly diverse and were never ever truly thought through and committed to paper. There was no overall blueprint, and it was mostly "off the top of his head" stuff, however with Ian Botham and Viv Richards as his celebrated clients, he became very much more in the public eye, sporting or otherwise, his private life also now being under scrutiny. His every utterance being greedily seized on by the press, Tim as ever thrived on media attention and was very soon using Botham's exclusively contracted column in "The Sun" to promote his rather unusual ideas about the game. This and his many other proclamations stirred up considerable alarm among both cricketing traditionalists and the game's governing establishment who now saw him as another Kerry Packer, the Australian media entrepreneur and cricketing catalyst, and someone who could compromise the games delicately balanced financial infrastructure and someone with the professed aims to fundamentally change the game for good.

Hudson's huge raft of ideas initially were naturally showbiz orientated, as one would expect from a man with a self proclaimed Hollywood background. They included rock and roll cricket festivals with his own Hollywood XI facing star studied sides assembled by say cricket loving Mick Jagger and Elton John. After having acquired his own super bowl stars, Botham and Richards, he proposed a travelling circus of one day cricket built around them. Going on to prophesy one man ownership of teams on a "my team against your team" basis in a super league of cricket. One must assume that much of this cricket would be played at the Birtles Super Bowl or on similar grounds equally unable to handle huge crowds and road traffic. To cap that there was the suggestion that pop and classical concerts could be promoted after games, which games? On a less frivolous front he suggested the abolition of county 2nd XI's to provide more money for first team players, player transfers and an extension to the number of county venues "to take the game to the people", an admirable supposition this, but logistically and financially suspect. He also suggested the individual sponsorship of players, added to this was the expressed belief that the super star is the life blood of the game, not a healthy premise this, but when one considers today's media pre-occupation with say Andrew Flintoff or Kevin Pietersen, not far off the mark.

More controversially, Hudson's most radical plan and one which was to bring him into conflict with the Test and County Cricket Board, was for the best players to abandon county cricket and compete in touring exhibitions and Test Matches only. Wait a minute! Isn't this broadly speaking what has happened? Exhibition games no, but are not the best players now contracted to play for England only during a Test series? Again, in and among the muddled jumble of Tim's ideas isn't there some evidence that in many ways he was almost on the right track? There is greater freedom of movement among players, certainly at the close of a season, and talented Australian and other overseas players seem to float freely between the county clubs during the season and to devastating effect at that. There is individual sponsorship available to players, even at minor county level especially if you take the motor cars that are made available to them, which is excellent. Most significantly the powers that be have introduced us to "twenty20" cup cricket, a briefer and more enlivened form of the game into which show business aspects have been added to attract and entertain a wider and family friendly audience. What do you think?

What of Ian Botham? He was no stranger to celebrity status, in the cricketing world he was a cult figure of heroic proportions and well wooed by the game's society and society in general. Tim Hudson though was something very different. He talked a similar language, they had much in common, not least flamboyance and a passion for cricket. Both had a love of pop culture and not too much regard for establishment authority. From that very first day at Birtles when Hudson staged his "heavyweight world cricket match" between Botham's Somerset and Boycott's Yorkshire, they gelled. Soon Hudson became Botham's agent, there was his initial success in negotiating Botham's lucrative new contract and from then on there was the continual promise of the greater riches to be had through the exposure he would obtain via Hudson's talent for securing publicity. Seemingly he had the world at his feet. Where did it all go wrong? To say that Hudson over gilded the lily would be one of the greatest understatements of all time. As well as endlessly massaging Ian's ego, his enthusiasm for his protégé began to take on ever greater proportions, amounting to hero worship which at times verged on the ludicrous. The world of cricket gradually seemed to be inextricably interwoven with that of show business. In a short space of time however, despite the obvious fact that cricket was the launch pad for any success, show business gradually took over and Hollywood became the ultimate destination.

In Hudson's vision, Ian Botham was a star in the making, and a trip was proposed to introduce him to Hollywood. According to Tim he was, and I again quote heavily from the Sunday Times of October 1985 and "You" magazine of the same year, going to be variously "King of the B movies, England's answer to Tom Selleck", a Biggles, Raffles and Errol Flynn all rolled into one, "a star, a natural shoot-em-up, drive the car, get the girl star like John Wayne or Randolph Scott", though it is hard to visualise Randolph Scott ever driving a car through the Texas terrain. He told the "Daily Mirror" in the summer of the same year that he thought Botham "should be the next James Bond". In a "Sun" exclusive that year he boasted that Botham had been guaranteed $1m by the Australian film director Gary Rhodes to appear opposite Oliver Reed in a feature film called "The Perpetrator", this Rhodes vehemently denied, saying he asked only for publicity stills, proof that Ian was taking acting lessons or a videotape proving that he could act, in return he received a request for $40,000. Ian must have read, heard and been advised most of what was being said. At what stage did the penny begin to drop and he wonder where all this was leading? What in fact was reality and how much further into the realms of fantasy was he being lured. Eventually he saw the light or good friends and advisers helped him to see it, and he very wisely shipped out. At roughly the same time, coincidently, the Hudson monies tragically ran dry. I have not seen either Tim or Maxi Hudson now for many years, but understand they still live in the Macclesfield area. For everyone involved with them over the years, myself included, it was an interesting if somewhat bumpy ride. There was plenty of excitement, many intriguing characters were met, but all in all there were cautionary lessons to be absorbed by everyone. Where ever Tim and Maxi are, I wish them well. They were always extremely kind and courteous to me.

The Tim Hudson experience in fact did me no harm at all, on the contrary, it served me well in the longer term. I had learnt a lot, particularly with regard to matters relative to the National sporting press. I knew both my way around and a lot of people that mattered then. The good friend and cricketing colleague who had introduced me to the Hudsons was at a later stage sitting in committee with the Cheshire County Cricket Club and was involved in a fund raising capacity with it. A wealthy business man in his own right, he had little time for day to day involvement, he suggested to the County Club that they took me aboard mainly to put some flesh on the bones of possible and proposed sponsorship deals. This the club was pleased to do so. I was delighted to be presented with the opportunity to assist my County Club in this way, I am a passionate supporter of the Cheshire County Cricket Club, and it's success means very much to me, as does the Minor Counties Cricket Association. The member counties play their cricket on the most beautiful club grounds in the country. Cheshire compete in the western division of the competition and to attend away matches in Berkshire, Cornwall, Devon, Dorset, Herefordshire, Oxfordshire,

Shropshire, Wales and Wiltshire is a sheer joy. The company that one keeps is delightful, extremely amusing, much of the time hilarious, always interesting and well informed. Most committee men are nearly all former minor counties players and therefore have considerable knowledge and experience of the game. I was never in their category as a player, far from it, but was always made to feel welcome and part of the set-up.

I was installed officially as the county club's press and publicity officer with the added responsibility for obtaining county wide sponsorship deals and having obtained them it was my further lot to service local business companies who had kindly agreed to sponsor our home games. Cheshire's home games were played on deliciously beautiful club grounds, the likes of Alderley Edge, Bowdon, Neston and Toft and historic towns such as Knutsford (where Toft are located), Nantwich and the fair city of Chester. With the generous and most times willing help of the home club who kindly loaned their ground for several match days, I was involved variously arranging marquee accommodation for the sponsor's guests, recommending and sometimes securing outside catering companies, ensuring that the highly visible sponsor's advertising hoardings were in place, produce a hopefully interesting match programme, again ensuring that the sponsor's advertising was equally well placed within it. I was kept extremely busy. I suppose it was highly appropriate, given my restaurant connections with the wine trade, that I had to negotiate with our major sponsor, the famous Spanish wine grower's "Marques de Caceras" for supplies of their wonderful produce. They had supported us loyally for many years, and what better county cricket club to support than Cheshire Country Cricket Club, who's appreciation of their product knew no bounds. Considerable quantities of the nectar was to be found in the boot of an appointed committee man's car on match days, ready for a civilised pre-lunch gargle which served to further enliven lunch time conversations – happy days!

My involvement unfortunately had to end in 1990, when I was offered the position of Custodian of Arley Hall, the home of Lord and Lady Ashbrook. The responsibility was such that it demanded my total commitment and I reluctantly had to resign my position. There was to be little contact with cricket for the next five years, though there could have been, as I often looked at the estate's sweet little cricket ground, envisaging greater use of it. It was under used, under prepared and would have made a great addition to the exclusive country house cricket circuit. However, I had plenty on my plate at Arley and kept my ideas under my cap. I had little idea of what my involvement with Cheshire had meant to the county club, but was delighted to be made an honorary life member, an honour I will always treasure.

Before taking up my position at Arley, I was still living at my flat behind the La Belle Epoque restaurant and working for the Mooney family to whom I had sold the business so many years before. They had asked me to stock control and buy the fine wines for the wine list, the composition of which I was responsible for, this to compliment the fine French food the restaurant was offering. It was then my further responsibility during the evening hours to recommend these wines to the restaurant's distinguished and fairly knowledgable clientele. At the end of each and every evening it was also my job to "tot up" the customer accounts. Among the many distinguished diners, and for one week only in the year, that being the week that the test match is played at Old Trafford, we were pleased to accommodate and feed various cricketing critics, writers, broadcasters and the occasional photographer at La Belle Epoque. For me this was pure magic, somebody to listen to and talk cricket with, and to be privy to the latest hot news on the subject from the ultimate sources. These included Trevor Bailey the former England all rounder, Scylde Berry of "The Observer", Patrick Eager, the game's foremost photographer, broadcaster and author Henry Blofeld and former England captain Tony Lewis, BBC Television's cricketing anchorman at the time. However, the hotel was not able to house everyone at the same time, as it had only a handful of very smart bedrooms. Messrs Blofeld and Lewis cannily laid claim to two of these on a more or less regular basis.

For the benefit of non cricketing readers, Henry Blofeld is one of cricket's most colourful and witty commentators and writers on the game. Cricket radio listeners will always chuckle at his "my dear old thing" phrase, no matter how many times they hear it. As you would expect "Blowers" is one of the most charming people one could wish to meet, and I suppose it was something, of a privilege, as I added up his generous accounts, to be nicknamed "Totters". Equally charming was

Tony Lewis, he had been captain of Glamorgan County Cricket Club between 1967 and 1972, played nine Test Matches for England, and captained the England team that toured India and Pakistan in 1972/73. Since his television broadcasting and La Belle Epoque days, he has been the President of the M.C.C and was formerly President of Glamorgan County Cricket Club. Together in the evenings they were a humorous and fascinating duo and I was lucky to be privy to their comments and company. I had the pleasure of entertaining them on several occasions for alfresco breakfasts served on the patio of my flat, having been in the restaurant business then for twenty years, I fancied myself as a cook. The favourite dishes were "kidney's Tobago", "haddock Monte Carlo" and "kedgeree", all being washed down with vintage champagne. We were invariably joined by other cricketing pundits from the adjoining hotels. The Sunday morning sun always seemed to shine and everybody was able to relax as there was no Test match cricket on the Sabbath in those days. They were lovely occasions and in autographing his book for me, "Double Century" written to celebrate the M.C.C's two hundred year old history, Tony Lewis expressed his fond recollections of "the brilliant breakfasts" we all shared.

Talking of books, Blower's chose the La Belle Epoque to promote his then latest volume "My Dear Old Thing". It was a good choice, the restaurant had a huge reputation and Knutsford was central and easily reached. I was responsible for publicising the event and for the sale of tickets. The dinner obviously demanded a cricket audience and I was in the ideal position to contact club cricketers throughout the county, still being the press and publicity officer for the Cheshire County Cricket Club. The response was huge, we had no trouble filling the place with an enthusiastic crowd of lovely cricketing types. The La Belle Epoque put on a superb meal, a lot of wine washed it down, and the speakers, Faroukh Engineer of Lancashire and India, and Blowers himself were in fine fettle. A really great cricketing evening was had by all and most importantly a lot of books were autographed and sold. Blowers was extremely generous in paying me perhaps the nicest compliment I have ever received, and there have not been too many of those.

Cricket has been a great adventure for me. Over thirty years of involvement in my small town way with the game has meant meeting fascinating people who shared my love for it. It all started at Toft Cricket Club in the 1950s and is ending at Toft Cricket Club, when on Saturday afternoons a bunch of older former players gather to watch today's young Lions perform. Nothing gives me more pleasure though, than jumping into my car, driving through beautiful parts of rural England and Wales to watch county and minor county cricket played on beautiful cricket grounds, a deckchair, a lunch time pint of beer in a pavilion bar, a chat about the game to some kindred spirit, an evening meal in a good pub on the way home, paradise on Earth.

Most rewarding of all however, is my son Clive's input in the game in administrative terms. He is flying the flag for the game in the Far East through his involvement with the Hong Kong Cricket Association. He is a chief inspector with the Hong Kong Police, joining the force when it was a "Royal" one prior to the colony reverting to Chinese ownership. His work in several positions has tried his organisational skills to the full. In his then capacity as chief drill and musketry instructor to the former Royal Hong Kong Police, he was responsible for planning the departure ceremony at Government House which was watched on television by millions of us back here in the UK and around the world. He commanded the parade and was both highly visible and audible, as the Governor Chris Patten, made his sad farewell. He has of late been responsible for the creation and now administration of a new forensics department.

For some time now he has been addressing his organisational skills to the game in Hong Kong and where ever else the game takes him in Asia and the East. Hong Kong is a founder member of the Asian Cricket Council, a now powerful and extremely wealthy force for the game in that part of the cricketing world, it is responsible for the administration of the Asian Cup Competition. Past winners of the cup most notably have been Sri Lanka and recently Bangladesh. Sri Lanka spearheaded by the phenomenal bowling skills of Muthiah Muralitharan and some of the most highly acquisitive and entertaining batsmen in the world, are a joy to behold and having achieved International and Test Match status, have of late stood higher in the world rankings than such former giants of the game as South Africa, the West Indies and New Zealand. Bangladesh continue to develop and improve, and one day will prove to be a force on the International Cricket scene. Cricket thrives in Asia and many more emerging and aspiring countries now compete in the cup, many enjoy "tiger economies", so there is no shortage of investment in the game. A few are small like Hong Kong and Singapore, with too little an infrastructure that will not merit further development. The case for Hong Kong though is thought provoking. No longer a colonial outpost for cricket, as it is of course now part of the peoples Republic of China, however there has been much talk and rumour that China might soon take up the game and develop it across the nation. If so then in the not too distant future it would become a major member of the Asian Cricket Council and compete in the cup. Now that is a sobering thought. If that were to be the case then the Hong Kong Cricket Association is most surely the body with which to start the process. Much is in place, the tradition and enthusiasm is there and so are the administrators. There are two fine cricket grounds, Kowloon Cricket Club which is presently the scene of International Cricket and the exclusive Hong Kong Cricket Club which has the dignity and decorum of a Chinese "Lords". Hong Kong could just be the beginning of an oriental cricketing avalanche, or am I just getting too carried away with the idea?

Clive, through his membership of the HKCA committee, has found the most wonderfully exotic platform with which to display his talent and enthusiasm for the game. This has variously meant managing the Hong Kong touring team in such unbelievably distant and remote regions as Nepal, incredibly Kathmandu itself has three cricket grounds. In the years from 2001 to 2003 he was the tournament director of the Hong Kong International six-a-side cup competition. This is now a regular and popular event on the International cricket circuit, and is an exciting and novel addition to the game at world level. He kindly invited me to attend the 2003 tournament in which teams from England, India, Pakistan, Kenya, Sri Lanka, Zimbabwe and South Africa competed, but not Australia and New Zealand, who after some deliberation about the benefits of the event, are since 2005 completely on board. In 2003 a very strong England side, captained by Matthew Maynard of Glamorgan and including team mate Robert Croft, Kabir Ali of Worcestershire, Dougie Brown (Warwickshire), Glen Chapple (Lancashire), Darren Maddy (Leicestershire) and Chris Silverwood (Yorkshire) beat Pakistan in an exciting final in front of a huge crowd at the Kowloon Cricket Club. I suspect I had been invited over not just to watch the cricket but for him to show his 'old man' his ability to organise, I was indeed terribly impressed and extremely proud. When he eventually retires from the Hong Kong Police and returns to the UK, he just might be a useful addition to the committee of a county or Minor County Cricket Club. I have found cricket in the Far East to be dynamic and full of ideas that could well be incorporated into a game sometimes a little short of inspiration. In 2005 he became Chairman of the HKCA and in that capacity in 2006 was that body's representative at the Annual International Cricket Conference at Lords Cricket Ground. Not seeing an awful lot of him these days, at his invitation I slipped down to London for a couple of days to enjoy his company, staying at his hotel just across the way from the ground, I was able to join him and other members of the I.C.C for the odd glass of champagne at the cocktail party which preceded the Annual Dinner for the council which was being held in the legendary Long Room. I confess to not being officially invited, but the M.C.C President Robin Marler, may not have minded too much, I did after all use to serve him wine at the La Belle Epoque in the days when he covered the Old Trafford Test Match for his newspaper column, however I failed to make the dinner!!

CHAPTER TEN

Restaurateur – Part II

Father's culture shock – an uphill task – a cockroach paradise – the wandering crocodile – nuclear company bedrooms – Gallileo's romantic heir – father's terrible end – art exhibitions – the Giftique – a licensee again – winter of discontent – disaster looms – a ristorante by night – Malcolm and Dominique – La Belle Epoque – killed by a drunken driver – George Best – the musical Smiths – gastronomique evenings – twin offers to buy – Ronnie Scott's and Jazz – Lyttleton, Melly, Grappelli, Adler, Earl Hines – Hereward Restaurant Developments – Scottish borders – De Quincey's Wine Bar – Cheshire Courier Cars – La Belle Epoque again – mother dies – family chapel of rest.

~

To go back in time to 1968 and my need to take over my father's business at the Kings Coffee House and of course the head lease from the owners of the building, the Knutsford Council. My father by now was undergoing very serious operations, the final one being for a cancerous tumour of the brain, the portents were ominous. He was released from Salford Royal Hospital, and came home to be nursed by my mother in what was a busy and noisy environment. Poor father, it had been only ten years since he had finally left the licensing trade behind at the eruptive Red Cow inn. He had not been there for that many years after spending a life time at the old and much loved White Bear. The move just 100 yards across Canute Square had been induced by a better wage offer from Chester's brewery, the owners of the Red Cow, and the fact that the inn had several guest bedrooms, which would allow my mother to gain profit from their letting. Then came the offer of the tenancy from the Knutsford Council. It must have been a considerable jolt to my father's lifestyle to leave the masculine for the feminine. All his life he had spent in the smoky low ceiling rooms of a public house, and he was by the way a heavy smoker himself. His customers were mainly men of varying social backgrounds from the cheerful grimy faced workers at the local gas works, to the city gentleman stopping off for a quick drink on his way home after a day spent in his Manchester office. My father, the complete sporting man, would have to miss out on conversations concerning cricket, football and horse racing. No bookies runner would be collecting bets from the Kings Coffee House, he would never hear a swear word again. Instead he would be offering a selection of fancy pastries and cakes to be boxed and taken home by young well to do housewives, whose clamouring children had been appeased by the selection of fine Swiss chocolate which was on offer at the counter. His largely feminine clientele would sit and chatter for hours on end over endless cups of tea or coffee, his day being briefly lit up at lunchtimes when local business men popped in for an inexpensive lunch and a quick "mannish" chat. Always a quiet man and a perfect gentleman he would have soon settled to his new way of life.

Pity though my poor father on his arrival at the Kings Coffee House, gone were the glory days of this enlightened business venture, time had taken a deadly toll. Opened in 1909, Richard Watt had endeavoured to ensure that the project harmonised with the thinking behind his building of the Elizabeth Gaskell Memorial Tower, which was the architectural cornerstone of the whole building. It mattered greatly to Watt that the Coffee House echoed the literary and artistic connection with the town's great authoress. To achieve this he engaged the talented and artistically inclined Wilson sisters, Alice and Ethel, who I have previously referred to in the chapter regarding Richard Harding Watt. Their success in achieving Watt's ambitions, is I hope, well noted. However from 1909 to the mid 1950's is a long long time to be running a business and maintaining high levels of excellence. The two bright young things in their twenties or thirties in 1909 were now well advanced in age and in their late seventies or eighties. I know nothing of their demise or departure from the coffee house, my father would certainly have known, but I was not aware of the circumstances, being married and busily engaged by Messrs Kendal Milne. Whatever the circumstances of their going it is not hard to visualise after so many years the immediate problems facing him. The familiarisation process alone would have taken months to absorb. Knowing my father as a thorough and painstakingly careful man, as befits a former draughtsman engineer, I also knew him to lack imagination in the business sense. He certainly was not the entrepreneurial type, however for the first time in his life he was no longer a wage earning public house tenant, with few opportunities to be expansive, at last he was in control of a business that offered him the chance of making capital gain and profit. He was his own man at last.

What though were the chances of making such profits? I am afraid I have to say in retrospect, they were minimal. His relatively short time at the Red Cow would have not allowed him sufficient time to accrue much capital from his hotel bedroom letting business. Above all, the run down Kings Coffee House was in great need of capital injection and tender loving care to restore it to it's former glory. Certainly he inherited a business that was up and running, unfortunately though, it was running out of both time and steam. It was being managed as well as it could possibly have been under the circumstances, by a Mrs Jones, again I re-iterate I have no knowledge of the whereabouts of the Miss Wilson's, though I feel sure that only Alice remained to the end as tenant, and owner, Ethel having married Manchester Guardian editor John Hall, had departed earlier. Vast amounts of money were needed to be invested in the business to modernise and bring it back to the real world, it still echoed the Edwardian period in which it was conceived. Father had not got the kind of money needed, so it became more of a holding operation, a gently, gently, see how you go affair, with most attention being paid to the cleaning and overhaul of the building, the Knutsford Council of course as the landlords, being responsible for maintaining the structural condition of it. Father though had to make do with the existing and outdated kitchen equipment, most of which needed replacing. The much vaunted model bakery with which it baked it's own bread and confectionery had long gone and was now part of the living accommodation.

As well as having to adapt to the existing way the business was conducted, he also had to give due consideration to the staff he was inheriting. These too of course were all ladies and if not well advanced in age, were mature to say the least. There was an able cook producing traditionally good but modest food, and an abundance of kitchen assistants variously employed with preparation and washing up. It was though, the front of house staff that demanded father's total attention. These were a brigade of formidably matronly middle aged ladies with minds of their own, who dressed in black with white aprons and caps, went about their business of serving morning coffees, lunches and afternoon teas with great solemnity and dignity. My father had for some time to exercise much patience with them, he was the new boy and they ruled this particular roost, if there appears to be an allusion to hens then it is entirely accidental. He eventually got on extremely well with them, after all he had been serving beer to most of their husband's in past years.

Such was the scenario that I too, with much trepidation, entered into. At the time I had little heart or enthusiasm for it, it was a step back in time, I had virtually inherited the same problems that my father had had on his arrival. There had been little investment, more restoration and replacement than progressive modernisation, he just had not the money or possibly the mind for it. Now I too was in the same position. After just three years of opening The Tavern and making it into a popular and successful restaurant, I had left it without either rancour or profit. It was unthinkable that I should ever demand capital gain from it, I left it without a brass farthing to show for my endeavours and with nothing to invest in the coffee house, I was starting from scratch all over again but at least there was a business that was up and running. At first I was a little too reluctant to get involved and perhaps feeling hard done by, it was after all a far cry from my beloved Tavern, full as it was of excitement and it's lively throng of interesting people to keep me on my toes. I was to lose my sporting and cricketing associations, no longer would I be buying and serving fine wines, the coffee house was "dry" and unlicensed. I would have to settle for serving coffee and tea instead, I had to grit my teeth and get on with it, for everyone's sake.

Gradually I grew to love the old place for what it was, I became somewhat absorbed in it's history and background. I came to understand much better the spirit in which it was conceived and so much so I resolved to endeavour to resurrect, however slowly, some of the things that the Kings Coffee House was famous for, other than serving home made patisserie. Along with that, some modernisation had to take place which would not compromise it's traditions and the spirit of the place. I had to invest in it, but with what, it was after all my father's business and it was his money I was going to have to use, he was going to have to trust me to get it right. It was risky business and a gamble, but I had gambled before at The Tavern and got away with it, but at The Tavern, both turnover and profitability were high, at the coffee house both were low and the risk greater. The business could not however mark time, I had to move it on. Time and future events would show that if it had not have progressed, it would have folded. Firstly there was some routine investment to be made, beautiful cane furniture was bought to match the existing art nouveau style banquettes and chairs, new pottery was required this time in the K.C.H livery, and in the kitchen Bains Marie were introduced, along with a replacement and most expensive slicing machine. At first no attempt was made to increase prices, decimalisation was shortly going to take care of that. This was the late 1960s and early 1970s and coffee was one shilling and sixpence or 7p in today's money, lunch (please refrain from smiling) was six shillings and sixpence or 32 pence for three courses, this has to be taken into context, as yet dishwashing machines, cold rooms, extra refrigeration, stainless steel cookers and much more were things of the future. The whole kitchen itself was hugely unhygienic with both the walls and floors in need of tiling, fortunately at that moment in time the health, hygiene and safety people were not so attentive, maybe they understood the problems of what was something of an institution and were kind to us, or at least patient. Worst of all though was the plague of cockroaches that I inherited. To switch the kitchen lights suddenly on at midnight, meant seeing a black mass of the little beasts scuttle away, seemingly in a flash. With the splendid help of "Rent-o-kill" we eventually rid ourselves of the infestation, until then my great dread was for one to pop out of the spout of a pot of tea, and into some poor unsuspecting old ladies cup!

By far the best way of increasing turnover and profit was through the letting of the hotel's few bedrooms. Father had entered into a contract with the Northwest Gas Board, which guaranteed the rooms would be filled most weeks of the year from Monday to Thursday, by young trainee employees. This at the princely figure of £2 per night per room, again please consider that this was the 1960s and £1 the rough equivalent to £20 or more today. Whatever, it was silly, and I cancelled the contract. I then did a fairly awful thing and converted the glorious old ballroom and exhibition room into five further bedrooms, but not before ensuring that they were of wood and plaster build and could be taken down again if necessary. I had sympathy with the gas board whose headquarters were at nearby Mere, they subsequently moved on, the building is now the fine Mere Court Hotel. I am completely convinced that it does not cater for young lively training gas board employees, whose nocturnal activities included placing the Coffee House's stuffed crocodile in each other's beds, godfather style. It was easy to detect in which room the poor reptile reclined by the trail of sawdust that led from the empty wall it had hung from to the bedroom door. Towards the end, it was becoming so emaciated that it looked like a huge empty gentleman's wallet.

Now with sufficiently enough bedrooms to make a substantial increase in the turnover via the introduction of a higher priced tariff, I could have gone public and catered for upmarket but occasional types of business, this would have been a slow process and in need of costly publicity material and advertising. I took the easy way out and entered into an agreement with the then thoroughly successful Nuclear Power Company, which was located in nearby Booths Hall and Park, and which overlooked Toft Cricket ground, they now being the club's landlords. They were extremely happy to pay the new prices and to have somewhere reasonably sophisticated, very adjacent, fairly historic and all theirs. Though the business did not serve dinner, they were quite delighted to be recommended to and be given special attention at our related business upstairs at The Tavern. All our rooms were occupied again from Monday to Thursday, leaving me free to coach the Toft Junior section on Saturday mornings, a liberty this, as Saturday was a very busy day at the Coffee House, we were closed on Sundays, which meant more cricket, as Toft were then heavily involved in the National Village Knockout Cup.

We were happy and pleased to be asked to entertain and cater for the needs of some of the Nuclear Power Company's more prestigious clientele. On one such occasion we were asked to pay very special attention to an Italian gentleman who turned out to be no less than the Professor of Astronomy at Pisa University and was then occupying the chair that the great and glorious Gallileo himself had sat in so many centuries before. He had been asked to lecture the scientists at Booth Hall. What an honour of course this was for us. I was duly briefed by the company and further pressed to attend to the Professor's every need, all stops were to be pulled. With the coffee house closed during the evening, the establishment was of course quiet. I usually was involved with books, ledgers and so on, and needed only one member of staff to act as receptionist and general factotum. To do this I employed part time Knutsford ladies, who were attractive, well mannered, intelligent and with plenty of common sense. They were ladies who I always knew fairly well and were anyway day time customers of the Coffee House, just a little pocket money and to get out of the house was their small need. One such lady was Jean, she was on duty on this occasion and my brief to her was to give the Professor everything he asked for and to pander to his every whim. On arriving and prior to going out for dinner that evening, he had asked for a bottle of brandy and glasses to be taken up to his room after he had bathed and dressed. I must point out at this juncture that the gentleman bore no resemblance what so ever to the average person's immediate vision of a learned Professor, not was he long haired, bearded, bespectacled or shrunken, but the most handsome of Italian men imaginable, my heaven's he was good looking and didn't he just know it. I did not see Jean wilt in his presence and she was duly last seen disappearing upstairs with her tray of brandy. Be assured that I was not counting in minutes, but noticed that after fifteen minutes or so, she had not re-appeared. Several minutes later she did, looking slightly dishevelled, highly coloured and extremely agitated. It appears that in following my brief to the letter to take great care of the fellow, she had been asked if she would care to join him in a glass of brandy, sit on the edge of the bed where he joined her and engaged her seemingly in harmless conversation which lasted some ten minutes. Then without much ado he pushed her back on the bed and attempted to kiss her. Jean, the sweet innocent housewife and mother that she was, duly panicked and fled the scene believing that accepting the amorous advances of the Professor was not quite within the remit of her instruction, for Queen and country maybe, but not for the Nuclear Power Company or Kings Coffee House. Of course we made nothing of it, the Professor appeared later immaculately turned out, as smooth and unruffled as ever. On the many occasions over the years when ever Jean and I bumped into each other, we always exchanged jests and I pulled her leg unmercifully. One conclusion that can be drawn with regard to Italian Professors is that Professors they may very well be, but first and foremost they are essentially Italian. Thank heavens!

To revert to much more serious matters and indeed a terribly sad one for my mother, my family and myself, this was the worsening cancerous condition of my father. His tumour must have been a terrible thing for him to have to endure. His speech was so badly affected that he could hardly communicate and he was now for the most part bed bound. My mother and I were doing our best to look after him which was difficult during the working day when we were both involved with running the business, myself front of house, she managing the kitchen. My father's mental torment must have been a terrible thing to have to bear. It was to manifest itself one working day. I had managed to slide away from the counter during a busy lunch hour to see how he was, only to find that he wasn't in his bedroom, but on hearing a splashing noise in the next door bathroom, entered to find him naked and trying to submerge himself in a very full bath of water. Had I been ten minutes or so late, he would have drowned himself. I pulled him out of the bath, wrapped him in a blanket and sat down on the staircase step with him, where we both cried our hearts out, he in recognition of the hopelessness of his condition, myself with the terrible pity for a father I loved dearly. He was shortly admitted to hospital and died there in great pain within a few weeks, so awful was his death that I admit that I wished I had been twenty minutes later going upstairs that day to see him. The piteous scene at his hospital bedside will live long in my memory. So died a man who had once been described as the "whitest man in Knutsford".

It was necessary to put this dreadful time for the family behind us, and for me to get on with the process of re-invigorating the Kings Coffee House. I was desperately keen to re-establish it's links with it's artistic past, this had eroded over the years through the aging process of the Wilson sisters. The music room had been variously, Knutsford Council Chamber, Masonic lodge and now The Tavern Restaurant. The library and reading room had become the resident's lounge, and I criminally had converted the upstairs exhibition room into bedrooms. Now I had a yen to hang paintings once more in the Miss Wilson tradition, both ladies having been well recognised and much exhibited painters in their day. To do this I made contact with various artistic groups and societies in the North West, mainly Cheshire, and invited them to hang their works in the coffee room, a room which everybody had to pass through. This worked well for a while and culminated in an exhibition given by members of the Augustine Studio, a very fine London colony of supreme artists, who had been recommended to me by my uncle, former Major Kenneth Lee, then doing business in Berkeley Square in the capital. I was right to accept his recommendation, for they exhibited a collection of paintings, sculptures, hand made gold and silver objects, pottery and jewellery, the likes of which I had rarely seen before. The craftsmanship was breathtakingly beautiful and it was a privilege to display the work. That they came to Knutsford was in no small measure due to the former fame and reputation of the Kings Coffee House and of course, to it's charm. This dalliance with painting was to lead me further with my desire to resurrect the links the K.C.H had with the fine arts, music also was to be not too far away in my thoughts.

The high quality objects that the Augustine Studios brought to the coffee house were again to act as a stimulus. My responsibility was to be able to display them to their best advantage and I had of course given due consideration to the matter. Richard Watt had designed and built as part of the façade of the building, the most beautiful bow window imaginable. It projected into the main street and had much fine detail and is considered the best in Knutsford, if not Cheshire, originally it had shown the patisserie that had been produced in the business's model bakery, and when that was demolished no further commercial use had been found for it, it was a worthy home for the studio's hand crafted artwork. The whole process of window display had the affect of re-kindling my now long gone retailing instincts. I had the opportunity to again don the former retail buying and selling cap that I had worn for Harrods, and had tossed away to enter the restaurant trade. The window and another window in the K.C.H courtyard that had lain fallow for so many years were quite patently the most advantageous areas in which to show fine merchandise. Taking a leaf from the Augustine Studio's book, it was obvious that art related items that were attractive, of quality and originality without being over priced could be displayed to good effect and would interest a mainly feminine and largely already captive clientele. In short this was to be gift type merchandise. I had myself an instant upmarket gift shop to which I gave the hugely unimaginative name of "The Giftique", an easy name to remember if you are trying to locate a gift shop. My logo was a black silhouette of the building on a white background, you knew immediately where the goods in the bag came from. The old Harrods buying principles were then put to good use, that is to search high and low and if necessary far afield for merchandise that was not available or not considered by other outlets within preferably a fifty mile radius and I was soon on the pre-seasonal road to trade fairs in London, Birmingham et al. Not for me fine Staffordshire porcelain or crystal glassware and the like, which could be found in Knutsford and other local towns ad nauseam. I sought out studio glass and ceramics, sculptural bronzes, high quality continental jewellery and hung the walls with quality prints. Where a noted manufacturer was not represented locally, I did take advantage. For instance it was amazing that Moorcroft Pottery was not available, I was able to gorge on it and wished now that I had held on to it as an investment. This was of course all being bought with accommodation and restaurant profits, I trod a fine line but the portents were good, then!

It was now high time to grasp the Coffee House nettle fully, to bring it forward to meet the requirements of that period's needs and demands and that without losing the charm of the place. In fact everything was done so as to enhance it's exquisite art nouveau and arts and crafts décor and traditions. Businesses of this type could succeed if tuned to the pace of the modern day. "Bettys" that splendid group of Yorkshire tea and coffee houses is the most prominent example, Swiss orientated they are able to bake their own delightful patisserie, our model bakery was long gone and we had been buying cakes from a local competitor and selling them at little profit, the fine chocolate also turned over very slowly. The 32 pence three course lunch was suicidal and had to go, and being unlicensed we could not serve a civilised glass of wine. I applied for and easily obtained a licence to sell beer, wines and spirits, but where and what from? Sadly out went the cake and chocolate counter, and in it's place we had built a good looking dispense bar, craftsmanship made, that was moulded in the art nouveau style and sympathetic to Watt's original interior design.

It was difficult for me to refrain from buying the finest wines, but there would have been little demand for them, not a lot of wines are consumed in the lunch period, and the Coffee House was not in the business expense bracket, our ladies, forever careful, would it was predicted, permit themselves just a glass of wine or sherry. The wine list was therefore limited to the more popular and reasonably priced wines, though I did stock the odd good bottle for the occasional male wine buff. To the horror of my regular customers, who knew a bargain when they saw one, I did drop the 32 pence lunch, but was unable to replace it with a modern and sophisticated menu. My cook was a lovely middle aged lady who had cooked in her own way all her life, and would have found "new fangled" recipes difficult to cope with, she was anyway part and parcel of the establishment, so we were unable to go the full hog. The menu was largely made up of light meals of grilled food and salads, the soup and puddings remained "wholesome" but priced separately. All was now in place and we were all systems go, however it was a high risk programme that I had adopted, I was treading a fine and protracted financial line, I was keeping a lot of fiscal balls in the air at one time and though the swinging sixties had shortly ended, there was no reason to believe that the seventies would not also be of the swinging variety, and I needed the buoyant trading period to continue to finance my ventures. It was not to be.

Disaster struck with a vengeance, and very quickly, we must have been blind not to see it coming. The economic and political situation under the governance of Ted Heath's Conservative Government was to prove inept under the challenge of the trade unions. The country's electricity network was vulnerable to mechanical failure and industrial action. In December 1970 hospitals were forced to function on batteries and candles during a "work to rule" strike, then in 1973 an oil crisis worsened the situation and caused Heath to attempt to impose a prices and incomes policy to cap rising inflation. The unions resisted, a series of miners strikes forced him to declare the awful three day working week to nurse the electricity system through the crisis. It is hard for anyone today to imagine how dreadful this all was. Unemployment became high, as businesses cut their staff in an effort to keep afloat. Recklessly I refused to do this. In an attempt to remain loyal to both my customers and my staff I chose to try to keep functioning as if all was normal. Business's throughout the country started to crash by the thousands. Small business's in particular were badly affected, the café trade was savaged and both my rivals in the town were forced to close, one of them never to re-open. The Coffee House complex including The Tavern restaurant was and is huge, and the heating and lighting bills enormous. Despite this I chose not to shorten my opening hours and remained open despite being without heat and light for hours and days on end. My elderly and mainly feminine clientele could be forgiven for not wishing to sit in a cold and darkened restaurant, so they stayed away. My giftware trade suffered accordingly as there were fewer ladies about to be tempted and less money for such luxuries. My bedrooms were empty, as my eggs were all confined to the business basket, and the Nuclear Power Company was pulling it's horns in. All this was not helped by the introduction at about that time of decimalisation which further added to already raging inflation. My feminine clientele had difficulty in coming to terms with the fact that the old one shilling and three pence cup of coffee or 6 pence decimal, was suddenly 10 pence. I reckoned that decimalisation meant a 50% increase across the trading board. Now you can pay £2 per cup of coffee, beware the full introduction of the Euro, which saw prices rise overnight in Europe.

My high risk investment in the business was soon to prove a threat to it's very existence. The period of consolidation needed was no longer available. Accounts became harder to pay and took longer to do so, trades people were in the same boat and in desperate need of their money, I had no capital to invest in new stock for the gift shop, which meant fatal stagnation, in short I was staring disaster in the face and had to do something fairly drastic and rapidly at that. The very obvious way out was substantially increasing my turnover without increasing my costs too much, but how? I could not do that within the confines and structured style of the existing business. It was hugely apparent that the way to do this was to increase the hours of opening, in short to open in the evenings. I had never ever contemplated doing this, as I would have placed myself in direct competition with my ex wife trading upstairs at The Tavern restaurant. I had no wish to hazard her operation or threaten what was proving to be her expensive lifestyle. Now I felt I had no other recourse, she would have been more under threat had I gone to the wall and had to surrender the head lease to the Knutsford Council, another landlord would not have been so sympathetic, I was after all, still asking her for the miniscule rent that my father had kindly asked me for.

I had much missed the excitement of my days of The Tavern, they were lovely working days and had been very successful and it had been hard to say goodbye to them. The Coffee House had provided me with a further challenge, but it had been much harder to change a business that had become so rooted in tradition, than it was to create one from nothing as was the case with The Tavern. I had little doubt that the Coffee House that my father took on in the fifties and managed through the sixties, would never have survived "the winter of discontent" as it became known. Now my luck had changed. We had come very far and stood at the threshold of something that could prove to be very good indeed. I was not going to lose the business that I had toiled to change and invested so much time and capital on. I now relished the prospect of again trading in the evening and meeting the needs of a wider, more affluent and demanding clientele. I knew this type of market like the back of my hand, it was one I had learnt during my buying days and earlier training with Harrods. I relished the thought of being once again involved in the buying of fine wines, to get to the crude point, customers in the evenings spend more on food and drink over a longer period then they do at lunchtime. The interiors of the Coffee House would be even more interesting and beautiful when lit at night, customers would be thrilled by it's splendid Art Nouveau/Art and Crafts décor. There would be little need of further investment in the front of the restaurant, we were licensed, had a bar, smart furniture, the kitchen still presented many problems in equipment terms and would have to be adapted to meet the needs of the new chefs who would prepare the food for whatever cuisine was chosen, but what cuisine? For me this had long been obvious, here in the middle of the main street of a lovely old market town, stood this amazing Italianate building, what better cuisine than Italian? I have to remind the reader at this point, that Italian food thirty odd years ago was not common place in the British high street, certainly there was a presence in the big cities, but it certainly would be the first in Knutsford, now at the last count there were five. This would be the only Italian restaurant in the country that traded in an Italianate building, it made very good sense. The quality of the building, particularly it's interiors, dictated that the food served should also be of the highest quality. I never ever would have chosen to serve pizzas, though they would have doubtless proved to be a raging success. The pizza house chains of restaurants were still not yet evident in the towns, we could maybe have been the first, no, certainly not a pizzeria or trattoria, the latter would also have been a sure-fire winner, either would have been easier to manage, easy to operate and less demanding all round. Not for me though the easy way, I just had to make life difficult for myself, I didn't want to court the popular trade, I wanted to be different however hard, it would have to be a "ristorante" and as unique and original as was ever possible.

I decided to endeavour to create a menu from the classic cuisines of the four north Italian provinces. The meat dishes from Emilia Romagna, the vegetable dishes from Tuscany, the fish from Veneto, the sweet dishes and other refined foods from Lombardy. I took myself off on a whirlwind tour of the great capital cities of Bologna, Florence, Venice and Milan, sampling the food, making numerous notes, absorbing the heady atmospheres of their best restaurants, believing the cost would be handsomely repaid in due course. At the same time I was placing equally costly personal advertisements in the relevant Italian press needing to attract the attention and interest of an entrepreneurial Italian superman who would give the project a very necessary authenticity. This had been an essential ingredient in establishing The Tavern as a "pukka" Danish restaurant. His main job of work initially would be to recruit an Italian crew including chefs. I had plenty of bedrooms to accommodate them with some over for commercial use. It all depended on the right chap reading the right newspaper on the right day. He didn't and time was running out, my only other recourse then was to tap into an increasing Italian catering population. The "Mario and Franco" group of trattorias had established themselves in the British cities by now and had gained a good reputation. I took myself off in an attempt to poach one of their bright and hopefully enterprising managers and succeeded in interesting one "Gianni" who looked the part and who I thought would be splendid. After some negotiation, we agreed to proceed, but the very next day his English wife told him she was not prepared to move to Knutsford. Good god this is a town in which people are prepared to spend a small fortune to come and live in. Maybe I was wrong in my judgement, he certainly was. A few years later with the La Belle Epoque up and running smoothly as one of the leading restaurants in the north of England, I bumped into him in his then role of manager of a Manchester bar, he confessed with great sadness to making the biggest mistake of his life.

I really was in trouble now, time was of the essence and I was certainly running out of it, then my luck changed. For many months on most Saturday afternoons, a small family sat on a corner table adjoining the bar, they were Malcolm and Dominique Mooney and their six month old little boy, Lauren. The Mooney's owned a very successful and authentically French bistro in a precinct in nearby Hale Barns called "The Borsalino". He was English and she Norman French from Caen. We obviously had restaurant interests in common, got on well and talked business. I had for many months been outlining my plans for my classic Italian restaurant to him, and he was so enthusiastic that he went as far as to venture that if I ever changed my mind, would I consider bringing him into the business as a partner as he believed the building would make an equally beautiful French restaurant. The dire situation I was now in left me little alternative other than to contact him with a view to doing just that. The Kings Coffee House was not to become the first Italian restaurant in Knutsford, that honour belonged to "Est, Est, Est" who's brilliant creator Derek Lilley, went on to build his chain of unique and classy restaurants. The La Belle Epoque was thus born and go on to mature into a highly reputable and renowned French restaurant.

Malcolm Mooney was quite a character being bright, progressive, enthusiastic and ambitious. I am sure that I am right in saying that he owned a menswear boutique in an area of Manchester then known as "the Village" and was behind Deansgate and to the rear of Kendal Milne. A colleague in the business was non other than the young George Best, the celebrated northern Irishman playing wonderful football in another great Manchester United team, he of course was also building a reputation as a bon viveur, if that is the way to describe George. They got on extremely well together, so well in fact that Malcolm became George's very first manager. His description of life with Best in that capacity was simply riotous, as George's services seemed to be in great demand the length and breadth of Europe, and not in his capacity as footballer. His exploits attracted the covetous attention of Manchester's not so illustrious smart set, including individuals who desired a slice of the Best life style, many jostling Malcolm for his position as his manager. He found this to be exasperating and very wearing, so much so in total disgust he relinquished his managerial role. He and Dominique then opened The Borsalino, a truly French bistro.

Not too much time was needed to get the business underway, a little fine tuning here and there in the front of the house particularly with the lighting, the restaurant never ever having been utilised in the evenings before. The kitchen however did need bringing up to date, another oven was purchased in addition to the one I had bought, a cold room was built and dish washing machines introduced. Most costly of all was the need to conform to hygiene regulations, much tiling needed to be done to walls and floors. The modus operendi at the newly created La Belle Epoque was for Dominique Mooney to establish the classic French cuisine. Soon we had engaged the services of a group of splendid local young ladies who nearly all were married, enjoyed a country lifestyle, and needed a vehicle in which to express their talent for cooking, in some instances to earn a little extra to keep a pony. All were fine cooks with Cordon Bleu training and all with experience in other good local restaurants. They were of course taking over the duties of the old coffee house cooks who had retired realising that change was inevitable, and who anyway were of retirement age, mercifully there were no sackings. The new cooks were of course in no need of lessons in how to prepare French cuisine.

Dominique was there to establish the overall French style of the menu. In addition we took on board a bevy of young attractive French girls who we would easily accommodate and employ as waitresses. The essentially French atmosphere was thus realised, with Dominique now working in Knutsford, Malcolm had to remain at The Borsalino to ensure it's continuing success. I managed the front of house, customer accounts and the wine service in La Belle Epoque.

Dominique and Malcolm lived at nearby High Legh, roughly midway between the two restaurants. With her kitchen management duties over by 10 o'clock, Dominique would leave to then go home and ensure the very young Lauren was well seen to. Malcolm of course, had to put The Borsalino to bed which invariably was very late. Naturally he wanted to see how we were progressing with the new restaurant, and would call on his way home, which meant a round-a-bout journey. We would then chat for half an hour over the evenings business and who had been in that he knew, and proceed on his way home. Then tragedy occurred. Just nine weeks after we had opened the La Belle Epoque, he was making the very same way home, only this time passing through the traffic lights at Mere corner with a green light in his favour, when a lorry driven by a drunken driver drove his vehicle through a red light and struck Malcolm's car broadside on, killing him instantly. Sadly I was the last person to see him alive. So ended a very brief but exhilarating relationship with a man who I found to be inspirational. The funeral took place at Knutsford Cemetery on a cold bleak November afternoon I was one of the four pallbearers who carried his coffin. At the rear of it were a wealthy business friend and old customer and a former Cheshire County Rugby Union three quarter. I took the right hand corner and linked arms with the man on the left who happened to be George Best. This was the nearest I would ever get to a footballing hero of mine, how I wish it could have been in less tragic circumstances. It was all so terribly surreal. Poor Malcolm was laid to rest in a quiet far corner of the cemetery seemingly, but I am sure, not forgotten as the years have rolled on.

I am sure that from the moment of Malcolm's death, Dominique felt that the move from The Borsalino to La Belle Epoque was ill fated, and with The Borsalino now without it's charismatic figurehead, also felt the need to take over the front of restaurant duties there. However difficult that was under the circumstances she bravely took the helm. Her good close friend Nicole Guerin and fellow director joined me in Knutsford to maintain the French style. Dominique eventually married again, this time a fellow countryman, and moved back to France to live in Paris. The Borsalino closed it's doors to become a dear memory as possibly the last of the true French bistros as we now become swamped by a plethora of Italian restaurants. I remained at the front of La Belle Epoque with that wonderful crew of Cordon Bleu cooks continuing to present truly excellent classic French cuisine. The restaurant very soon rightfully earning it's entry into the almighty "Good Food Guide".

Before Malcolm was killed, his killer incidentally only receiving a six month prison sentence for his heinous crime, we had discussed the possibility of presenting classical music in the restaurant on a once a month basis along with an equally classic French meal of several courses. We knew that the block of bedrooms that I had constructed a few short years earlier in the concert/exhibition room could quite easily be taken down and become a venue for musical events. I was thrilled at the thought of music again returning to the lovely old building, the artistic wheel would then have turned a full circle. All would be as Richard Watt and the Miss Wilson's had intended more than half a century earlier. The concert room would be restored to it's late 19th century glory, with Malcolm gone the onus was on me. I cannot, for the life of me, remember how I came upon Nicholas and Sally Smith. I needed someone who could take my hand and lead me through what might have been a musical minefield. I am not a music buff, but classical music was not exactly foreign to me. In the past I attended Halle Orchestral concerts in Manchester's Free Trade Hall, lunch time concerts in St. Ann's Church and in Manchester Town Hall. I had also gone along to concerts given by students at the Royal Northern College of Music, where a wonderful array of talented young musicians perfected their skills. This must have been the path that led to the Smith's who, Nick Smith in particular, was highly involved and in contact with and had access to their burgeoning talents, which is what I was seeking, but had little idea until I met them, how to go about it. I have an idea that Nick Smith had been or was involved in a teaching capacity at the R.N.C.M.

I was able then to roughly outline my plans for bringing classical music to the La Belle Epoque, the Smiths were delighted at the prospect, and together we mapped out a programme, with them acting as agents for these brilliant and up and coming musicians.

These commenced with a choral concert given by the BBC singers and then were followed in sequence throughout 1975 by the Sartori String Quartet, the Northern Chamber Orchestra, the Festival Brass Consort who played their music on the roof garden, the Alfreton Hall String Quintet, and ended the year with Alan Cuckston delighting everyone on his harpsichord. In the summer of 1976, Chetham's Hospital School of Music Chamber Orchestra played for us again on the roof garden as had the Northern Chamber Orchestra, it was then it was realised that if we were to expand our activities in a grander musical scene, the sooner the five temporary bedrooms occupying the old concert room came down, the better for us it would be. The classical music programme ended on what turned out to be the most beautiful of piano recitals given by Nicola Gebolys who had won the British National Piano Competition at the age of thirteen, made her first appearance at the Proms when age seventeen, had broadcast many times and played piano concertos with leading orchestras all over Europe. Tragically she was to die shortly afterwards and a great talent lost to the world of music, sadly this also brought an end to our association with Nick and Sally Smith and we began our association with popular music and also with Jazz with which I have a considerable affinity with and love of. Nicholas Smith became the inspiration behind the formation of the Performing Arts Symphony Orchestra, for which he was the conductor. The orchestra also included many of the young stars that played at the La Belle Epoque. It played the country house "Last Night of the Proms" concerts at such venues as Harewood House, Ragley Hall, Shugborough and Arley Hall the latter being when I was Custodian at Arley Hall. I last saw the Smiths' when the orchestra was playing at Erdigg in North Wales. I think it right to say that after so long a time, we were pleased to see each other.

It was in the mid 1970s and possibly a year or two after Malcolm's death that I received an offer to buy my share of the business, Dominique of course retaining her half share of it. This was from Malcolm's identical twin brother Keith, which at the first time of meeting was a strange experience. Now Malcolm was to be replaced by another Malcolm, A.K.A Keith, quite disturbing! I had now for what seemed an eternity, been starting, acquiring and developing restaurants, taking a gamble or two and huge financial risks, most times never seeking or seeing a penny for my endeavours. I had never considered selling my share of the business, capital gain was not on my agenda. I had given The Tavern to my ex-wife, had not thought of any distant future and was possibly naïve. I never saw myself as entrepreneurial, now here was this offer out of the blue. I was though, at that time, somewhat careworn and a little unhappy with the restaurant way of life and was in fact very tired. I like change and challenge and the La Belle Epoque was by now running beautifully smoothly. The thing that was keeping my interest alive was the prospect of developing the musical side of the business. Initially I was not interested but after further consideration I accepted, agreeing to stay with Keith and his wife Nerys for a two year period as part of the deal, also that when I eventually did leave I would give an undertaking not to open another restaurant within a certain mile radius. Keith and Nerys were also anxious to develop the musical and gastronomic evening side of the business, which suited me wonderfully well. I was given the rather grand title of artistic director, they however could call the shots because it was now their money we were investing in them. They had complete confidence in me locating and recommending the artists that were to be engaged, down came the bedrooms and we were off on our new musical adventure. Another huge bonus was of course that I was to continue buying the very fine wines and compiling the exclusive wine list.

With the blessing of Keith and Nerys, I was now able to begin a relationship with Jazz and the musicians that played it. Since my late teens, I had kept abreast with the developing trends, and my interest ranged across the whole spectrum, from traditional to modern, a modest record, disc and tape collection reflects my taste. I was now thrilled at the prospect of being able to engage the talented services of some of the best bands and singers in the country, if not Europe, and yes, eventually from the USA. At the same time we had to be cautious and to some extent commercial, not everyone is a jazz lover, never the less we had a reputation to build, and the field was quite open. Not every jazz venue was like the La Belle Epoque, the music has a tradition for being played in seedy, smoky cellars and the like, which was fine for me and all jazz lovers, now it was going to be presented in one of the most glamorous and beautiful settings imaginable, to an audience that were not necessarily jazz fans, and who were largely interested in the classic French food that was being served prior to the music. Where and how though to establish contact with these bands? Way back in the 1960s when on my menswear buying trips to London on behalf of my Harrodian employers and which usually lasted weeks on end, I was glad of the opportunity that presented itself to visit Ronnie Scott's Jazz Club. It was to them that we now turned to as agents acting on behalf of some, if not, most of the bands and singers available.

We at first tested the water by hiring a few good local Jazz groups, before taking the plunge and hiring no less a band than Humphrey Lyttleton's in the February of 1976. He came again on New Year's Eve, famously saying that it was infinitely more preferable to play and then eat at La Belle Epoque on New Year's Eve than it was to sit on an upturned Guinness crate eating fish and chips at Shoreditch Town Hall. Then came George Melly as wonderfully outrageous as ever, unbelievably I had gone to the Band on the Wall club in Manchester to determine the suitability of booking him, it was not that his jazz and his singing were unsuitable, it was of course tremendous, it was to see if his programme was possibly a little too raunchy for a sophisticated Cheshire audience. It was very near the knuckle but we still booked him, we held our breaths but it went down spectacularly well. It did help that on the front row of the audience were numerous members of the Wilmslow Rugby and Prestbury Cricket Clubs, a little raunchy themselves. On the morning following the performance, with the band up reasonably early and finishing breakfast, a ravished looking Melly appeared on the balcony staircase clad in silk dressing gown and clutching a cigarette holder. He then was greeted with a shout from the band of "what are you going to have for breakfast George?, George's throaty reply was "a large gin and tonic please". Echoes of Noel Coward! Later and on many occasions the fabulous American jazz songstress Marion Montgomery came to enchant us all and become much adored by everyone. Sadly she is no longer with us having died in the early 2000s. Britain's leading exponent of the Jazz piano and composer, Stan Tracey, brought the jazz suite he had composed to the words of Dylan Thomas's poetic masterpiece "Under Milk Wood", played by his quartet. The poem was narrated by that fine welsh actor Donald Houston, it was a truly riveting occasion. That gentle, lovable, Frenchman Stefane Grappelli delighted everyone with his magically swinging violin backed up beautifully by the Diz Disley Trio.

It was impossible to categorise Larry Adler. The music he played on harmonica crossed over from jazz to classical music in a twinkle, a great raconteur and humorist, he regaled us with great jokes and wonderful stories. Amongst the latter was the fact that he used to be asked to play for the notorious New York and Chicago mobster, Al Capone. When Capone felt the need to listen to the then child prodigy, he would ask his most trusted lieutenant to "get me da kid", "wot kid boss"? Was the question, "da kid wid da tin sandwich" was the answer. Adler had been living in England for many years having escaped from the clutches of the witch hunting anti-communist senator, Joe McCarthy. Not exactly my idea of a "red under a bed", Adler had a penchant for the British aristocratic classes and was renowned as being something of a social climber. He was also a lawn tennis lover, and it was my job to try and find a court or two to play on during his visit, preferably with people of a "superior social standing". This was not a difficult task as any number of my old Tavern customers had their own tennis courts, if they could not oblige, one of Toft Cricket Club's wealthy vice president's would. On the subject of America, by far the most exciting of occasions, and speaking from a jazz purist point of view, were the visits of two legendary American jazz pianists. Teddy Wilson had been part of the illustrious Benny Goodman trio and quartets in the 1930s and 1940s. He had also been pianist, arranger and conductor of the jazz groups that had backed that renowned jazz songbird Billie Holiday. For Earl "Fatha" Hines, we gave a European premier to, which was something of an achievement. He considered himself to be the father of the jazz piano, hence the "fatha" part of his title. Doubtless many others, including Jelly Roll Morton, would have disagreed with this presumption. Never the less, Hines in fact had played with the great Louis Armstrong's Hot Five in 1928. I was deliriously happy to be involved, it spoke volumes for their fame that jazz fans from all over England arrived on those occasions just to stand outside the restaurant doors and windows in an attempt to catch a few snatches of their music, I felt extremely sad that they couldn't come in on those dark winter nights.

By the middle months of 1977, my two year liaison with Keith and Nerys Mooney was coming to an end, but was proved not to be over. I still after all lived in part of the building, retaining my flat as a base and home for any future endeavours. I was still only in my mid forties, and my head buzzing with plans and ideas, any form of taking it easy or becoming part retired was entirely out of the question. I however had no wish at the time to become an employee. I had for far too long then, been self employed and was still of the restless free wheeling frame of mind. I had of course since selling the business, known that this situation would arise and made plans accordingly. During the two years with the La Belle Epoque, I had worked on a plan for forming a small limited company of the consultancy variety which would largely relate to the problems facing individuals, with no experience who had the desire to open a small restaurant. I believed that after so many years of involvement I had sufficient experience and was well enough qualified to do so. I was ready to start immediately and did, thus was born "Hereward Restaurant Developments" or HRD. I became a wandering one man band prepared to travel to any part of the United Kingdom and spend upwards to one year on site working on the given restaurant project or problem. Initially I had hoped to be dealing with the many people who would wish to start from scratch, secure a premises for them after advising on the likelihood or not of the chance of it succeeding. The restaurant with everything going for it can fail miserably if it is not in the right location, it is possible that being several hundred metres out of position or on the wrong street can bring this about. In Knutsford, the many restaurants situated on the lower street all do very well, a restaurant opening on the upper street is nearly always doomed to failure. Having secured the premises I would then advise on the interior design and décor of the restaurant itself, evolve the kitchen layout, advise on the selection and purchase of the necessary equipment, locate the suppliers of all commodities, choose the wine list, design a bar, and work in situ until such time the business was ready to trade. The theory I thought was good, however it did not quite work out like that.

I was occasionally engaged on a false premise and then found myself in more of a managerial role than an advisory one. If the people who were employing me were of a nature that I could identify with, and the location of the restaurant or hotel was pleasant enough then I would indulge and immerse myself in their venture. One such place was the Philipburn House Hotel located on a hillside overlooking the River Tweed just north of Selkirk in the Scottish Borders. Jim and Anne Hill were the charming owners and had entered the hotel business after pursuing other careers. Jim Hill was an Edinburgh architect with a yen for owning a hotel. The couple, full of marvellous ideas, had enthusiastically thrown themselves into their venture at the same time enjoying the social side of hotel life. This can be an exhausting process if over indulged in, particularly in Scotland, numerous Edinburgh friends had visited them over a period of years and much fun had been obtained during endlessly long hours, which usually ended at dawn in the hotel swimming pool, a necessity if like Anne Hill, you were a swimmer who had represented Scotland on numerous occasions. They were now more anxious to spend less time entertaining and wanted more time with their lovely family and developing the architectural attributes of the business. I weakly accepted the position of manager, and threw myself into the Borders way of life, which was a dream. The hotel was also located above Selkirk Rugby Football Club ground. They were then captained by Scottish International half back John Rutherford, so it was rugby in the afternoon, work in the evening, which always ended up with a dip in the pool, along with the customers. This was truly lotus eating stuff and one came quickly to adore the beautiful and historic Border countryside and everything that went with it including the highly social rugby event of the year, the "Melrose Sevens" where a whiskey perfumed bouquet hung over the ground and where brilliant rugby was being played.

De Quincey's wine bar however was a different matter, that was everything I had set my stall out to achieve. Fellow Knutsfordians Brian and Chris Hewitt and their family of boys, had departed to the Lake District and bought the Regent Hotel at Waterhead at the northern end of Lake Windermere. An extremely ambitious and adventuresome family, they were anxious to develop the hotel fully. An adjunct of the hotel, was a run down barn stuck on the end of the building like a carbuncle. The

Hewitt's had long realised that as well as the fact that it did nothing to enhance the attraction of the hotel, it did have huge potential for a wine bar. It was magnificently situated, an outdoor area almost stretched into the lake itself and the views were spectacularly beautiful. Remembering the success of The Tavern the Hewitt's sought out the services of yours truly. I was thrilled at the prospect and gladly accepted the challenge, moving north with all speed. I truly appreciated their confidence and I was given absolute freedom of action. I worked from the drawing board with their trusted architect and we designed what I still consider to be my very best endeavour next to, of course The Tavern. It opened with a flourish and went on to win a wine bar of the year award. With the job done, I was unfortunately expected to manage it, however I had been too long away from my mother and her long suffering new husband, their healths were deteriorating and it was necessary for me to return to Knutsford which was very sad. Initially the Hewitt's were upset but soon forgave me and we remain good friends. With their splendid trio of boys now grown up, I would not mind betting that they own a good slice of the hotel business in Ambleside. They deserve every success.

What to do next? I could no longer spend months and years away from my mother, and there was a life of my own to be lived in Knutsford. With Hereward Restaurant Developments now fully tucked up in bed for good, I still needed something to occupy my mind. I was still extremely restless. For sometime I had been developing the idea of forming what I hoped would be an individualistic and very private travel company, working the business from a home base in Knutsford. So I formed a one horse business and called it "Cheshire Courier Cars", cars in the plural being something of a liberty as I had only the one car. The business was an indulgence on my part, it was geared to meet the very special needs and whims of a monied and sophisticated clientele that were to be lured across the Atlantic from the eastern seaboard of the United States. I was prepared to tackle anything and everything that was asked of me, in tailoring terms it was to be a truly bespoke service, tailored to meet every need of the client, however it was relatively easy for me to see that it would not bring me a small fortune.

The financial situation however was somewhat cushioned by a good offer that I was to receive from Keith and Nerys Mooney who, seeing me back at home loafing around waiting for some contact with the U.S.A, asked me if I would like to return to my job as wine buyer and sommelier. The La Belle Epoque was then still trading as a classical French restaurant, the quality of the food was still of a high standard, and the wine served with it needed to be of the similar quality. I was also asked to oversee and control the preparation of the customer accounts during the evening trading, I had their trust and they my complete understanding of what was required. However what was of great importance to me was their understanding that if and when the services of Cheshire Courier Cars were needed, I could shoot off without any problem, as it was, this was not to be on too many occasions so the restaurant was not badly inconvenienced.

The choice of touring with Cheshire Courier Cars depended entirely on the requirements of the client concerned. One Bedlington terrior owning couple wanted to visit Bedlington in Northumberland, a quilt making lady required to meet quilt making ladies in North Wales. In all such instances it was necessary for me to research the subject of their special interest, at least so I believed. This always meant that not only did I plan the journey to meander along the most picturesque routes, but that fittingly, exclusive hotel accommodation was found as were good food restaurants en route. I also endeavoured to include historic sites, buildings and museums where ever possible. I set myself some pretty steep tasks coordinating these tours. More over I could not leave anything to chance, and shortly prior to my American clients arrival in the country, I would take myself along my planned routes. This of course verged on the ridiculous, the exercise costing money and valuable time could be laid at the door of inherent Harrods related perfectionism. I could not build this indulgence into my tour costs and always ended up by breaking even, which was not really the point of the exercise. However it was great fun, truly absorbing and I made many good friends, amongst whom was a nuclear scientist with his wife and sister who basically were tracing their ancestry which lay among the cotton mill towns of Lancashire. They were then going on to York to visit the public school that the sister's dearly departed husband had attended as a boy, and as a boarder. The visit to the dormitory where he had allegedly slept proved to be emotionally disturbing and the ensuing meeting pre-arranged with the headmaster in his study, proved to be beneficial to the tune of a £10,000 gift. I obtained not one glance of appreciation from the headmaster. However the lady concerned did enquire if I might accompany her on a proposed boat journey up the River Orinoco in South America, oh my! what potential bliss. The lovely lady's pleasant attitude differed greatly with that of the wife of an oil billionaire who required to visit historic sites in the south of England. She expected her tour guide to drive a Rolls Royce, be clad in livery, betopped with a peaked hat and to keep a respectful distance, which was all a far cry from the way I chose to operate. We were both glad to eventually reach her London home in Sloane Square, which was huge and palatial. Her rich husband however was a poppet and appreciated all that I had done to make his journey interesting, she unfortunately was too dim to understand half of anything that she was being shown.

The trading life of Cheshire Courier Cars, like that of Hereward Restaurants, was all too short lived, which was very sad, I had been in my element. Touring the country with by and large, charming people was very rewarding indeed. The situation at home with regard to my mother's health was not promising, and I deemed it essential to end my wanderings with the travel tour business and stay closer to her even though I was usually never more than a week away at any one time. This meant of course a much closer and more responsible association with the La Belle Epoque which was in fact much fairer to the Mooney family, I was now working on a full time basis for them and more to the point able to keep a closer eye on my mother living next door but one to my flat. Sadly in 1987 she lost her second husband, and from then on things had been going downhill. Being alone had brought about a drastic deterioration in her health which was not helped by an addiction to alcohol, which was her way of dealing with the situation. It had become necessary for her to be cared for at Bexton Court the local day care centre where I walked her to every morning and which was a blessing for both of us. They were magnificently kind to her despite the fact that she was quite a handful to manage. I tried to look after her at night by sleeping at her cottage, but this was a nightmare experience, and I felt it better that she should move into my flat where better care could be taken. I had by then re-married to Susan who, poor girl, was left to look after her until I returned late from my duties at the La Belle Epoque. She coped extremely well with the situation providing the company and attention that mother needed. During daytime hours it became my responsibility. With Susan having left for work, it was my duty to look after her. Her condition had deteriorated to such an extent that the day care centre was now no longer an option, she needed one to one constant care and attention which was very difficult under the circumstances but never the less essential. So began a two year period of feeding and bathing her, the latter accompanied thankfully with the professional supervision of a visiting nurse. Mother soon became bed bound. I had been earlier advised that her mental condition and hyperactivity would eventually lead to burn out within three years, she passed peacefully away after two years. The emotional stress was considerable for all concerned but we did not let her down. My mother had truly been one of Knutsford's more colourful characters, she was of course a member of the controversial and flamboyant Lee family. She was at times larger than life, outspoken, difficult, often outrageous, completely natural and quite beautiful. I think that as mothers came she was in a category of her own, often disturbingly so. My quiet gentle and gentlemanly father was her alter ego and had much to endure. Shortly after her death and when being treated by my very good local doctor, he ventured to say that I was deserving decent medical attention as I had looked after mother so well, which was exceptionally kind of him to say so.

Mother's death appeared to coincide with a huge shift in the La Belle Epoque business policy. Since it was established in the early 1970s, it had traded as a classical French restaurant, on this it's reputation was built. It was now felt that a change from classic French to bistro style food might be more appropriate, and in line with the less formal eating habits that were becoming ever more fashionable. Consequently a much more streamlined and simplified menu was introduced, with David, the eldest of the new generation of the Mooney family being responsible for its creation and implementation. This he succeeded in doing admirably. Subsequently his younger brother Mathew joined the business in an administrative role, and has taken the restaurant pleasingly forward. It delights me no end to see that the menu now includes a greater number of ambitious dishes which are what this charmingly original building demands and deserves. To revert to the time of the change of policy. It was quite obvious that there was little need to carry a wine list of the size that I had designed, and a much briefer and less expensive one was introduced that would not require the services of a wine buyer/sommelier.

Thus ended an association with a building and it's predecessor the old Hat and Feather inn which both sides of my family had been involved on and off for 140 years. In 1850 my great great maternal grandfather Tom Lee had bought the Hat and Feather along with the next door Rose and Crown inn. In 1874 Tom Lee willed the inn to my great grandfather Fred Lee then aged eleven years. In 1884 Fred duly took up the licence, and was married from there to Jeannette Jones. In 1895 my grandfather Thomas Livingstone Lee was born there, as was his brother Oliver Lee in 1892. In 1895 Fred Lee sold the inn to Richard Harding Watt allowing him to build the Elizabeth Gaskell Memorial Tower and the Kings Coffee House in 1907-1909, and for Fred to make his disastrous move along the street to the White Lion. There was then a lapse in the family connection with the Kings Coffee House until 1958 when the owners, the Knutsford Council asked my father Harry Howard if he would care to take the lease and the business opportunity that went with it. He did so bringing his wife Bessie nee Lee back to a place where her father Tom Lee II had been born seventy-three years earlier. The Lee's were thus reunited with their past, sadly though, from then on the building served only to become a re-occurring final resting place for members of the Lee family, but in the most uncanny set of circumstances. In 1959 my mother brought her mother Annie Lee, my grandmother, there to nurse her through a terminal cancer, she died there that year. In 1970 my father died in hospital after being admitted there just weeks after his attempted suicide in the Coffee House bathroom. That same week my uncle Maurice Victor Lee died suddenly in a Coffee House bedroom while attending my father's funeral. In 1975 my mother's brother, my uncle Geoffrey Lee, collapsed and died of a heart attack when working for the La Belle Epoque restaurant, by which time the transition from Kings Coffee House to La Belle Epoque had been concluded. Finally in 1989 my mother passed peacefully away there. The final family death toll was by then four and included Annie Lee and her two children Bessie and Geoffrey and their cousin Maurice, all of whom were not actually residents, but were either brought there to be nursed through the final months of their lives or in Geoffrey Lee's case to come in to do just an hours work. Maurice Lee had only arrived to stay for a couple of days. In retrospect the building had served to be no more than a huge private family chapel of rest, it was all so very bizarre. I have rarely visited it since 1990, but the relationship is now cordial enough for me to do so. Maybe under the afore related set of circumstances it is possible that I would be tempting the fates, I am not as young or as fit as I used to be, in any case I only live next door but one to the building, and just over the rear wall of the La Belle Epoque, it would be very handy!

CHAPTER ELEVEN

Country House Custodian

Arley Hall – the Brewhouse flat – hall custodian – the west wing – tour guides – the Egerton-Warburtons – Olympia – television at Arley – Cluedo – a bevy of T.V beauties – not hip hooray – retirement – no to boredom – Lee family history – video presentation – "Knutsford in Portrait" – Venetian Achilles tendons – wheelchair bound – Bexton Court – pen to paper – an end.

~

My wife Susan and I had a flat in the town which we rented but were unable to take possession due to there being a year to run on the leasing agreement. Temporary accommodation was therefore needed for just one year. We then had a rather special slice of luck in that the splendid local estate agents Meller Braggins found a flat for me at nearby Arley Hall. It was located in a new and sympathetic development at the rear of Arley Hall itself. Named "the Brewhouse flat" for the very good reason that it was situated on the site of the former Victorian brewhouse where the Egerton-Warburton family had brewed their beers for home consumption some one hundred and fifty years earlier, and indeed possibly many years earlier than that. We then enjoyed a memorably social year sharing the good company of the friends that we made with the residents of the adjoining houses, which were only a handful, and who fitted nicely into each others homes on the occasions of the various house parties that were given. Those given on Sunday lunch times being particularly memorable and were often attended by Lord and Lady Ashbrook and their family. Being a former restaurateur meant that the food and wine that I provided had to be to a relatively high standard, I hope it didn't let anyone down! The days spent were idyllic, I had access to what must be the loveliest country house garden in the north of England and wandered idly through it at all times of the day and season. It was breathtakingly beautiful and I was able to have it all to myself after the general public had departed. Though I had much pleasure from it, when the gardens were officially closed for the winter season, it was well worth getting up early on winter mornings to see the sun rise on a garden laden with a hoar frost.

Even at Arley, despite the reverie, I felt the need to do something. I had not long left the restaurant business and it was still very much a part of me. I needed an active interest and so looked for part time work in restaurants and hotels in the evenings. I did obtain a couple of jobs with reasonably prestigious business's but found their idiosyncratic owners too much to bear, and decided then that the catering industry no longer held me in thrall and paid my final goodbye to it. I then had another stroke of amazing good luck. Approximately when my one year lease at the Brewhouse flat was due to expire, I was approached by the Arley estate with a view to me becoming Custodian of Arley Hall itself. The Arley estate manager, an admirable man if there was ever, had decided to retire. The new manager happily ensconced in a nearby cottage had no wish to reside in the hall which was normally an essential part of the job. So the estate decided to accommodate his wishes and appoint a Custodian responsible for all the events that took place in it which variously included mostly weddings, private parties of every description including birthdays, christenings, funeral wakes, receptions, corporate dinners and lunches, trade fairs, antique fairs, exhibitions, musical events et al. In short I was performing duties that were not too far removed than those demanded by the hotel trade. I had also unknowingly over the years developed the social skills to deal with the public that we were now entertaining. The stalwart retiring estate manager had to cope with all this as well as to administer to the estate proper, he must have been exhausted.

My accommodation too was of dream proportions and was comprised of almost the whole of the west wing of the hall. The west wing traditionally being where the owners of the hall resided, and prior to the estate manager, had been occupied by the now late 10th Lord Ashbrook and his wife. The rooms were of wonderfully large proportion and very grand. We rattled in them like peas in a very large pod, and were able to entertain family rather grandly from time to time. My son Clive and his family were able to spend Christmas with us during seasonal leave from his Hong Kong police duties. My American relatives were more than suitably impressed when they visited on a couple of occasions. Of the duties I was responsible for, non gave me greater pleasure than that of organising the schedules and rotas for the house guides that were employed on obviously a part time basis, being mainly housewives but also having a small number of men, some with farming and estate connections. They were a good bunch and I learnt a lot from them. It was however essential that I become thoroughly acquainted with the history of both the estate and the family who owned it, this in order to conduct tours of the hall myself. As you already know I have had a keen interest in British history since my school days, this interest was re-kindled when I formed my small touring company, Cheshire Courier Cars. I was now in my element. The Arley estate and it's history really did provide a vehicle with which I could drive myself along in and very enthusiastically at that!

Piers Warburton moved the family seat from Warburton, where the family had lived since the late 13th century and built a moated timbered house in the woodlands of Arley in 1469. This stood exposed to the elements for nearly three hundred years, when in 1758 Sir Peter Warburton decided to encase the decaying exterior timbered walls with new brick ones which were then stuccoed and further embellished to create a Gothic house. The scheme proved to be ill considered and by 1818 the house was again in need of extensive repairs. In 1826 the twenty-one year old Rowland Egerton-Warburton inherited the estate and commissioned George Latham, a young Nantwich architect, to design a new house. Work commenced in 1831 and the house that can be seen today was finished between 1840 and 1845. Named by Latham as his "Queen Elizabethan" style, it contains some of the finest ceilings of this style in England. If you have not yet visited Arley Hall and it's beautiful gardens, I urge you to do so as I am beginning to sound like a tour guide. I lived at Arley Hall for five years, years that I consider to have been the most rewarding in terms of enjoyment and satisfaction with the work involved, leaving there in 1996. I visit it regularly now as a "friend of Arley", so much a friend that I am currently helping to restore the ancient books in the magnificent library. I find it impossible to describe the feeling of pleasure I obtain the moment I step foot on the estate.

That is not to say that during my time there I did not feel that more could have been done to promote the estate in a more commercially artistic manner and style. At the time it was not possible for me not to think of ways to do this, it was just in my nature to do so. I had had, after all, some little success in creating business's for example the La Belle Epoque, The Tavern and De Quincey's wine bar. I could also claim to be at ease with the arts and had numerous good contacts within the artistic professions. I also had an obsession with barn conversions long long before today's stampede to convert every agricultural building in sight. During that first year before taking on the responsibilities of Custodian, I had come to admire a huge empty but quite beautiful barn grandly named "Olympia", it had colossal potential. I could not resist the temptation of thinking how best it be used to the benefit of the estate. Putting on my snobby Harrods hat of necessity I came up with the idea of converting it into an exclusive residential hunting lodge, to be used by the well to do lovers of country pursuits, the like of riding, shooting, walking and fishing. Hunting lodges after all were not strangers to the best of country estates, it would have been a truly splendid place to enjoy a luxurious country holiday. Readers of advertisements in Harpers and Queen magazine and Country Life would have been much attracted.

Olympia could also have doubled as a seasonal theatrical venue, being fractionally narrow it would have needed a first floor corridor to give access to the bedrooms. The idea would have been to erect a wide wooden structured staircase and landing, covered, but with an exposed side which would double as a balcony overlooking the 'U' shaped and enclosed courtyard. The structure would then have echoes of the Globe theatre in style and compliment temporary seating in the courtyard. The estate would then have had something quite unique and which would further enhance the good reputation it already enjoyed. If the idea had been accepted, the Arley Hunting Lodge could by now have grossed a couple of million pounds, all things being equal. My figures are now rough and from long memory, the estate having retained my written thesis. For fifteen years since then, and further stymied by the moratorium on barn conversions, Olympia has lain fallow. I was not asked to further enlarge on my suggestions, had I been given the opportunity to do so, I would have offered my services for very little reward in an effort to make the scheme succeed going on to manage it, I would have staked my life on making it a success. Recently plans were approved to convert the lovely Olympia into a further facility for entertaining, it is sure to be a huge success.

Shortly after this I was offered the position of hall Custodian and threw myself whole heartedly into the job, so much so that the physical side of it caught up with me with a vengeance. The hall by now being converted on an almost daily basis into whatever use was required of it, with myself and only one or sometimes two of our male tour guides to assist. We made much light of it and there was often considerable pleasure to be obtained. In particular the days when the hall was utilised by the various television companies as a backdrop for some of their ongoing productions. Cleudo springs immediately to mind, when a whole host of TV stars descended on us for weeks at a time and we were thrilled by the likes of such lovely ladies as Jerry Hall, Rula Lenska, Koo Stark, Susan George and amused by Ruth Madoc, Molly Sugden, Liz Smith and June Whitfield. We all fell in love though with the beautiful and so gracious Joanna Lumley. The men obviously didn't quite catch as much of our attention, and included amongst many others Tom Baker, Richard Madeley and Richard Wilson.

I had developed a back problem at Arley which, coupled with an arthritic hip, began to make work extremely difficult, and I deemed it necessary with considerable reluctance to tender my resignation. It was a heartbreaking decision to make, I had made a great many friends there and the Ashbrook family had been kindness itself to me, in particular I will always have fond memories of my dealings on her behalf of the late Lady Elizabeth Ashbrook whose life was an object lesson in goodness. I have however never lost interest in the estate and contrive to be as actively involved with it as my life allows. I hope I am able to remain a friend of Arley for the rest of my days. We returned to our flat in Knutsford, but it was not long before I was called into Macclesfield General Hospital for a hip replacement operation which reduced my mobility fractionally but not my desire to find something interesting to occupy my mind. How now to spend my days and engage my brain cells? Do I read books all day, and play with D'arcy my black cat? I missed the historic aspect of the work at Arley and addressing the groups that toured the hall. I missed people and the excitement and stimulation that they brought. I then began to think of my own family history and what fun it might be to research and investigate what were to all intents and purposes were the rather disturbingly lurid and colourful stories about the Lee family as related by my Indian army uncle, Major Kenneth Lee. If they were true then I might just turn them to good use by compiling them into lecture or talk form. This preferably with slides, providing I could find sufficiently interesting photographs to compliment it, fortunately I was able to do this. Thus was born my talk "More Lees Than Cheshire Fleas" which I began to hoick around Cheshire and Greater Manchester hoping to amuse and sometimes shock the members of the various history societies, probus clubs, women's institutes, towns women's guilds and the like. I estimate that I must have talked to some 5000 people over a short period, and it is because of their professed interest and obvious enjoyment that inspired the book of the same name which you will have now read.

During the same period of time that I was busily researching my family history, I was approached out of the blue by a remarkably nice chap by the name of Peter Wildin, this with a view to co-present a video he was proposing to produce about the history of Knutsford. Initially I was a little hesitant, not wishing to become involved with anything that would not do justice to this beautiful and historic town. However, when I learned that Joan Leach, a very serious historian indeed, and a lady now with an OBE to her name for her work with the Elizabeth Gaskell Society was going to be the consultant historian and co-presenter, I gladly joined the team. The outcome to my mind and satisfaction was a quite comprehensive lovingly well finished and produced item. For anyone interested in Knutsford, and there are thousands of people out there that are, it is on sale in local bookshops and stationers, it is called "Knutsford in Portrait" and well worth a look at. It is something that Peter Wildin can be extremely proud of.

I was shortly to have more problems with my health, however this was more my fault than due to any deterioration in it. Firstly I dislocated my replacement hip by merely falling off the couch when sleeping through a late movie, very painful but more embarrassing than anything. More seriously when on holiday in Venice, I attempted to escape from hot deep sand by breaking into a run. Unfortunately my ankles did not feel the immediate need to join me and the Achilles tendons stretched to almost breaking point, this not unlike the beach scene in Dudley Moore's film "10". Foolishly I chose not to pay too much attention to the ensuing pain and on my return home was asked to help out at Arley Hall after the Custodian's wife had fallen down a staircase and been tragically paralysed by the accident. I was thus temporarily back in my old job. The best intentions however were not to be realised, and being already unsteady on my feet, was knocked off them by a heavy swinging door when entering the hall to interview the parents of and bride to be about their wedding arrangements, managing to snap both tendons, though I was not aware of this at the time. There was a certain irony in the situation in that the father of the bride was permanently wheel chair bound which did not auger well. He was then being pushed around the hall and garden by his wife, while I wobbled unsteadily in agony by their side listing the available facilities. I then had to motor home, which I knew would be a risky business. I crawled to the car and began the six mile journey, proposing to drive straight to the doctors surgery. Fortunately, the journey from Arley to Knutsford is a country one, and it was still only late afternoon. The trip, slip of the tongue, brought to mind the tired old joke about using kangaroo petrol, as without any control over my feet, I went quick, slow, quick, quick, slow all the way. Arriving at the surgery I fell out of the car, crawled up the surgery steps and lay there tapping furiously at the base of the glazed door in a frantic desire to be noticed. I shall never forget the quizzical expressions on the faces of the receptionists at their desk, all they could see was a head and a hand. Was it a dwarf? Was it a drunk? Or even a drunken dwarf. My good doctor duly confirmed that both Achilles tendons had snapped and I was immediately taken to Macclesfield to see what were by now my old friends in the Orthopaedic wing. I had set out that afternoon to do a job of work and be back home for tea, I did not return home for nigh –on three months.

With both legs now in plaster up to the knee, I also became wheelchair bound, temporarily of course, which was not too much of a problem under a normal set of circumstances. As the fates would have it, my circumstances were not normal, our flat was a first floor one of two and entered via an open outside stone staircase which was hardly wheelchair friendly. This triggered a frantic search by the social services for somewhere to put me. The solution turned out to be a room in Bexton Court, a residential home for the elderly and infirm, many of whom were very old and infirm indeed, and a day care centre for people like my mother who needed just that. I could have died a slow mental death there I suppose, but being of a reasonably cheerful disposition, resolved to make the best of it and throw myself into their activities with some enthusiasm. I had a jovial relationship with the nursing staff and life was made even more bearable by almost daily visits by good friends bearing gifts, most of which were in liquid form and much appreciated. I left after three months with nothing but the greatest respect and affection for the staff of Bexton Court and the sterling work they do.

I was very soon out and about the county, peddling my "More Lees Than Cheshire Fleas" talk, but coming under some pressure to put the Lee family history into print and throw in some Howard stories for good measure, which began to feel like a half decent idea. I was by then anyhow becoming a little tired of listening to my own voice, I subsequently put the talk to rest. At about this time I began to feel the effects of my hip and ankle problems, becoming non too steady on my feet and learning the literal meaning of the phrase "I bumped into Joe Bloggs in the street the other day" once knocking a fellow pensioner off his feet. I refuse to use walking sticks in case I ever feel the need to use it to enforce my point of view! My wife and I have now parted, I wondered at the time why her visits to Bexton Court were less frequent and more reserved than one would normally expect under the circumstances. I soon found out why when she sued for divorce, which even suspecting her real reason for doing so, I did not contest, the marriage having been somewhat arid for some little time. She subsequently married a friend, as you do, and I am sure is far happier and better suited to him than with me. I live now in the terraced cottages that my great grandfather Fred Lee built in 1886 to celebrate his marriage which was a happy one, despite it's tragic White Lion finale. I have a splendid view of my old Egerton School and the Knutsford Parish Church and it's churchyard packed full of long gone Lees. This has been the backdrop to these personal ramblings, being alone has given me the time and space to put pen to paper, and now with the family histories committed to print, I must look for something new to keep me occupied. Never ever say die!!

~

Footnote

The magnificent Olympia at Arley Hall has now been beautifully converted into the most superb all round facility for hire.